REBELS

MY LIFE BEHIND ENEMY LINES
WITH WARLORDS, FANATICS,
AND NOT-SO-FRIENDLY FIRE

ARIS ROUSSINOS

arrow books

1 3 5 7 9 10 8 6 4 2

Arrow Books
20 Vauxhall Bridge Road
London SW1V 2SA

Arrow Books is part of the Penguin Random House group of companies
whose addresses can be found at global.penguinrandomhouse.com.

Penguin
Random House
UK

First published by Century in 2014
First published in paperback by Arrow Books in 2015

www.randomhouse.co.uk

A CIP catalogue record for this book is
available from the British Library.

ISBN 9780099590798

Printed and bound by CPI Group (UK) Ltd, Croydon, CR0 4YY

Penguin Random House is committed to a sustainable future
for our business, our readers and our planet. This book is
made from Forest Stewardship Council® certified paper.

REBELS

*To Mama for making all things possible,
and to Katie for putting up with me.*

INTRODUCTION

Living in Britain kills me. Everything is so safe, so sani-
tised and regulated, life here feels like being shut into
a tiny box. But when the Arab Spring began in the winter
of 2011, a whole new world opened up to bored young
journalists like me. Ordinary guys my age were demonstrating in the streets against their governments, and when
their governments gunned protesters down beside them,
they took up arms and fought back. The world these guys
created isn't necessarily better – in many ways it's much
worse than the oppressive regimes before them – but it's
wilder, realer, freer ... for them if not for the civilians
they now rule.

From Sudan to Syria, Libya to Mali, I've hung out
with the men who took up arms against their governments, and with the government forces trying to hunt
them down and kill them. As a freelancer, I followed
the wars that would sell and tried to sell the wars the

world doesn't care about. The closer to the action you get, the more death and mayhem you can capture on screen, the more money you are paid. It's not wise, and it's not healthy, but it's my job. This is what the world looks like to me.

LIBYA

October 2011

The hidden awful truth about war is how much fun it is. Everything else becomes an afterthought, dragged into the slipstream of its exhilarating violence. However they begin, whatever their ostensible aims, wars are fought by young men. In a technological age this needn't be the case, but it is. A pregnant housewife or an elderly man could easily lean a Kalashnikov out of a high-rise window to shoot a burst of suppressing fire into the street below, but they don't. A doddering grandmother has enough strength to push a button and send four 107mm rockets shrieking through a hedgerow into the enemy's forward trenches, but she doesn't. Young men do this, and they enjoy it. This is the essential fact of war.

If you watched the Libyan War of 2011 on television, then for you the eight-month slog of slow, bloody attrition will have been telescoped into a succession of distinct, visually exciting images. The initial protests. The sense of hope, and the bloody crackdown. The threatening speeches. The chaotic retreat back along the desert road from Brega, and the siege of plucky Misrata. The first NATO airstrikes. The sudden fall of Tripoli, after months of stalemate. The capture and sudden, violent death of Gaddafi. The End.

But that wasn't how it was, and it wasn't the end. All these things happened, but they weren't the truth of the war. The real war, perhaps like all wars, revealed itself slowly, coyly, in a slideshow of jarring, captivating images. A kitten eating human flesh after a rocket strike. The unearthly beauty of tracer fire fading slowly back into the desert night. A child dancing on the smouldering wreckage of a car bomb. But if the Libyan War could be distilled into one image, it would be that of a handsome youth, in Ray-Bans, posing with self-conscious, reckless heroism on the back of a stripped-down pick-up truck, with one hand cradling his machine gun and a Marlboro jutting from his lips. The Libyan war loved the camera, and the camera loved it right back.

As for most journalists who covered it in depth, Libya was my first war. It was dangerous, sexy, and only a day's travel from Western Europe. Like the Libyans who actually fought it, we picked up the war as it went on, and fell in love with it. And like the Libyans who fought it, we shared the secret sense of grief as the romantic, hopeful revolution soured.

In Tripoli, late in 2011, with Gaddafi gone, we'd talk shamefacedly about how we missed 'our war'. When the sound of gunfire barked through the dark streets, I'd rush to the window hoping it was *something*, and it never was. It was always just a wedding, or a petty argument descending into shooting in a city awash with automatic weapons, or simply young Libyans wanting to hear the joyous percussion of gunfire once more, for old time's sake. I was interviewing a young rebel commander in his cavernous office one day soon after the war had ended when his mobile phone rang with a startling, familiar sound – the synthesised rattle of heavy machine-gun fire. I laughed. He shrugged. As Libyans have now learned, war's a hard drug to kick.

The Libyan War began, as far as the journalists covering it were concerned, at Sollum, a bleak border crossing on the westernmost edge of Egypt's Western Desert. In Libya the desert didn't have a name, it was just 'desert'. *Sah'ra*. People would shrug quizzically, dismissively, if you asked them what a particular stretch of it was called. For all their pride in their Bedu[1] roots, in a country composed ninety per cent of desert, the Libyans aren't desert people. To them it is just somewhere to drive through at crazy speeds, air con on full blast and hip-hop blaring, somewhere to throw rubbish out of the SUV window.

---

1 Bedu, or Bedouin, are the descendants of nomads from the Arabian Peninsula

It had been a full day's drive from Egypt's coastal city of Alexandria to the border. In the lobby of the Cecil Hotel – chosen for its prominence in Lawrence Durrell's *Alexandria Quartet* which I'd loved as a sixth-former rather than for convenience' sake – I'd haggled with a taxi driver until we settled what seemed like a fair price. It was three times the going rate. Past the honking traffic, past the eternal bustle, crowding and hassle of Egypt, the Nile Delta lost itself in sand, the litter and the gimcrack concrete high-rises fading into bright whiteness, heat and silence. Through El Alamein, Marsa Matruh, Buqbuq, Halfaya, we drove across the scorched landscape where British and German armies had crashed headlong against each other, back and forth, for years. War cemeteries loomed white in the burning sun. To our right, the sea glittered unfeasibly blue. I was going to Libya as a freelance reporter. It was my first war, and I wanted fame and glory.

As the Libyan border drew near, the desert sprouted checkpoints. Bored teenage conscripts in desert camouflage poked about in the boot, dawdling, waiting for a few coins or a cigarette before letting us through. Past the coastal village of Sollum, the road swept up sharp switchbacks above the bay towards the Green Mountain. During the Second World War, British artillery officers would wait for the flash of sunlight reflected from vehicle windscreens as they zigzagged down this barren slope, using it as a signal to fire further down the road, blasting lorries full of Italian troops, burning them alive. Now Egyptian tanks, Vietnam-era M60s, studded the border to both sides like fat desert beetles, their barrels pointing vaguely but unarguably at Libya over the barren sands.

This arbitrary border has always been a contested one. In the 1920s, the Libyan guerrilla leader Omar Mukhtar led his people here for their last stand. Trapped between the Italian colonisers and British Egypt, thousands died here of starvation. Mukhtar had fought for an independent Libya to be governed by the leadership of the Senoussi dynasty, and in 1951 the British occupation government established an independent Senoussi kingdom, the Kingdom of Libya, under British tutelage and host to sprawling British military bases. The three provinces of Libya – Tripolitania in the west, Cyrenaica in the east and the southern Fezzan Desert – were combined into a single political entity for the first time in history.

Until the discovery of oil in the 1950s, Libya was literally the poorest country on earth, its entire economy based on salvaging wrecked British and German tanks for scrap metal. The Senoussi dynasty was weak and unpopular outside its Cyrenaican Bedu heartland. When the twenty-nine-year-old Captain Muammar el-Gaddafi launched his military coup in 1969, many Libyans loved him for it. After all, the very first thing Gaddafi did was to expel the unloved British and Americans from their vast bases. But the new dictator had never been popular in Cyrenaica, and especially not in its capital, Benghazi. The Cyrenaicans were the monarchy's bedrock. Cyrenaican Bedu nobles filled the highest ranks of the Libyan army, and prospered from the king's largesse. So Gaddafi punished them for it. Promoting himself to colonel, he purged the armed forces of anyone holding higher rank. Fearing a military coup, he kept the army weak and poorly trained. Officers were so underpaid, most took second jobs to support their families, rarely ever showing up in their bases, never training their men. Gaddafi had successfully ruined his military. As if to prove it, he launched it into war after disastrous war.

Gaddafi had never suffered from lack of ambition – he began plotting his coup at the age of fourteen – but other Arab rulers had always held him in contempt. His bizarre outbursts in Arab summits led Egypt to back away from the proposed union of the two countries. In response, in 1977 Gaddafi launched a short, disastrous raid across the Sollum border into Egypt. Within days, the Egyptian army had hurled the Libyan army back with four hundred dead and dozens of armoured vehicles lying burned out in the desert, had bombed Cyrenaica and captured Libyan border towns. Only Arab League mediation convinced Egypt's Sadat to withdraw from Libyan territory, grudgingly, distrustfully.

Humiliated, Gaddafi switched his ambitions south, reinventing himself as the King of Black Africa. His 1978 invasion of Chad saw the weakened Libyan army suffer defeat after defeat at the hands of civilian volunteers in pick-up trucks. In 1986, after eight years of inconclusive desert war, French airstrikes and a Chadian counter-offensive saw the Libyan army flung in headlong retreat back across the southern border, leaving over 7,000 dead and 1,000 prisoners behind them. Libyans would always say that Gaddafi abandoned the prisoners- of-war to their fate, blaming them for his defeat. This wasn't quite true. Really, he blamed the French and Americans for his defeat. The petulant revenge he would take in acts of terrorism would see Libya and 'the mad dog of Tripoli' quarantined from the outside world for decades.

One night, after the war of 2011, driving down the empty road to Tripoli, Mahood, a petroleum engineer in his fifties, threw up his hands and sighed in the back of the car when I asked him about this. 'Gaddafi was good at first, until the end of the seventies. He threw out the colonialists, he helped us gain skills abroad. Look at me, I studied in London, and Hastings, and Fife. You know Fife? I had an Irish girlfriend, a Catholic from Belfast. A nurse. I had a Mini Austin. Good memories.' Mahood smiled wistfully, then frowned.

'Too much power, it corrupts, it is like a sickness. But the sanctions of the past twenty-five years are what ruined Libya. Not the buildings – we can make new ones – but *in here*, you know? In the *suq* in Tripoli, when I was a boy and the *azan* sounded for prayers, the shopkeepers would all leave their stalls unguarded. They'd just place a piece of wood across, like this, to say they were closed. Now they have to leave their sons there to watch, maybe also some Africans, and still they can't stop people stealing. America, the West, they did this to us.'

———

At the Sollum border, a one-kilometre-long concrete passageway separated military-ruled Egypt from revolutionary Libya. On the Egyptian side, a grumbling cluster of Egyptian refugees huddled around a dingy shed, desperately trying to fling their passports through an iron grille to the passport officers inside. They had fled from the fighting, left their hard-won jobs and possessions behind them, and just wanted to get back into Egypt, to their homes and worried families. The border guards affected not to notice them with exaggerated calm. Rolling their eyes in pantomimes of boredom, they lit cigarettes, put them out, checked their watches, idly picked up a passport, yawned, and tossed it back on to the desk. The guards had time. The refugees had cash. It was the eternal Egyptian story.

My taxi driver barged through the refugees, clearing a path by waving my maroon European passport above them like a fly swat. Guiltily, I hung back. This wasn't fair, but then, I was in a hurry. In any case, the refugees seemed to accept it as part of the natural order of things. Exit visa stamped, I was waved through the passage to Libya.

In the narrow concrete no-man's-land between Egypt and Libya, hundreds of sub-Saharan refugees were camped out in squalor. They had made flimsy tents from grey UNHCR[2] food sacks, or lay underneath lurid polyester blankets in an abandoned passport office. Kids with braided hair darted by around the sleeping men, and past the tired-looking women washing clothes in plastic tubs. Long-limbed and red-eyed, the Africans had sat for weeks in no-man's-land, waiting. They barely spoke. In his self-styled role as King of Africa, Gaddafi had imported hundreds of thousands of African migrants to work in Libya. They cleaned the streets, built the apartment blocks and glittering new hotels and government buildings, carried Libyan loads. Their remittances kept countries like Niger afloat, and their presence en masse a day's sail from Europe gave Gaddafi a bargaining chip with nervous French and Italian politicians who feared the dictator could send a vote-losing Biblical exodus of black refugees their way. Now, they were trying to flee the war, for anywhere that would take them.

---

2   United Nations High Commission for Refugees

Gaddafi was genuinely popular in black Africa, with the leaders who pocketed his handouts and the ordinary people who scrabbled for the crumbs of Libya's oil wealth. But the Libyan people didn't share the dictator's paternal benevolence. Isolated from the world for decades, even liberal, educated Libyans would blandly make staggeringly racist statements about 'the Africans' as they called them, as if Libya lay somewhere on the North Sea. *They're lazy, they steal, everywhere they go they cause trouble.* People would always say that if Gaddafi could, he'd expel the entire Libyan people and replace them with Africans. *They love him*, they'd say, *they owe him everything. He knows we hate him.*

Certainly, wobbly mobile-phone footage of black African men in yellow construction helmets stalking the streets of Benghazi, wielding pick-helves and machetes, made blacks unpopular in rebel Libya. Accused of being drafted in as an emergency riot police, of raping women and murdering unarmed demonstrators, Libya's African migrants had outstayed what little welcome they had in Cyrenaica. One mobile-phone clip showed a captured African trussed from a rope on the steps of Benghazi's courthouse in the first days of the uprising, then slowly beheaded with a glittering knife before a baying crowd, their camera-phones held aloft like lighters at a rock gig. And so they fled here to the Sollum tent city. Libya didn't want them, and Egypt certainly didn't; they were the UN's problem now.

I lugged my rucksack through the concrete passageway, past the Africans, to the first rebel checkpoint in Free Libya and my first war. Four or five bored rebels were leaning against concrete bollards, smoking and idly playing with their Kalashnikovs. I handed the oldest one my passport, beamed widely and trotted out my Arabic spiel that I was an English journalist. He asked me something in Arabic. *Sorry, I don't speak much Arabic*, I answered in Arabic, smiling awkwardly. He tilted his head and looked at me. In his fifties, with a neat grey beard, he was clearly the officer of the group. Like the others, he wore mismatched uniform: jeans, a camouflage jacket and sandals. The decision on whether or not I could enter Libya rested entirely with him.

'You,' he asked in English, glancing at my date of birth, 'how old?'

'Twenty-nine.'

He pinched my cheek, and laughed.

'You look young. Too young, ha-ha!' He checked my passport again, flicking through the stamps. Bahrain, Tunisia, Japan. It had been a busy year so far, and I hoped it proved I was a journalist. He asked where I was going, and I said Benghazi.

'Benghazi *inshallah*,' he corrected. Benghazi if God wills it. New to Libya, I corrected him in turn.

'No, *not inshallah*. I am going to Benghazi.'

He sighed. 'You have friend in Benghazi?' If I had someone from the rebel capital to vouch for me, he was thinking, I would be a safe bet to let in.

'Yes, I do. In fact, he should be here now, just that way,' I said, pointing past the checkpoint vaguely into Libya. I'd been sent to replace the last correspondent after his month-long stint in country, and to his distaste, I'd insisted on being met at the border by a driver. Because Gaddafi had severed the lines of communication between the outside world and rebel Libya, Benghazi and the whole of the east was cut off from the international banking system; no money transfers were possible, no ATMs were functioning and no one would accept credit cards. So journalists entering Libya had to carry with them all the cash they would require for their stay; in my case, a month. In what my predecessor considered rank cowardice, I felt wary of transporting thousands of dollars in cash – which represented maybe two years' worth of a middle-class Libyan salary – across hundreds of miles of an objectively lawless war zone where I knew no one, and didn't speak the language. As it transpired, he was right. I didn't yet know that Libyans are the most scrupulously honest and hospitable people on earth. The driver, however, may have been a rare exception. After many unanswered phone calls, it became clear he was not here, probably would not come, and as far as the officer was concerned did not exist. The purported driver's name was Sharif – 'Omar Sharif?' asked the commander sarcastically, to his men's laughter – and without him my situation did not look good. It was getting dark. A few rounds of rifle fire barked off somewhere in the distance.

The officer sighed.

'First time in Libya?'

'*Na'am*,' I nodded. *Yes*. He nodded back, pityingly.

Picking up my rucksack, he threw it on the flatbed of his pick-up. He opened the back door for me, shut it after me, and beckoned for one of his men to join him in the front. Both sat with AK-47s between their knees. Fumbling in his jacket pocket, he pulled out a pistol and plonked it on the dashboard, then found the packet of cigarettes he was looking for. He turned round, gave me a cigarette, lit it, and we drove off. I had no idea where we were going. We drove through empty desert while they discussed me, occasionally looking at me curiously. It was clear they strongly disagreed about something. The commander turned round again with a concerned frown on his face.

'Why have Islam phobia in the West?'

I babbled an earnest disavowal of the very idea.

'Islam very good religion,' he went on, 'No kill women. No kill children. No kill trees. Only Gaddafi kill women, children. First one ever in Islam.'

'Gaddafi *majnoon,*' I said. Gaddafi's crazy.

They both laughed. 'Gaddafi *majnoon*. Kamron good,' the commander said, giving me a thumbs up, 'Sarkozy very good. Thank you, Britannia. Thank you, Fransia. Welcome in Libya.'

I was in.

The Funduq Imsaad, about ten minutes' drive from the border, was the best hotel in Imsaad, which wasn't saying much. When the commander's SUV pulled into the car park, he turned to me and said, 'Now in Imsaad. Imsaad first town in Libya' – a geographical rather than a qualitative truth. Seedy in a way only North African border towns can be, Imsaad's clusters of idle youths and muddy, unpaved streets were the perfect illustration of Gaddafi's neglect of Cyrenaica. Now every vertical surface was scrawled with revolutionary graffiti, and rebel flags – the red, green and black of the old Kingdom of Libya – flew everywhere. Dusty Toyota pick-up trucks mounted with heavy machine guns sped up and down the road. In the hotel lobby, past rebels sprawled sleeping on divans, their rifles resting against the walls, I was ushered into a side room. A waiter brought me the best Turkish coffee I have ever had. A group of rebels were fiddling with a large wall-mounted flat-screen TV, trying to make the satellite connection work. The commander pointed at the screen.

'Wedding soon. William, Kate. Very good.' He gave me a thumbs up, patted my shoulder like a reassuring uncle and walked off. When he came back, he had a translator with him, a gentle-looking guy in a black leather jacket. The translator smiled and shook my hand.

'I am Mahood,' he said. 'I am geography teacher in Imsaad. Tonight you will stay here. Road to Benghazi is not safe now. Tomorrow we take you. How old are you?'

I told him.

'How old you think I am?' Forty, I thought, and said thirty-five. He nodded sadly.

'Thirty. Gaddafi very bad to Libyan people. But now we are free! Come with me, we go for a walk. But first you must call your family and tell them you are safe.'

I texted my fiancée, and called my boss. I'm a journalist.

To anyone who has worked in the Arab world, Libya comes as a surprise. But for anyone who has crossed the border from Egypt, entering Libya is like entering a parallel, inverted universe. In Egypt almost every single social inter-action is concluded with a whining, persistent demand for a gift. After agreeing a fee in advance, a taxi driver will ask for a gift at the end just for originally agreeing a low price, or for getting you there on time, or because we are friends now, yes? Soldiers and police will hold out their hands for bribes for letting you through a checkpoint, or for stamping your passport. But once across the border, a completely arbitrary line drawn in the sand by European colonisers, the traveller is humbled by the earnest, solicitous hospitality of the Libyan people. Complete strangers will go out of their way, often at significant disruption to their own plans or placing themselves in physical danger or at financial disadvantage, to ensure your comfort and peace of mind. Never once in rebel Libya was a bribe suggested; to have offered it would have been an unthinkable insult. Now Mahood was determined that my first night in Libya would be comfortable. He chose me a good room in the hotel, negotiated a fair price for me and insisted he would buy me a pizza and be my guide around Imsaad.

First, he took me to a wire-mesh enclosure where teenage boys were playing football in the mud. He pointed at a handsome, barefoot kid with a floppy black fringe.

'He is Ayyub. He is fifteen years old, and the best footballer in Imsaad. Ayyub!'

Ayyub came over. Mahood ruffled his hair through the mesh. 'Very good boy, Ayyub. Look, he has no shoes. Because of Gaddafi.'

Ayyub stood there awkwardly until Mahood waved him back to the game. We watched him play for a while. Every time Ayyub touched the ball Mahood clapped delightedly.

'Do you teach Ayyub?' I asked. Mahood looked surprised, and said no. He sighed and we walked on until we passed a stall selling pirated CDs. Mahood asked me if I wanted a CD. No, but thank you very much, that's very kind. Mahood looked sad. 'Please,' he said, 'I want to. It would make me very happy.' Well, OK then, thank you. Inside the shop, a concrete cubbyhole completely lined with lurid floppy plastic sleeves, Mahood asked me what I wanted. I had no idea, and suggested Umm Khultoum. They had none of the classic Egyptian diva's albums in stock. Mahood looked distraught and demanded that the stallholder should look in the back until I insisted that it was OK and I didn't have a CD player with me anyway. The next shop was a small grocer's, and Mahood offered me dates, cheese triangles, orange juice, chocolate. We settled on orange juice, and he handed the chilled can to me after examining it carefully.

'Korean juice,' he said. 'Good Korea, Seoul Korea, not Pyongyang Korea. Gaddafi is same as Pyongyang. Same Bashar al-Assad,[3] same Iran.' As a representative of Iran's state news channel, I felt a terrible, fraudulent shit.

Nowhere was selling pizza, and it was dark. Loitering youths gave us suspicious looks as we wandered up and down Imsaad's single muddy street. I was exhausted. I had left all my money back in my hotel room, and there was no lock on the door. Gently, guiltily, I told Mahood I

---

3   The Syrian dictator Bashar al-Assad, then facing the beginning of the revolution against his rule

was tired. We went back to the hotel, where the bearded commander was snoring on the lobby divan. Mahood gave me his email address and solemnly shook my hand. I went upstairs, wedged a chair against the door handle and curled up beneath a grubby polyester blanket. Gunshots rang out in the street below. I turned off the light and fell asleep in Free Libya for the first of three months' worth of fitful sleeps.

———————

I was woken before dawn by a long burst on an anti-aircraft gun somewhere nearby. I couldn't go back to sleep, and needed to get to Benghazi as soon as possible. Downstairs, the commander was still asleep on his divan. I sat next to him reading until he woke up. He blinked blearily and lit a cigarette. '*Sayara*,' he said, 'Benghazi.' He had fixed a car for me. Tiny glasses of sweet black tea were brought to us, and I paid the bill as he made a phone call. A taxi arrived within minutes and he shook my hand. 'Welcome in Libya,' he said, then shuffled back inside the hotel.

It was a shared taxi, and I made my introductions to the occupants, pretty much using up all of my Arabic by wishing them peace, and saying that I was an English journalist heading for Benghazi. The driver, a greying gold-toothed man in his sixties, shook my hand and wished me peace also. In the back, a fat, sweating man slightly older than me growled something about Iraq through his straggly beard. He was wearing black robes and a Gulf-style chequered headdress, and sat flanked by two silent women wearing the full black *niqab*.[4] They were heading, it transpired, for the coastal town of Derna, about halfway to Benghazi.

A few days before, in a widely publicised report that caused consternation amongst the rebel leadership, the commander of US military intelligence asserted that the Pentagon had detected 'flickers' of al-Qaeda activity within the rebel forces, centred on Derna. The town had a long history of Islamist activism. It was the centre of the Libyan Islamic Fighting Group, a Salafist insurgency which had long tried to overthrow Gaddafi and establish an Islamic emirate in Libya. In one 2007 study of killed and captured jihadists, Derna had, incredibly, sent more fighters to Iraq than any other town in the Arab world, two more than the next in the list, Riyadh, which had forty times the population.

A couple of weeks after my journey, I made friends with an American journalist who'd raised this point with his Dernan taxi driver. No, not at all, the driver had said, we are a very liberal people, we have no al-Qaeda here. Fair enough, thought my friend. About half an hour later the driver mentioned how much he missed his brother. Where's your brother? asked the journalist. Oh, in Afghanistan, said the driver. Yeah, he's been there for

---

4 The full, modest, black Islamic body covering

years. In a slightly shaky voice my friend asked what his brother was doing there. Oh, you know, said the driver, fighting Americans. That might just be a Dernan joke. Unfortunately, the Dernan in the back seat with me wasn't in a joking mood.

For the next uncomfortable hour, the chubby Salafi[5] behind me lashed invective and spittle against the back of my head in a stream of furious Arabic, as he outlined, as far as I could make out, his disapproval of American and British foreign policy in Afghanistan, Iraq and, most of all, Palestine. Pointing at me, he loudly insisted that I was an Israeli. At one point, in the middle of a passionate rant about Gaza, he grabbed the driver and insisted that we stop here in the middle of the empty desert, right now, for a purpose I did not understand but had no wish to ascertain. The driver looked at him, then me, then back at him, horrified, and shouted that he was taking me to Benghazi and that was that. Turning round, I insisted as calmly as I could in broken Arabic that I was not Israeli, that I was British, and that Britain was supporting the revolution. Squinting narrowly at me, the Salafi then told me in Arabic that he knew I was a Jew, helpfully adding with a pointed finger the single English word *Jew*.

I turned to the driver and shrugged my shoulders, palms out, in the internationally recognised gesture for *Is it me or*

---

5 Literalist, or fundamentalist Muslim

is this guy a complete dick? The driver kept his eyes fixedly on the road. The two women squinted through their *niqabs* at the empty desert. No, I said, I am not a Jew, I am a Christian, I am a journalist, I am going to Benghazi, OK?

'Is there a problem here?' I asked the driver.

'No, no, no problem,' he said, looking deeply nervous and apologetic. 'You go to Benghazi, everything OK.'

Still the guy in the back studied me. He saw I was wearing a turquoise ring of the type worn by religious Shias, and remarked upon it in a sardonic tone to the driver. In fact, it had been given to me by a Shia revolutionary in Bahrain a couple of weeks before, when I was working undercover there. He'd told me it would bring me good luck, though the fact he'd locked me in a room a couple of days later and solemnly informed me he would have to kill me for being an Iranian spy seemed to mitigate against its efficacy. Certainly, it wasn't a good look in this taxi.

Mr Derna clearly identified with the Sunni insurgency in Iraq, which had a dark record of slaughtering the Iraqi Shias they saw as puppets of a heretic, expansionist Iran. He may even have fought in Iraq himself – he was the right age for it – and if he hadn't, then being an unusually angry radical from a small town with a history of sending jihadists there, he would have known people who had. In any case, he now began a long and angry speech about Iraq, Iran and – pointing at me – Shias. He asked me, in suddenly flawless English and with a feline smile, which British news organisation I worked for. I paused. In my pocket, with my money, I had a sheet of paper which, in Arabic, informed whomsoever it may concern that I was the Benghazi correspondent for the English-language subsidiary of Islamic Republic of Iran Broadcasting. Summoning up my fast-dwindling reserves of courage I answered him.

'The *Daily Telegraph*.'

I added in shaky Arabic that the *Telegraph* considered Tony Blair a very bad man indeed.

He shut up.

As soon as we reached Tubruq, a few hours' drive from Benghazi, the driver screeched into a parking lot full of taxis, reached over to open my door and shoved me out.

'I will get you a new car here for Benghazi,' he said, adding in English, 'I am very sorry.' He looked mortified. He found me a driver, handed over the fare for Benghazi I had given him just an hour or so earlier and shook my hand. As he drove off, my bearded nemesis scowled back at me through the rear window before the car was lost in a cloud of dust.

He was an appalling aberration in Libya. During three months spent living with the rebels I met only two Libyans I wouldn't entrust my life to. Gaddafi's killer was one, and my fat Salafi companion on the road to Derna was the other. I needed a cigarette badly and the first thing my new driver did was give me one. He shook my hand vigorously and beamed.

'Welcome in Libya.'

As we headed back on to the desert road, it began to rain. Hossein, my new driver, swerved back and forth at speed over the flooded surface to overtake the herds of camels drifting across the featureless landscape. The road to Benghazi was studded with checkpoints, where bored rebel fighters manning anti-aircraft guns cursorily checked ID cards and huddled around petrol campfires to escape the rain and chilly fog. The spring downpour had carpeted the gravelly terrain with a sea of violet wildflowers. Once, a jackal skittered across the desert, bedraggled and mangy-looking. Coaches hurtled past, horns blaring, with teenage boys inside, seventeen, eighteen years old at most, waving rebel flags, banging on the windows and making V for Victory signs. Off to the front, a few hundred miles down this road, with only a couple of weeks' training. Off to the war.

The war for Libya was, essentially, a war for this road. From the border with Egypt at Sollum, Libya's coastal highway snakes 1,000 miles to the west, all the way to the Tunisian border. Almost all of Libya's population lives along this narrow coastal strip. The remaining ninety per cent of the country is desert, of unremitting, inhospitable uselessness above ground and a covetable storehouse of oil and fresh water below. Along this road lay the capital, Tripoli, the oil fields of Brega and their port at Ras Lanuf, the vital container ports of Tubruq and Misrata, and my destination, the rebel capital of Benghazi.

No traveller entering Benghazi from the desert, pushing his way through its crowded *suq* and first discerning the majestic sweep of its bay, can suppress the thought: *what an absolute shithole*. In the drizzle, weary-looking men with sodden shopping bags picked their way through the muddy, unpaved streets; great hulks of container ships rusted forlornly in the once-busy port like mammoths in a tar pit. Benghazi had been a cosmopolitan city, once. The city had been founded as Berenice 3,000 years before by Greek traders, and the stubby ruins of a Doric temple could still be discerned on the seafront, behind metal railings and beneath a pall of litter. The invading Arab tribes had renamed the site Bin Ghazi, *Son of the Holy Warrior*, and let it sink into torpor. The Ottomans had made it a prosperous slave port, leaving strangely Baroque mosques and bath houses behind them. The Italians had built the largest church in Africa here, and a crumbling stucco grid of boulevards and colonnades. In their back-and-forth desert tug-of-war, the British and German armies had destroyed almost every building of note.

Like Alexandria, Benghazi had been a city where Africa met the Mediterranean, and traded slaves and salt and gold for silk and spices. Under the Italians and later the Libyan monarchy, the city had supported a polyglot population of Jews and Greeks and Italians and Maltese. But Benghazi's glory days were long gone, and its affluent and sophisticated minorities had fled with them. A city that lived by trade, Benghazi had been crushed by the West's sanctions, a decline compounded by Gaddafi's policy of studied neglect. As the capital of Bedu Cyrenaica, the deposed monarchy's heartland, and as the scene of two failed assassination attempts, Benghazi had always been suspected by Gaddafi of harbouring a lingering disloyalty to his rule. In this, the dictator was entirely correct.

Just two months before, on 15 February, crowds had gathered in the centre of Benghazi to protest the detention of a human rights lawyer, Fateh Terbil, who had campaigned for justice for the families of the 1,000 dissidents murdered by Gaddafi's henchmen in the 1996 Abu Salim prison massacre. It had been a wet winter, the wettest people could remember in many years. As the protests began, tentatively at first, people huddled from the rain in the city's Italianate arcades, waiting to see how many would come, whether it was safe to join in. Just a week before, the Egyptian president Mubarak had fallen, the second dictator to succumb to the Arab Spring. To the west and to the east, Libya was now bordered by revolutionary states. In Tunisia, President Ben Ali had fled to Saudi Arabia after just ten days of street protests. In Egypt, the struggle had taken longer. Thousands had camped in Cairo's Tahrir Square for weeks, braving rocks hurled by government thugs and snipers on the rooftops. Hundreds had been killed. No one in Libya wanted the shooting to start here. No one doubted that it would.

Driving to the Hotel Ouzu, the seedy journo hangout, my taxi had swept through brown pools of rainwater, past burned-out government buildings then private houses riddled with bullet holes and scarred with rocket-propelled grenade bursts, to a vast shattered compound of high concrete walls reduced to rubble and twisted steel. Rags of ripped canvas fluttered from hollow metal rectangles in the breeze. It took me a few seconds to realise that these had once been billboards, where Gaddafi's omnipresent face had grinned or glowered down at Benghazi. Now his many faces, all slashed with knives or pierced with bullet holes, stared muddily up at the sky; images of him in sunglasses or turban, robe or uniform, proud, defiant, forgiving. Spent cartridges littered the ground, abandoned scraps of uniform lay splayed in darkly human poses. There had been a battle here.

This vast expanse of rubble, shaded with scrappy euca-lyptus trees, had been the *katiba*, the feared military base placed here by Gaddafi expressly to keep Benghazi's civil population from rising. When the protests began, the soldiers based here fired into the massing crowds, killing a handful of demonstrators. When thousands gathered angrily for the funerals on the following day, more were killed. Over those two days, Gaddafi lost Libya. His troops, untrained in crowd control, had used too much force to mollify the protesters, and too little to crush them. By 17 February, the protests had become a revolution. Defecting soldiers from local tribes joined the crowds, turning their weapons against their former comrades in the *katiba*.

Across the eastern province of Cyrenaica, protesters armed with hunting rifles, shotguns and home-made grenades launched raids against government outposts, capturing automatic weapons, vehicles and government soldiers. The weapons were then rushed to the fighting in Benghazi. The soldiers were jailed, or hanged, according to their luck. Rural Cyrenaica had fallen to the 17 February Revolution.

The Benghazi *katiba* held out for a few more days. Protesters braved snipers to lob home-made bombs over the high concrete walls, or ram them with bulldozers in a desperate attempt to breach an entrance. Dozens were killed, many shredded by high-velocity anti-aircraft cannon fired into the crowd. The pockmarked, burned-out houses and apartment blocks surrounding the barracks bore testimony to the wild abandon of the Libyan War's first bitter firefights. The end, when it came, was a typical, morally ambivalent tale of Libyan heroism. Without informing his family of his intentions, Mahdi Ziu, a middle-aged businessman, quietly packed his car with gas canisters and drove it into the *katiba*'s reinforced metal gates, blasting them wide open. As the dazed soldiers hid inside the compound, hundreds of protesters stormed inside the *katiba*. Mahdi Ziu was the first and only suicide bomber of the Libyan War. Through his sacrifice, the battle of Benghazi was over. The war for Libya had just begun.

There was a strange, sadly comic, Graham Greene atmosphere in the Hotel Ouzu in those spring days. Entering, you would walk through a metal detector, and be waved through it by bored guards cradling their Kalashnikovs and slurping sugary cappuccinos from paper cups. It was never once switched on, but at least it looked impressive. There were two choices of room: either those facing the foetid artificial lake Gaddafi had dug as a monument to his own genius, or those facing the roaring flyover and ringroad below with the port beyond. It was a tough call. The erratically guarded roadside was an open target for car bombs; on the other hand, the far side of the hotel faced the Hotel Tibesti on the opposite side of the lake. The rebels' shambolic NTC (National Transitional Council) government, composed of former political exiles and newly minted dissident politicians, had based itself in the Tibesti, and its car park was therefore the ideal spot for enthusiastic tribesmen to gather and fire their heavy machine guns into the air over the lake in long, morale-boosting bursts. Perhaps they thought the massive bullets would land harmlessly in the water; perhaps they didn't care. In any case, their shells daily whooshed a worrying few feet above the Ouzu's upper floors. At night, their tracer made an unnerving firework display as it shot towards you over the shimmering water. Guests rarely used the balconies on the lake side.

The downstairs lobby was crammed with Western journalists, spies and arms dealers, competing for space with the Libyans who huddled together to use the appalling internet connection, one of only three remaining in Benghazi. Every night, miserable-looking NTC spokesmen would gather the journalists together in the downstairs conference room to relay the latest news from the desert front, some one hundred miles to the south. The news was always unremittingly bad.

After a month of startling, unexpected victories, the rebels had been crushingly thrown back from the oil fields of Brega and their terminal at Ras Lanuf. Every day, unco-ordinated convoys of untrained volunteers in pick-up trucks had rushed down the road to the front, beeping their horns and firing wildly into the air. And every day, within minutes, they would be ambushed from the sides and would flee for dozens of miles in screeching, bloody chaos. A month before, as the revolutionary convoys fled headlong back to Benghazi, the rebel capital was about to fall. Only NATO intervention saved the revolution, and only just in time. On the road to Brega, in Benghazi's western suburbs, the charred hulks of government tanks and armoured personnel carriers littered the roadsides just a few minutes' drive from the city centre.

Nerves were still fraught in the city. No one had been paid for two months, the price of food had soared and a sullen stalemate had settled on the desert front. Almost everyone who could afford one had bought a Kalashnikov. Western politicians and journalists had begun murmuring about dividing Libya into two unequal parts. Gaddafi held all the oil, and all its decades of accumulated revenue. The Benghazi rebels had never expected it to be like this. They had thought they would win their revolution within days. Now they found themselves at war, running an impoverished statelet unrecognised by the outside world, too poorly equipped and trained to seize ground and dependent on a controversial NATO mission of uncertain length and dubious political enthusiasm to hold what ground it had.

If the situation in eastern Libya was bad for the rebels, that in the west was far worse. Early risings in Tripoli and the western city of Zawiya had been crushed within days. Only the Libyan port city of Misrata, the country's commercial capital, had held out, and Misrata looked set to fall within days. The city was, by some margin, the most dangerous place on earth. On three sides, it was surrounded by Gaddafi's best-equipped and most reliable armoured divisions. In the city centre, tanks and armoured personnel carriers roamed at will. The rebels, armed with only hunting rifles, home-made bombs, and the weapons they had captured from Gaddafi's dead, had been pushed back to the port of Qasr Ahmed, a few kilometres to the east of the city centre. The only ground they firmly held could be measured in square metres. Their only means of resupply was by sea from Benghazi, hundreds of miles to the east, and the port itself, constantly pounded by mortar and artillery fire, was a writhing, fearful hell of thousands of desperate refugees. I'd shared my taxi to Benghazi from Tubruq with one of them.

Ali al-Basri was a nineteen-year-old student whose parents had fled Saddam's Iraq for the dubious security of Gaddafi's Libya. He was studying medicine at Misrata University when the city suddenly became the world's fiercest battleground. For the next two months, his parents would know nothing of his fate. When I met him back in the taxi in Tubruq, he had just landed from an aid ship chartered to evacuate Misrata's refugees, clutching a holdall stuffed with textbooks and a laptop case. On the way to Benghazi, he told me that he had just informed his family he was alive. He smiled.

'My father lost his car because of me. Every time a ship came to Benghazi from Misrata, he would drive to the port and look for me. One day he left the car door unlocked as he ran to the ship, and someone stole it. But he said he can buy another hundred cars, he can never buy another son.'

Ali was in a good mood. When we stopped at a roadside café, he insisted on buying me a lunch of grilled sheep's liver and *harissa* baguettes while he mused on his experiences.

'Misrata was very bad,' he said chirpily, 'many people were killed. Too many. There are snipers in the high buildings who shoot anyone in the street. So people stay inside, and have no food to eat. I know one family who could only eat the grass from their courtyard for days, they didn't even have flour.'

He pressed another baguette on me. 'The Gaddafi tanks are dug into holes so NATO can't see them. When they hear NATO coming they cover them with sheets. You know, NATO should go to Misrata, not Benghazi. The English and French NATO ships let small fishing boats come from Benghazi to Misrata with fighters, maybe a hundred, two hundred, on each boat. But the Turkish NATO ships don't. I think maybe Erdoğan[6] loves Gaddafi.'

Ali pulled out his laptop and started to play a video file. 'These are my friends from university. Look!' I looked.

---

6   Recep Tayyip Erdoğan, Prime Minister of Turkey

Teenagers in jeans and Chelsea football shirts were ducking through alleyways under a crackling, whistling hail of rifle fire, resupplying mortars with desperately needed ammunition and clearing houses of snipers with wild AK bursts. Every time they fired, they shouted *Allahu Akbar, Allahu Akbar*, God is great, God is great. 'They never used to pray, my friends, but now ...' Ali shrugged. 'Look, you see this container lorry? It is full of sand. Watch!' The lorry was revved up, its gearstick wedged down with a brick, and sent trundling into a crossroads where unseen government soldiers peppered it with anti-aircraft fire. Bright yellow sand spilled out, making an instant barricade, shoring up another few metres of Misrata for the revolution, another few hours of survival for the city.

I've watched this footage of Misrata's first days of fighting dozens of times since then, used it in news packages, pored over its tiniest details. Those students – those kids – fought with impossible, insane courage, standing exposed in the middle of a street to spray a burst of machine-gun fire into a window, or running up an alley without cover to clear a machine-gun nest at point-blank range. I spent years in the Territorial Army learning nothing but how to assault enemy positions, over and over again, and this was exactly the way not to do it. Any Western military officer ordering his men into an assault in such a way would either see them all killed or else mutiny beforehand. But without any training, with minimal equipment and against overwhelming odds, the young Misratan rebels in jeans and flip-flops assaulted a mechanised army head on, and won. They taught themselves guerrilla war as they fought, scattering ball-bearings into the streets to seize up the tanks' caterpillar treads before launching home-made rockets into their vulnerable bellies at point-blank range, incinerating the soldiers inside. They took horrific casualties and still pressed on, holding off Gaddafi's army and reclaiming their city, house by house, street by street. And I knew, right away, that I had to join them. Benghazi could wait.

MISRATA

April 2011

I'm standing on a rooftop, stoned, watching a city burn around me. I've been locked by accident on the flat roof of the villa, in the middle of a bombardment, by a jumpy, greying Al Jazeera reporter, his nerves shot by days of incessant shelling. In every direction huge fires blaze, and streams of red tracer swing in giant lazy loops across the city, like a drunk giant pissing fire. Invisible NATO jets circle overhead, rumbling like looming angry storm clouds. An archetypal liberal *Guardian*-reader, I now find myself wishing them on, praying for them to bomb the fuck out of everything around me. The sound of heavy machine-gun fire barks in staccato bursts across Misrata as government troops try to shoot the jets down. I can hear the rebels in the room below cheer every bomb that lands, crashing like vengeful thunderbolts into the government positions where soldiers wait to kill us. It's the most beautiful thing I've ever seen.

———————

Over a thousand years of political thought, Islam has divided the world into two opposing zones: the house of submission and the house of war. In the *dar-ul-islam*, the house of submission, every Friday sermon in every mosque commands the faithful to obey their ruler and prays that God may guide him to enlightenment. For forty-two years, this was Gaddafi's world. He ruled his cowed nation like a medieval caliph, even amending the Qur'an to suit his own eccentric whims. But in the space of days, everything changed. Suddenly every male old enough to carry a gun was fighting to overthrow Gaddafi. From every minaret in the city, loudspeakers called the men to war and to exalt the day's many dead as martyrs. The ruler had set himself against God, and against the people: he had to be overthrown. The revolution had become jihad. Welcome to the *dar-ul-harb*, the house of war. Welcome to Misrata.

The city is Libya's trading capital, built around the country's largest port. Even before the war, it had been a dour, conservative place. There were no centres of entertainment, no women in the streets; the *Rough Guide to Libya* dismisses the city in a couple of lines. As I arrived in April 2011, it had become the most dangerous place on earth, and the harbour was the only thing keeping Misrata alive. Surrounded on all three landward sides by government armoured brigades, the rebel enclave was living on the last of its hoarded reserves. Every crumb of food eaten and every bullet fired would be brought here on the day-long sail from Benghazi or would have to be captured from dead government soldiers.

Misratans have a reputation in Libya for being shrewd, taciturn businessmen, quick to find an opportunity and stubborn in negotiation. Their quick wits and sheer bloody-mindedness would have to take the place of the weapons they so desperately needed. They despised their fellow revolutionaries in Benghazi as self-aggrandising, feckless braggarts, wasting bullets by spunking them into the air hundreds of miles from the frontline at every opportunity, to celebrate or show off. The fighters in Misrata were going into battle every day with ancient shotguns and a paltry fistful of ammunition. Some of them had taken on entrenched positions with home-made grenades, hatchets and butchers' knives. Back in the east, a vast expanse of empty desert separated the opposing sides; in Misrata the frontline was marked by the gaps between houses and shops on a single street. The rebels could hear their enemy chatting to each other, could smell them cook their rations as their own families starved at home a few hundred metres away. This was Libya's civil war at its closest quarters, the brutal fulcrum on which victory hinged.

I'd arrived from Benghazi by sea at dusk, in an ageing passenger ferry suddenly pulled from the Italy-Albania route to the mute protests of its crew. Drawn from across the Balkans, they sat in a corner smoking nervously throughout the voyage, watching with sad dark eyes as Libyan exile doctors converted the ferry into a hospital ship, shrouding its passenger lounges in sterile plastic sheeting, shifting mattresses along its corridors as IV drips swung listlessly from the ceilings. When the ship docked in the deserted port, sliding in past the shell-battered ruins of warehouses, plumes of black smoke hung heavily on the horizon. A couple of pick-up trucks mounted with machine guns as improvised battle vehicles, known as 'technicals' in military jargon, moved up and down the empty quay like anxious beetles. The constant crackle of machine-gun fire from each perimeter revealed the vulnerability of Misrata's lifeline. Government forces were probing the port's weak defences constantly, trying to force a breach and cut the city off from the outside world. If they succeeded, the rebels expected a massacre, with no quarter given and no way out.

My lugubrious Israeli cameraman and I smoked ciga-rette after cigarette as we watched our ship load up with wounded fighters before slipping back out to safety in the dark. 'We're trapped here now,' I said. 'We may as well make the most of it.' I certainly intended to.

———————

My entire life so far had led up to this shell-pocked quay-side in a city under siege. All my male progenitors had been soldiers or insurgents as far back as history records, though in rural Greece and Ireland this admittedly isn't very far at all. Photographs of uniformed Roussinoses clutching increasingly antiquated guns stretched back from colour to black-and-white to sepia along a long wall of the ancestral farmhouse in Corfu. More distant (and no doubt fictional) ancestors, I was told, plied their swords and axes as chieftains or warlords across the Ulster bogs and Balkan mountain fastnesses in some savage hairy past.

As a child in suburban Hertfordshire, I turned every stick I could find in the playground into a sub-machine gun, and every pinecone into a hand grenade. I read *Commando* comics with a child's avid thirst for blood, and amassed vast armies of plastic toy soldiers, which I pitted against each other in day-long living-room carpet offensives. Shoddily painted Airfix Spitfires and Messerschmitts circled comfortingly from my bedroom ceiling as I fell asleep and dreamed of war. The wealth of gore and severed limbs in my primary school doodles would, if painted by an adult, have seen them committed to an institution. Thanks to the strange scale of priorities of the English public school system, I learned to strip, reassemble and use an assault rifle at the age of fourteen; at sixteen I joined the school rifle club.

At the end of my first year of university, two jets struck the Twin Towers, cutting off *Neighbours* mid-episode and opening up a world of thrilling possibilities on live TV: I immediately switched my degree's focus from the drudgery of measuring ape crania to the anthropology of the Middle East and Islamic world, nurturing vague daydreams of leading a native insurgency on horseback somewhere dusty and romantic at an unspecified future date, and making a mental note actually to learn to ride a horse.

On graduating I applied to join the army, and after a surreal series of interviews was accepted by a cavalry regiment based in the former SS officers' mess at Bergen-Belsen. The Hussar colonel screening my group of applicants at the cavalry mess in Bovington had asked me why I wanted to join the army. The other applicants had all given earnest, compassionate-sounding reasons about doing good and spreading democracy in benighted far-flung places from the top of a tank turret. Taking a deep breath, I told him I supposed it was a question of temperament; that I'd always wanted to go to war, I imagined I'd enjoy it very much and thought I'd be quite good at it. 'That's the first sensible bloody answer I've had all day,' he barked approvingly. After sailing through the army's odd assortment of character assessments that determine one's fitness or otherwise to lead men into battle, I fucked my knee on an assault course before taking the final stage of my entrance test for Sandhurst.

That was it for my dreams of adventure and a dashing uniform. Instead, I got a job in television, thinking up ideas for documentaries; the ones I wanted to watch were never made, and the ones that were accepted I would never dream of watching. The banal idiocy of commercial television tortured me. Instead, I watched enviously as friends and acquaintances went off to fight in Iraq and Afghanistan, and came back bronzed and sated.

After a couple of years of drugs and boredom, I joined the Territorial Army as an officer cadet, and spent the next three years practising route marches and night patrolling and how to capture a Surrey trench held by two insurgents and a notional machine gun using just thirty other cadets of wildly varying ability and a dummy hand grenade. It was a sort of rain-lashed Open University version of Sandhurst, held every other weekend, seemingly for ever, on soggy Home Counties heathland, where the tactical exercises were repeated over and over again to drum them into the ever-changing cohort of part-time volunteers like a heavily militarised purgatory, and the prospect of ever seeing action seemed to recede further and further away. This wasn't going anywhere, I decided. I left, quit my office job, and got one at a news channel who offered rapid career advancement to those willing to risk sudden violent death or broadcasting slow suicide. Within six months I was in Misrata, headily coming up on my first dose of war.

The handful of bearded, turbaned fighters watching al-Arabiya[7] in the dockside Portacabin, absent-mindedly dandling their machine guns, seemed an anticlimactic sight at first. As their city burned around them, they watched the day's fighting on satellite TV. Perhaps they'd have preferred to be at the front; perhaps they just dreaded the rumble of approaching tanks. It's hard to say: only one would speak to us. Adnan, a cheerful wispy-bearded nineteen year old, unbuttoned his shirt to show us his bandaged chest. 'I was shot here during the battle last Thursday,' he said to us. 'Me and my two mates got up and went to fight one morning, and just before we reached the front, a rocket hit our car. I was hit here, my friend was hit in the stomach, and that was it.' He shrugged offhandedly, in a *shit happens* sort of way. The other rebels who were gathered around, all in their twenties and thirties, rolled their eyes as if Adnan was being a drama queen for the camera.

A clean-shaven officer dressed in a tan leather jacket and jeans strolled over, introduced himself as Ahmed, and explained that the port's defensive cordon had been pushed to the very edge of the vast complex, with the expected huddle of refugees kept far outside its meagre sanctuary.

'They were a security risk, we need to keep it clear here in case we have to fight.' He looked at us suspiciously. 'Where are you going to stay now?' Well, I don't really

---

7   Saudi satellite news channel

know, I said. I shrugged innocently. He sighed. 'Come with me.'

Ahmed spoke good English. An engineer, married to a Croatian woman, he lived in Zagreb, but came back for the war. Ahmed wasn't his real name, he told us. At this stage of the war, with the outcome still uncertain, many rebels chose to use pseudonyms. As his driver took us to his suburban command post, Ahmed lit us cigarettes and pointed out houses along the route wrecked by tank and shellfire.

'They don't come to fight with us,' he complained, 'they stay in the buildings and only the snipers shoot. The snipers are very difficult for us, because we don't have enough resources to flush them out. And then, NATO!' He shook his head angrily. 'There are some rockets here. Three times they bombed the same place – and nothing. Without any result.'

This was to be a common complaint in Misrata. NATO had interpreted the UN resolution authorising them to protect Libya's civilian population in the widest possible terms, but it still wasn't enough for the rebels. Legally, the Western military alliance was limited to enforcing a no-fly zone. In practice, NATO was acting as the revolutionary air force, bombing any armoured vehicle it could see and destroying Gaddafi's scattered network of command and control centres. Yet still, for the hard-pressed rebels, the results weren't visible quickly enough.

We drove through the quiet dusk along streets punctuated by improvised checkpoints, whose poorly armed defenders waved and made V for Victory signs when they saw us. The two-lane highway had been divided into one lane for civilians and an emergency lane for rebel vehicles. Beeping convoys of pick-up trucks overtook us, with machine guns mounted on to their beds and rebel flags and shouts of *Allahu Akbar, Allahu Akbar* fluttering in the air behind them as they drove to the front, swerving around the checkpoints made from shipping containers that bulged into the road and the crates of Molotov cocktails stockpiled as a last pitiful defence against Gaddafi's armour.

Down a quiet suburban street we parked outside a walled villa compound. Ahmed banged on the metal door with his fist and a bearded face and rifle barrel poked out curiously. We were home.

───────────

The Muntasir clan had been the most powerful Misratan family under Ottoman rule, and had preserved their position under the Italians by betraying the Misratan rebel leader Ramadan al-Swehli in return for colonial patronage. This time round, they were firmly in support of the revolution. Now we were staying in one of their villas, converted into a command post and hostel for journalists. In the main living room, a cluster of young rebel media activists sat uploading videos to YouTube while middle-aged commanders deployed their fighters around the city using the sort of two-way radios you'd see in a minicab office. Other commanders sprawled asleep across the divans on the floor, their rifles leaning against the walls, or argued heatedly over the next day's strategy. On the floor above, a couple of photojournalists and a BBC news crew had set up home. On the floor above that, the Muntasir family lived, crammed into a few rooms beneath the flat roof.

As the main rebel command centre for this district, the villa was a juicy target for Gaddafi's artillery, and according to the laws of war a legitimate one. Any modern army would be able to locate the building through its communications signature, the constant flood of radio and internet and satellite signalling marking the villa as a communications hub to any prying scanning devices. But through accident or design, any shells that smashed their way through the roof would have had to plough their way through two layers of civilians and Western journalists before they hit the rebel officers. Mangled civilians grab headlines in the Western press, but martyred white journalists are an even bigger splash. The trouble with embedding with rebel groups is you're often worth far more to them dead than alive; while I doubt the Misratan rebels wanted us to die, if we had, the thrilling tragedy of dead white journalists would unquestionably have led the bulletins back at home, with the mitigating fact that this was a rebel command centre mentioned much later, if at all.

We were ushered into a room next to the kitchen, which we were to share with the *Sunday Times* journalist Marie Colvin, and given a couple of mattresses. Marie was to be killed in just such a media centre-cum-journo hostel in Syria less than a year later, as government rocket launchers zeroed on to its tell-tale signals bloom. I'd always admired her writing; now I found I admired her more in the flesh. She trudged off to war every day with the matter-of-fact resignation of a London commuter, and cheerily transmuted the day's horror into gripping copy and affecting Skype interviews each evening as rockets exploded all around us. More than this, her eye patch and long blonde hair added a certain piratical glamour to proceedings. My cameraman was less impressed; she snored, he complained. Worse than this, he added with narrowed eyes, he suspected she was Jewish, an affliction he was convinced she shared with the BBC's distinctly unfriendly producer on the floor above.

On our arrival, curious officers kept popping in to greet us and ask us where we came from. 'England?' said one, a swimming teacher before the war. 'I went to England to see my friend. We went to too much festivals – WOMAD, Eminem at Reading … too much drinking, fighting, very much cocaine.' He grinned widely. 'But now just war for you!'

A junior officer, Jawad, peered in and handed us two steaming bowls of spicy mutton soup. He was short and bearded, with bright blue eyes and a tumble of curly hair. 'English,' he said happily, 'you must know Tim? We are very sad about Tim.'

The film-maker Tim Hetherington had been killed in Misrata with his friend Chris Hondros a few days before. The evening I arrived in Benghazi, the NTC's press officer had informed the nightly press conference of his death, and a Spanish journalist ran wailing out of the room to her room, next to mine, where she cried loudly for most of the night. His death had focused world attention on Misrata, and the rebels were keen to capitalise on it. For weeks afterwards, NTC press officers would tout PR events like a choir of Benghazi schoolkids singing revolutionary songs in his memory, keen to utilise him as a sort of Byron of the Arab Spring, a TV-friendly hook for increased NATO intervention. But in Misrata, the rebels saw his death as a tragedy rather than a PR stunt.

'Tim used to sleep here,' said Jawad, looking around the room with a frown. 'He was a very good man, very kind and gentle. And funny!' He shook his head, chuckling to himself. 'He was an English gentleman. It was very sad how he died. He was in a very safe place, maybe a hundred and fifty metres from the frontline. But a mortar landed next to him and killed him, and Chris too. I was there.' Jawad shrugged. 'It was very sad. But it is written.'

In the living room, over the hiss and crackle of the radios and activists giving Skype interviews to Al Jazeera, a bearded sixty-something doctor, Mohammed El Fortia, showed me footage of the fighting on his mobile phone as we squatted cross-legged on the divan. He was the director of the central hospital before the war; now he was a frequent contributor to rolling news channels, the lynchpin of the city's civilian revolutionary committees and a politician in waiting.

'The first thing,' he said, ' is that the *thuwwar*,[8] the *shabaab*,[9] must take power after the war, not the old men who worked for the regime. They are the ones who are sacrificing themselves, not the politicians in Benghazi. You know, I see these kids … before the war they drank alcohol, they stole things, they believed in nothing. And now they pray five times a day, they say *Allahu Akbar* before they go to fight and die, armed with nothing. Look at this,' he said, showing me a photo of a car mounted with a heavy machine gun, shrouded with home-made armour made from steel sheeting. 'We call this a Misratan tank. You see how we fight? But we are clever in Misrata − all Libya says we are the clever ones, we always have been. The Italians called us the head of the snake, they needed to crush us before they could take the country. And now

8   Revolutionaries, rebels
9   Guys, youth, lads

we Misratans are the ones fighting Gaddafi, and we are the ones who will win the war.'

He looked me squarely in the eye.

'But you are a journalist? For Iran, I know, but never mind. You are British. I need you to help us. I need you to tell NATO to bomb Misrata Hospital.' I must have blanched, as he added, 'Where is the problem? It is just a building only. I am the hospital director, and I am asking you to bomb it. It is a brand new hospital, it costs millions of dinars, and it has never had a patient. Only Gaddafi snipers live in there, and they kill civilians every day. What is more important, buildings or people? Tell NATO to bomb the hospital, so we can save our city.'

———————

My first morning at the villa, I woke up early to the sound of machine-gun fire and the clinking of teaspoons. In the kitchen rebels were blearily making mugs of acrid instant coffee before heading to the front. I went over to Jawad, hunting fruitlessly for fresh eggs at the back of the fridge. 'The most important advice I have to give you,' he said earnestly, 'is that you must do your own washing up when you have finished. Other journalists, they leave their dirty plates and cups in the sink. What is this? This is a war, you think we have time to clean your plates?' He shook his head in amazement. 'Now are you ready for the fight?'

The front was five minutes' drive away. Little hillocks of sand bled into the road every ten or twenty metres along the route, last-ditch barricades to buy the rebels' hard-won enclave another few minutes of life. In the bright morning sunlight, Misrata revealed itself as a drab city of roundabouts and flyovers and tall Soviet-style apartment blocks pitted with shell and rocket scars, a sort of post-apocalyptic Watford with palm trees. A thick plume of black smoke marked our destination, Tripoli Street.

This was once Misrata's heart, a broad shopping thoroughfare about the length and breadth of Oxford Street between Tottenham Court Road and Oxford Circus. Now it lay in ruins, its elegant Italianate arcades vomiting rubble and broken glass. As we stepped out of the car, Jawad reached for his rifle and cigarettes. 'Go, have a look, but be careful,' he said, pointing down the road, 'Gaddafi's soldiers are up there, about two hundred metres away.' As he chatted with fighters smoking *shisha* in the blown-out window of a bank, my cameraman and I explored, crunching gingerly over shards of glass, ducking instinctively at every nearby burst of rifle fire. Behind the ruins of a shop, a couple of teenage fighters beckoned us over to a cluster of stained brown blankets thick with flies. One began to peel back a corner to show us the corpse within then recoiled, gagging at the sudden stench. He waved us away in embarrassment as his friend laughed. Other rebels, teenage boys or tubby middle-aged men, milled around, seemingly aimlessly, staring wide-eyed at the ruins of their own city or shooting jubilant Kalashnikov bursts into the air for the camera. Jawad came over to us.

'You see this?' he said, pointing to a tall office block looming above us. 'This is the Tameen Tower, the tallest building in Misrata. We captured it yesterday. Now we will win the war for sure.' For two months, government snipers based in the bullet-riddled insurance office had used it as an eyrie from which to shoot anyone moving in the shattered streets below. Dozens of fighters and civilians had been killed from this vantage point. Now the rebel flag fluttered from its rooftop, the first tangible success in Misrata's two-month-long war.

When the fighting began in February 2011, it looked like the Misratan rebels' momentum would carry them to Tripoli within days. The world's longest-ruling dictator seemed to wobble on his throne, until Gaddafi ordered his best troops to crush the city. Armoured columns from the elite 32nd Brigade, commanded by his son Khamis, snaked into the city from three sides, pushing the revolutionaries back to a narrow sliver of land around the port. As his tanks positioned themselves on key intersections, snipers infiltrated the city's shops and abandoned apartments, denying ground to the rebels and their civilian support base. Misrata was days away from falling, until NATO trod onstage as Libya's history-altering *deus ex machina*.

Now the charred and rusting hulks of tanks and armoured personnel carriers littered Tripoli Street like mysterious relics of a long-lost civilisation. Only a few days ago, these pathetic and strangely affecting wrecks had been Gaddafi's mailed fist. Now it was hard to believe that men had ever lived and fought in them, and that other men had ever feared them. One T-72 tank turret had been blown from its chassis the width of the street and stood leaning crazily against the front of a shop like a guitar against a wall. An armoured personnel carrier, ripped open like a tin can and still warm to the touch, sat squarely beneath an undamaged billboard advertising diamond rings. The aerial bombardment was NATO's gift to Misrata, and it turned the course of the war.

With Gaddafi's armour destroyed and its crews burned alive or vaporised in secondary explosions, the government snipers were abandoned to unenviable fates as the main body of infantry pulled back to the city's outskirts. Now the rebels cleared the snipers from Misrata house by house, shop by shop, building by ruined building. Eager for a dramatic piece to camera, we ambled blithely down Tripoli Street towards the sound of gunfire. A wall of black smoke about fifty metres in front of us marked the centre of the day's battle; rebels crouched behind walls refilling their magazines, as long bursts from heavy machine guns and single aimed rifle shots provided covering fire. We realised we'd strayed too close to the action and scuttled back down Tripoli Street to a bullet-shredded road sign on a roundabout where, inordinately pleased with myself, I made my first-ever piece to camera with smoke and gunfire behind me, until a horrified Jawad ordered us away.

We got into his car and he cheerily drove us a few hundred metres away to Misrata's main field hospital, Al-Hekma. Before the war, it had been a private clinic; now it had become the world's busiest trauma hospital, as exhausted medics struggled to cope with the constant flood of casualties. Two marquees had been set up to deal with the overflow of dead and dying fighters. Every few minutes, ambulances roared screaming into the car park, while fighters hurriedly offloaded friends from the back of technicals, where they lay slumped in thick pools of congealing blood and spent bullet casings. At this stage of the war, twenty-five or thirty rebels died here every day. The whole process – from screeching arrival to frantic surgery to blanket-shrouded exit – seemed absurdly condensed in time, as if the wedding-like marquees were smoothly efficient death factories. Every half an hour or so, bored-looking orderlies sloshed buckets of water on to the marquee floors to clean them until the entire car park was awash with soapy blood. Dozens of fighters splashed around in this, smoking, cleaning their weapons, chatting, waiting for news, as more and more casualties were rushed in and bodies wheeled out.

We filmed one sequence that illustrated the process perfectly. An ambulance blares crazily into the car park and orderlies scurry out of its way. Behind it, a captured sniper cowers in the back of a pick-up truck surrounded by furious rebels. The ambulance doors are thrown open and rebels carry out their injured comrade, shouting at people to make way as they carry him into the tent. His abdomen has been ripped apart, his wet grey guts spilling out of his belly like an octopus trying to escape a net. The camera pans to the sniper huddled in the back of the truck, his eyes wide with terror, then to the back of the empty ambulance, pooled with blood. In the tent, to the maddening beeps of medical machinery, an Italian aid team struggle with the patient, pumping hard on his chest to restart his heartbeat with what seems like unbearable force. I go out for a cigarette. The injured fighter's brother, in a brown sweater and flat cap, waits outside the tent for news, frantically walking up and down. Every time he tries to enter the marquee, bearded fighters pull him back outside. A few minutes later, a body is wheeled out shrouded in an orange blanket. The brother rushes over and pulls back a corner of this, then shrieks and collapses, crying on his knees, his face in his hands. Other fighters surround and hug him, saying, *The holy warrior is beloved of God.* He stands up shakily and says, *I swear to God, he did nothing wrong, he was just an ordinary guy.* A doctor in blue scrubs hugs him, patting his back, and leads him slowly away. Did you get all that? I ask the cameraman. He nods. Fucking great sequence, I say.

It was just one death among twenty-four in Misrata that day, one family's tragedy in somebody else's war. I'd seen it on TV a thousand times; perhaps that's why it didn't seem real to me at the time. I felt absolutely no emotion other than a vague, dazed sense of wonder at watching it all unfold right next to me. If anything, I was mildly bored for most of it. Back in London, weeks later, I watched the fighter die over a dozen times again as I edited the footage into a documentary. The first time I began trembling and wanted to be sick. By the end I just wanted to get spectacularly drunk, alone, and cry, and at the end of the day I did. The deaths of strangers never seem real at the time somehow, but watched again on screen they become unbearable: the magic of television.

––––––––––

After the initial shock of being at the centre of the action, the first day of war was like doing a massive line, only more so. After that, the days began to bleed into each other, as the sound of gun and rocket fire outside the villa became normality. We'd drink our coffee, eat a *pain au chocolat* and head off to war each morning; each dusk, when we came back, we'd see Al Jazeera's reporter glumly chainsmoking after another day spent locked indoors. His

Australian security adviser wouldn't let him go outside; it was too dangerous. So he'd spend a full day listening to the war, then climb heavily up to the roof each evening to film another live broadcast in his body armour and helmet, edited with thrilling combat footage shot by some unnamed, glory-less freelancer to fill up the gaps.

I spent a lot of time at the Al-Hekma Hospital over the next week or so, observing the accumulating death, smoking cigarettes and waiting for things to happen. We didn't have a security adviser and as my cameraman consistently resisted trips to the very tip of the rebel spear-point, to my and Jawad's frustration. He was getting old, he had a family; ultimately he was right. But every day the rebels captured a new, important position and every day he found an excuse not to visit it until the fighting had burned itself out. At least at the hospital we could get accurate casualty figures and some TV-friendly carnage at relatively low risk.

One day a French journalist wearing full body armour and a helmet crossed the road in front of the hospital and was hit in the neck and paralysed by a stray round. The chances of this happening were infinitesimally small. 'You see,' shrugged Jawad, our constant companion at Hekma. 'Everything is God's will, so why fight it?'

Jawad was as frustrated as I was. Because he spoke English, he had been ordered away from his frontline unit to a relatively cushy billet babysitting journalists, a task he found vaguely shameful. He kept trying to palm us off on one of the English-speaking media volunteers who'd arrived from Benghazi, and each time he managed it his commander rebuffed his attempt to return to the front. To cheer him up, we filmed a brief interview with him sitting cross-legged on a rug in the villa's garden, a *keffiyeh*[10] artfully arranged around his neck and his rifle leaning against the wall beside him as he discussed the war.

'Now the Tameen building is free,' he said, 'we will try to put out all Gaddafi's soldiers from Tripoli Street. I think we can do it – we can! Because we have the true case. We need freedom. I think this is not difficult. But should be the freedom needs expensive cost, and we do that with our blood.'

The interview over, he beamed excitedly. And this will be on TV? he asked. Yes, I said, all over the world. When they are old enough to understand, and they see this, my children will be very proud, he told us. Once we'd cut the package together, he watched it with us three or four times, calling in the other officers to hear him speak, and they patted him on the back as he studied his sound bite, frowning, in silence. We copied the package on to his USB flash drive so he could upload it to his Facebook wall, his undreamed of cameo role in his tribe and city's

_____

10 Chequered Arab scarf

59

history recorded for posterity. After that, Jawad didn't mind babysitting us so much.

The insatiable hunger of twenty-four-hour news meant we spent more time in the rebel command villa than at the front, editing and sending footage back to Tehran or filming live stand ups on the rooftop to a backdrop of the burning city. Every day we were taken out on a tour of Misrata for a few hours, mad thrilling day trips into a world of violent death and unimaginable destruction. The safer Tripoli Street became to explore, the more the scale of the devastation revealed itself. The city's shopping district, a vast complex of office blocks and low shuttered stores, had been entirely levelled. Misrata seemed to be a vast wilderness in every direction of grey rubble and twisted steel. Thin bands of people wandered around the ruins, looking absurdly small as they gathered bullet casings and searched for booby traps.

In the hollow shell of one building we came across a medical team in yellow plastic raincoats and surgical masks, searching the ruins for bodies. They'd just found a dead sniper and had wrapped him up in fluorescent green bin bags, dumping him on the back of a truck, retching into their masks. One foot in a white gym sock peeped out, black and green with rot. A volunteer squirted disinfectant on to the ground. An oval patch of white and black mould, like that on a rotting orange, marked where he had been. A green cap lay forlornly on the ground next to it. The doctor in charge came over to speak to us, wincing at the stench when he removed his mask. 'We found four of Gaddafi's snipers today. Step by step we are cleaning the city, and sterilising the area.' Are they Libyan, I asked, or foreigners? The rebels had claimed that Gaddafi's forces were primarily sub-Saharan mercenaries, though the only captives we'd seen – like the terrified sniper at the hospital, a twenty-year-old conscript from Tripoli – were Libyans. He shrugged. 'Because they have been there for days, it is difficult to tell. One was Libyan, I think, and the others are Africans.'

Doctors, especially, frequently claimed to have come across the bodies of African mercenaries. They often told us stories of finding bloodied wads of long-worthless French francs on volunteers from Chad and Mali, or bundles of poorly photocopied US dollars. If it was true, they never showed us any proof. Certainly it was psychologically easier to believe that they were fighting savage outsiders rather than fellow Libyans from nearby towns.

Greyed out by concrete dust, silent save for the crackle of rifle fire and crump of mortars, Misrata's ruins had an eerie beauty impossible to capture on film. It felt like we'd stepped into a television rerun of *The World at War*. No civilians were visible anywhere, just poorly armed hand-fuls of rebels kicking spent shell casings out of the road, and smoking. 'Look at this, this is anti-jet machine gun,' one said to us, holding up an empty case the size of a board marker, 'it is not for people to kill people. All of us are simple people, civilian people,' he added, adjusting the Kalashnikov at his shoulder, 'we are looking for just freedom, just freedom only.' As he spoke, a wave of rockets came crashing into the city centre. 'Listen,' he shouted. 'These are Grad rockets – you can hear the rockets here.' As the explosions came closer, the men began to shout *Allahu Akbar, Allahu Akbar*. One held up his mobile phone to film the barrage. 'These are Grad rockets, in the hospital. In Misrata Central Hospital.'

We rushed to the car and drove to Misrata's main hospital through a web of side streets as Jawad casually enquired about the process of acquiring a British visa. 'I am an air-conditioning engineer, I studied in the technical school in Misrata. Now Gaddafi's soldiers are hiding in there. But it's OK, we will free it from them soon. I speak English, but not well, all because of Gaddafi. He did not let us learn things. Now, when Misrata is free, I want to go to London and Manchester, and learn English in England. You think you can help?' I can try, I said. 'And I help you, I take you the safe way,' he said, tapping his forehead like Asterix to emphasise his cunning, 'away from snipers.'

In the streets down from the hospital, a group of fighters, some patchily bearded teenagers in tracksuits and *keffiyehs*, others middle-aged men in oddments of camouflage, stood clustered around their vehicles, prepping their weapons for battle. The hospital, just fifty metres ahead of us, was one of the few buildings in the city centre still held by government snipers; it was here the doctor had pleaded with me the night I arrived somehow to direct NATO airstrikes. The government snipers fired occasional desultory shots at us as we introduced ourselves. Abandoned by their own commanders, and shelled by their own rocket batteries, it was hard not to think the last few government troops had a certain doomed courage. The rebels, equally, disdained cover and insisted we interview them in the centre of the road.

'It was very strange, they were using weapons we have never seen before,' said one. 'Even now, until just before you came, they were firing Grad rockets at us.' He shook his head in wonder. 'I am a student, and some of us are just simple workers. God is great, God is great, God is great.' At just that moment, a mortar shell exploded with a sharp zinging crack a couple of dozen metres away from us. A hot shard of razor-sharp shrapnel the size of a runner bean landed plinking at my cameraman's feet. The rebels didn't even flinch.

'You see?' said one, laughing. 'You can even hear it yourself. They flee the hospital and then they fire rockets at us, like now. Even until just before they surrender, they keep shooting. They have destroyed so many buildings and it keeps getting worse. You can see it yourself.' He turned to face the camera and grinned. 'But, *merci, Sarkozy!*'

It was odd to see grimy, bearded Arab insurgents earnestly praise Cameron and Sarkozy, but the rebels' gratitude was well deserved. Every night, the rebels in the command post pointed in the air and laughed when they heard the first NATO jets circling over the city. We would go out on to the roof and watch the air strikes, listening in hushed awe as the sky burst open with a thunderous crack and plumes of dust rose from the shaking buildings around us. I never once saw a NATO jet, and nor had any of the rebels I asked, but that only added to their unearthly power. The ordinary fighters on the ground spoke of NATO with awe and sometimes impatience, as if the alliance was a capricious sky god, sometimes munificent and sometimes deaf to their pleas. Fighters sprayed small yellow Ns on to the bonnets of their trucks to ward off friendly fire, as if a speeding jet could discern such tiny talismans from thousands of feet above. But the officers commanding the rebel war had little need of such magical thinking: they were in direct communication with the storm god himself.

Months afterwards, the senior rebel leadership, the Misrata Military Council (MMC), took me to the coastal bomb shelter where they fought and won the war. It was a damp, claustrophobic concrete chamber, littered with empty batteries, dead biros and cigarette butts. Lit only by the light on our camera, the officers – in neat tweed jackets, pressed white *jellabas*[11] and green bomber jackets all studded with pens – led me around the dismal dungeon. I was the first journalist to see this place, they said. They looked around it themselves with a sort of nostalgic wonder, as if they were visiting their old school. How small it seems, their faces said, how vivid the memories. The war had ended a few weeks earlier.

Most of them had been middle-ranking air force officers before the revolution, based at Misrata's Air Academy. Unlike Libya's neglected army, many of these officers had spent happy months learning how to fly and maintain their fleet of Mirage jets in French airbases, before the sanctions plunged Libya into gloomy isolation. They had a window to the West, and knew how NATO worked. As soon as the revolution began, they made contact with the Western alliance. It was hard to avoid the impression that the first days of the revolution, in Misrata at least, were as much a failed air force coup as a popular revolt.

'I swear by God,' said Colonel Omar Gaied, the MMC's overall commander, stroking his neat moustache, 'most of the officers here in Misrata joined the revolution on the nineteenth of February. By the day after, we were in this

---

11 A loose, hooded cloak

shelter, talking to NATO. Because the war here was so fast, and communications with Benghazi were so slow, we didn't even take orders from Benghazi. We just spoke to NATO and told Benghazi what we were doing once we had done it. One officer, Fatih Ali, spoke to NATO for us, because he was a pilot and he could speak English. Every day we spoke to NATO and gave them new GPS co-ordinates, and every day they would bomb everything they could see beyond those points. But I swear to God, we had no NATO soldiers here to help us.'

The view from our command post in the rebel-held villa, months earlier, was markedly different. Some of the officers, coming to us individually and swearing us to secrecy, informed us that a handful of French and British Forward Air Controllers were based in Misrata calling in air strikes. They showed us the villa in which the controllers lived – a tall handsome pink building with a commanding view, a few minutes' drive from our base – then bitched at the uselessness of its British and French occupants. One day at the rebel command post, I overheard another air force colonel, Salahadin Badi, arguing over his crackly Land Cruiser radio with a disembodied, almost comically French-accented voice. 'I tell you again,' said the voice impatiently, 'once we have the co-ordinates we will attack, but without them we can do nothing.'

A junior officer shook his head angrily and beckoned me over. 'Every day we give these fucking French important targets to bomb, and every day they say their maps aren't good enough. And every day we tell them to use fucking Google Earth!'

The greatest frustration for the rebels was NATO's slow progress in destroying the Grad rocket launchers, which began pummelling the city as soon as Gaddafi's troops had been pushed back from Tripoli Street. The rockets, a barely updated version of the Soviet Katyushas that had struck terror into German soldiers on the Eastern Front during the Second World War, were wildly inaccurate and struck the city in long salvoes every few minutes. If a NATO jet flew overhead, the Grad trucks stopped firing and sidled into ruined buildings for cover. As soon as the jets flew away, they sneaked out again and resumed their barrages. Incapable of discerning between military and civilian targets, they were militarily more of an annoyance to the rebels than a tactical threat; but as the rockets slammed into civilian homes and wiped out entire families, they tore at the rebels' morale.

Once, the rebels took me to where a family of four had been killed in a Grad salvo. The family had fled to a relatively safe part of the city at the beginning of the uprising. After Tripoli Street had been liberated, they'd returned home briefly to pick up food and clean clothes when a Grad landed on their house, demolishing a room. They ran to their car in terror and were pulling out of the driveway when another Grad landed directly on their vehicle, killing them instantly. The youngest, a girl, was just three years old. Their incinerated bodies had been moved away by the time we reached the scene; only the burned-out car, surrounded by rocket craters, and a few pitiful remnants of their last moments survived: a bloody child's sock on the ground, and close by, a fluffy kitten gnawing on a dusty gobbet of human flesh. As we were filming, a patrol passed through shouting that another Grad barrage was on the way. We ran to our car and drove away. On the way back to the villa, we heard the dull repeated thuds of rockets striking that neighbourhood for the second time that day.

We came across a shopkeeper one morning, about a week in, as he unlocked the shrapnel-pitted shutters of his food store and hurriedly loaded tins of tuna, bottles of fizzy drink and shrink-wrapped croissants into his pick-up truck. 'This is my shop, closed for two months,' he said, stuffing cans of almond milk and packets of crisps into my hands. As he spoke, the sound of rocket salvoes crashing into the streets around us boomed like a rapidly gathering storm. 'Now all my family are coming here taking everything for *mangiare* … for eating.' His two young boys played in the street, peering into the bullet holes that peppered every nearby house. He hadn't spoken to his extended family in Manchester since the start of the revolution, so we lent him our satellite phone and listened as he reassured them he was alive, then started to complain about the shelling. He frowned often, as he was handed from cousin to cousin and had to begin his story over again, and he looked heavenward, shaking his head slowly as if they were asking him stupid questions. After a few minutes, he seemed glad to hand the phone back. A loud impact nearby made us all flinch.

'The people of Misrata have no food because of fire, fire, fire,' he cried in broken English. 'No stop fire! Stop fire, please, Muammar, stop fire!' They all called Gaddafi by his first name, as if scolding an errant child.

Nodding absent-mindedly, pretending to listen, Jawad poked through the back of the man's truck for goodies to bring back to the house. Like all the Misratan rebels, our command post lived on whatever it could scrounge from local shopkeepers: endless dry baguettes filled with tuna and cheese triangles, and cartons of sugary mango juice. At this stage of the siege, the rebels were running on empty. The few aid ships and dangerous-looking fishing boats coming into the harbour were reserved for medical supplies and ammunition, with only the occasional truck full of rice from Benghazi breaking the siege. A packet of cigarettes now cost $50 on the open market, though they were dished out, sparingly, for free to the men at the front, and, at the cost of a disapproving look, to me when I guiltily asked for one. Commanders detailed units to break into abandoned pharmacies and grab whatever medicine they could find, and hospital foyers were littered with a mismatched carpet of brightly coloured pharmaceutical heraldry as junior doctors sorted through them on their knees, trying to find something, anything, of use.

One afternoon, I was sitting under the shade of a palm tree in the garden, eating a melon and reading a novel, when a Grad whooshed over my head and exploded nearby. My cameraman and I drove a few hundred metres away to the geriatric hospital where it had landed. A doctor and a handful of fighters were inspecting the crater in the car park where it had struck, mangling the nearby generator and spraying shrapnel and broken glass across the ward-rooms. 'Our patients are afraid,' said the doctor, 'some of them have minor injuries, but they are very lucky. They are old women, they come here suffering from chronic diseases and suddenly they are bombed by a missile.' Do you want NATO troops here? I asked him. He looked around nervously at the fighters beside him. 'Well, everyone has different opinions. Me personally, I'd like UN soldiers in the blue helmets, just to make it safe for the civilian people here, and maybe some French and British if they wear blue helmets, but not American soldiers shooting at people on the road. This is not Iraq.'

It took ten minutes of negotiation to convince a patient to give us an interview. The elderly women were huddled for shelter in a basement with their adult daughters. Only one heavily tattooed old lady would talk on camera. The others masked their faces with their veils and turned away from us angrily. 'I was resting,' she said. 'Suddenly lots of glass landed on me, and dust. He is destroying us, and I pray that God will destroy him. Oh, Muammar, how can you do this to your own people? Our lives are ruined, we are always frightened. Oh, God, let the revolutionaries see victory, give our sons the strength they need to win. This is all we ask,' she said, and burst into tears. She was the only Libyan woman whose face I had seen in my whole time in Misrata.

We were wandering around the corridors, trying to find a casualty to film, when a young media volunteer from Benghazi told us to wait for a minute before motioning us into a side room. A young rebel with no discernible injuries lay on a stretcher covered by a blanket. He'd been hit by a mortar, the volunteer told us, and was horribly wounded in his abdomen. Can we see? I asked, adding that it was important for the world to know what was happening in Misrata. The two glanced at each other for a split second; the casualty stifled a nervous giggle. Oh, no, said the volunteer, they're all internal wounds, from concussion. There's really nothing to see. In a city where dozens of people were being killed daily, this little propaganda farce was entirely needless. We trudged back angrily to the rocket-struck ward.

My cameraman was filming arty cutaways of the damage when a middle-aged man came into the foyer crying, next to a body on a trolley. It was his son. His head had been smashed open by a high-velocity round, and the exit wound was strangely beautiful where his skull had folded open on itself like a pink rose. His mouth hung slightly open in a last expression of surprise. I shouted for my cameraman to come, and he shouted back that he'd be along in a minute. The man was crying for his son, and the media volunteer shoved him sharply on his arm and told him to stop talking and wait for the camera. He did, and stood there weeping silently until we'd filmed the close up. I hated myself and my intrusive, heartless job. They put his son into the back of an ambulance, and called him a *mujahid*, a holy warrior, giving his crying father deep hugs and kissing him on his cheeks before driving him away with the body.

Afterwards the volunteer nodded, satisfied. Good, he said, you see?

It wasn't good. We couldn't use a shot like that on TV, not for a Western audience: manufactured fantasies of carnage replace, for us, what Arab audiences see on their TV news every day, and our television coyly shrouds from us. But you film it anyway.

————————

After we'd spent days chasing him down, the rebel commander in our sector, Salahadin Badi, finally gave us an interview. He was an air force colonel before the war, and in his pilot's jumpsuit, grey beard and chequered turban, looked like a strange post-modern Saladin. 'You see?' he fumed, genuinely pissed off. 'They still shoot rockets and mortars at us from far away, because he and his soldiers are cowards. They can only fight us from a distance. Gaddafi is a maniac and a fraud, and he is using his last weapons. Now he and his soldiers will run away from Misrata like rats.' I asked him how the war was going. 'Good, good, all praise be to God. We have divided Tripoli Street into different sectors, so we can liberate the city from different directions. This is how we will trap Gaddafi, like he trapped us for forty-two years.'

But the heady rush of victory after the recapture of Tripoli Street was fading under the constant bombardment. Only that morning, Jawad had come into our room and happily informed us, pumping his fist for emphasis, how vigorously he had fucked his wife on his first night home for two weeks. But as the Grads smashed into the houses around us, closer and closer, he had begun to lose his nerve.

73

'I am scared for my family,' he admitted, once we were alone. 'I know I have to stay here but I want to go home to see they are still alive.' Swearing us to secrecy, he drove off for an hour to check up on them. His wife and children were still alive, thank God, he told us when he returned. He looked sheepish, as if his worry was somehow unseemly.

The bombardment was exciting, from a distance. I enjoyed watching the firework show with the same detached curiosity crinolined ladies watched Gettysburg or Waterloo through ivory spyglasses. But the closer and closer the shells came, the less fun it began to seem. The Grads were landing on neighbouring houses now, gouging out huge holes or flattening them, for hours and hours on end. Whenever our windows flexed and bedroom shook, my cameraman and I would look at each other and grimace comically, our ironic terror a mask for genuine anxiety. In the mosque next door, a tag team of children endlessly sang *There is no God but God, Muhammad is the prophet of God* from the minaret in high frail voices, to shore up morale or prepare us all for martyrdom. We're in the best room, I lied to myself, ground floor, facing away from the launchers, we'll be fine. Nerves were becoming frayed in the villa; the rebels bickered about small things. I began to think about home.

I desperately wanted to talk to my fiancée, which was problematic. Not wanting to frighten her, I hadn't told her I was in Misrata, not least because I'd explicitly promised

I wouldn't come here. But because Gaddafi had cut the communications network, I could only use the satellite phone, which entailed a trip on to the roof to find a signal. During the bombardment, no one went outdoors if they could avoid it. Every time I trudged unwillingly on to the roof I found more shrapnel dotted about. One afternoon, in the half-hour space between two fruitless calls, the rooftop water tank was punctured by a nearby shrapnel burst and I stood in a puddle of dusty water listening to her answerphone again, and to the swoosh of rockets landing all around and the sickening, ever-nearer thuds of their impacts. Eventually, I stopped calling.

Like the rebels, I came to love the sound of NATO circling overhead, and to fear its absence. We all felt a clammy wave of dread when approaching storms drifted over, making air raids impossible. A sort of enforced jollity washed over us as we awaited the inevitable pummelling to come. We'd sit and watch satellite TV in the operations room as the radios squawked in the background, eating Nutella on stale baguettes and chatting about the Premier League or music. Marie would sit at the dining table, typing up her notes; a young fighter would unroll his prayer mat now and again, and quietly, undemonstratively, prostrate himself in a corner of the room before sitting down and lighting up another cigarette. Officers would lean against the kitchen cabinets drinking mugs of instant coffee and debating politics, or reminiscing about their time spent studying in Budapest or Prague, or fighting in Chad or Lebanon. It felt like being back at university.

One evening Jawad solemnly shook our hands and told us that he'd been redeployed to work with a different news crew who had just arrived, and introduced us to our new driver, Omar, a young volunteer from Benghazi. We were the same age, Omar and I. He liked Chelsea, rap and smoking weed, and increasingly found the war a strain. Often, we'd sneak round the back of the villa and smoke hurried joints together. He'd empty a whole cigarette into his palm, crunch it together with granules of hash one-handed, and suck it back into the empty paper cylinder in a way I've never been able to replicate, his eyes darting around as we smoked to make sure no officers were creeping up on us. 'I know I shouldn't,' he'd always say, 'but I'd go crazy if I didn't. How can you not get high in a place like this?' He had a point.

Omar was always stoned when he drove us to the front. He'd switch on his car stereo to terrible American rap, adjust his baseball cap and check his bloodshot eyes in the mirror, then hurtle off along the bumpy, shell-scarred roads to war. I soon learned to check the safety catch on his Kalashnikov before we set off. Unlike in Benghazi, weed was frowned upon in Misrata, where the rebels, fighting for their homes and families, were more disciplined and perhaps more puritanical than in the NATO-defended east. It was hard not to laugh, one morning, when an officer discovered evidence in his car that one of his sentries had been skinning up spliffs on duty. *But this is war,* he said angrily, *it's not a party. This shit comes from Gaddafi to make us weak.* But the Misratan rebels were not weak. They were the most motivated and instinctively disciplined soldiers I have ever seen, willing to fight and die against over-whelming odds with ludicrously inadequate weapons. I saw one fighter with a single-shot hunting shotgun, entirely useless in a war like this, as he broke it open before battle, wedged in a shell, and slammed it shut with a shrug, as if saying, what else can we do?

Another fighter, a middle-aged man in a leather jacket, with grey curly hair and a beard, came over to my camera once during the battle for the hospital with tears in his watery blue eyes. He raised his Kalashnikov and said, 'This was my brother's gun, he was killed two days ago. We are sorry about him, he was a brave man. All the men know him, ask anyone here.' He looked around at the teenage boys alongside him in Ralph Lauren rugby shirts and hooded tops. One, with dark tousled curls, was surely no more than fifteen years old. He turned his face shyly from the camera's gaze. 'He went to die to get one thing only,' the man continued, 'to get Libya free. To get

Libya free. We want one thing only, to get Gaddafi out. No more Gaddafi. If only one Libyan man remains, he will kill Gaddafi and he will live alone and free.' He bit his lip, eyes welling up, but instead of crying shouted *Allahu Akbar, Allahu Akbar,* and the fighters around him, men and boys, thrust their rifles in the air and shouted that God was great, God was great. The holy warrior is beloved of God, I said, placing my hand on his arm. It was a phrase I'd heard a lot recently, the formulaic requiem for the day's dead. He looked me in the eye doubtfully before he and his friends cocked their weapons and went to storm the hospital at the end of the street.

They buried that battle's dead the same day. Teenage fighters loosed long rat-a-tat bursts of automatic fire into the air in the improvised graveyard by the villa as male relatives carried the cheap plywood coffins over the dusty ground. There were no women at the funeral. Grey-bearded fathers and grandfathers wept silently, muttering the prayers for the dead over the graves while young fighters saluted their dead friends as mujahidin, gripping their rifles tightly, tears streaming down their smooth faces. When it was over, the teenagers clambered back into their technicals and sped off back to the front for revenge, beeping their horns as they went. Workmen poured wet concrete over the graves to seal the contents from scavenging animals. As we trudged back home past the rows of fresh graves, only the imam remained, praying silently, looking at his hands before he faced the setting sun.

We'd spent ten days in Misrata, and it was time to go. My cameraman's contract was nearly up, and he had no intention of staying an hour longer than necessary. It was hard not to resent him for what I saw as cowardice, but I had no right to force him to stay; he had a family, and had promised them he wouldn't go anywhere or do anything dangerous while in Libya; he was working for little pay and with no insurance, and the encroaching barrage and endless factory line of death had tarnished what little lustre Libya's civil war had ever held for him.

But our lift back to Benghazi was subject to delay: in recent days, Gaddafi's artillery had switched its murderous attention to the port in an attempt to starve the city into submission. Grad rockets plunged in never-ending white plumes off the harbour's shore to frighten ships away from docking; cluster munitions deployed from artillery shells skidded across the quays to render them unusable. In actual fact, the rebels' war effort continued much as before, with gaily painted wooden fishing boats disgorging their dribs and drabs of fresh ammunition and reinforcements from Benghazi unhindered. Grinning officers would say that they were off to the port for a fishing trip – 'to get food for Gaddafi' – before returning hours later with a truck full of crated bullets. Only the relief effort suffered, as the single aid ship plying the sea route waited for days offshore and out of range for a break in the shelling.

The bombardment of the port was a nuisance for the rebels; but it was an ongoing, methodical massacre for the hundreds of African guest workers huddled in a squalid makeshift camp along its perimeter. Unwanted useless mouths in a city under siege, the Africans had no choice but to wait in their flimsy shelters of plywood and plastic sheeting for the shelling to lapse long enough – through Western aerial attention – to allow the ship to dock. Gaddafi's rocket shrapnel scythed mercilessly through their pitiful tents; trapped in someone else's war, the Africans were now decimated by it.

Hekma's ER tents began to fill up with mangled black bodies. I watched a doctor sew a gaping face wound back together without anaesthetic as his African patient stared fixedly ahead, his teeth gritted, at some distant, imaginary, clearly preferable point. When he was finished, I asked the doctor if anyone had been killed in the morning's shelling. 'No, no, no one!' he cried exultantly. 'Just five Africans. It is a miracle actually. We don't know how many rockets landed today, maybe fifty, sixty, seventy in ten minutes. I tell you, we are very lucky, we are seeing miracles here every day.'

An agnostic eye would firmly attribute Misrata's brush with the miraculous to NATO's increased activity. Royal

Navy warships were now dredging the harbour entrances of the sea mines government speedboats were laying every night, and French and British fighter jets circled the city constantly, hunting the last surviving rocket launchers. One night, panicky-looking rebels came into my room asking if I had any night-vision goggles they could borrow. I didn't; and if I had, I shouldn't have given them to them, though by then I definitely would have done. They shook their heads as if I was useless and wandered off into the dark, informing me that an armoured column had smashed through the city's outer defences to retake the port. Only a handful of volunteers at an improvised checkpoint were holding them at bay while the rebels cobbled together a scratch force from whatever men they could spare for a desperate counterattack.

A video released by the RAF reveals, as if from the view of a vengeful God, what happened next: as the T-72 tank spearheading the column slowly traverses its turret, aiming at the rebel checkpoint, a British pilot in a Typhoon jet unhurriedly zeroes in on the unsuspecting monster. A flash of white on the black-and-white video marks the death of the tank and the crew inside it; a dozen technicals full of Gaddafi's loyalist troops speed away in confusion and terror through the suburban streets, like woodlice who've found their log suddenly disturbed. It meant that the port was safe, and that our ship could dock. We were going home.

We shook hands with Omar and Jawad, hugged them, promised we'd come back, and declared we'd see them all in Tripoli soon while thinking they'd all be dead within weeks. On the drive to the port, the black cloud of burning fuel from a rocket-struck oil-storage tank hung over the quayside, smutting our clothes. Fires smouldered across the unloading bays; wrecked cars and shredded shipping containers full of plastic goods yielded a thick white haze of toxic smoke. A couple of IOM[12] volunteers at a desk slowly processed the hundreds of African refugees standing silently in the smoke and blinding sunlight, carrying what remained of their lives on their heads in chequered plastic shopping bags. None of them spoke to each other, and they spoke slowly to our camera in halting French as French jets circled overhead protecting them; the Arab aid workers herded them this way and that like sheep, with impatient shouts and clicks of their fingers.

We dumped our bags on board and waited. The few remaining Indian and Pakistani migrant workers still trapped in Misrata were ushered inside the ship to find sleeping spaces with the European journalists. The Africans were ushered to the outside decks. A Pakistani woman next to me spent the day-long journey wailing endlessly at her unhappy husband, while the Africans outside crouched in

---

12 International Organisation for Migration, an NGO handling the global flow of refugees

silence. I went out on to the deck, and handed out a few cigarettes. They crowded round me, shouting, wanting more than I had; I kept most for myself; my one-man aid mission sputtered into failure as I went back inside.

As night fell, and the thinly clothed Africans on deck huddled together, shivering, we edited footage on a table in the ship's café, with only a porthole separating the warm white journalists from the freezing, black refugees outside. They peered through the window at us for hours as the cold sea wind whipped across them in the dark, pleading with hungry bovine eyes as we ate our hot spaghetti. Eventually I shut the curtain. We reached Benghazi the next afternoon.

BENGHAZI

April/May 2011

Zooming to the Ajdabiya frontline from Benghazi, my driver Saadi turns to me. We're driving at 160 k.p.h., and he's simultaneously pressing on the gas, lighting a cigarette and trying to find his MP3 player on the back seat, but it's OK, we're in the desert. For the past two hours we've been driving through a flat sea of scrubby sand, punctuated by rows of pylons stretching out to oil fields, and herds of camels wandering, wavering, seemingly untended, across the road and endless desert. The road is straight; we're all on autopilot. A few dead camels, casualties of war and black with rot, stick their legs up in the air like dead spiders, or 1950s television aerials, as we drive past. The car is full of tiny, aggressive flies: I'd thrown our gigantic spliff out of the window before the last checkpoint, and a hundred angry sand flies had flown in.

'I fought at the front, you know,' says Saadi, a handsome, stocky nineteen year old. 'You know, my father is a rich man, a professor of medicine? I told him to give me money for two *Kalash* and then I went to the front with my friend.' And then? 'Oh, we stayed a few days and then we left. It was dangerous, you know? For real, people were being killed! So I gave the revolution my guns and went back to Benghazi and became a driver. But you know I'd die for the revolution, right?'

In that sentence was encapsulated the difference between Benghazi and Misrata. Where the Misratans died to procure weapons, the Benghazi rebels traded them on the street for petty cash: no decent home went without an assault rifle or two. While the Misratans hoarded every bullet, and aimed each shot at a precise target, the fighters of Benghazi spunked thousands of glittering bullets into the air almost every night: celebrating victories, celebrating rumours of victories, scaring away portents of defeat like savages would an eclipse, or marking their personal tribal sheikh's entrance to the war. It was hard to avoid, after Misrata, the sense that Benghazi was a city of idiots. Unfortunately, the idiots were running the war.

The frontline, as it happened, was a serious misnomer. By this point, two months into the war, journalists were only allowed a few kilometres past the giant ugly gate Gaddafi had erected as the entrance to Ajdabiya, a hundred and fifty kilometres of empty desert south of Benghazi. Beyond this, a checkpoint stopped us all by a Portacabin where a few rebels, slurping tea from plastic glasses, waved us down. One, maybe seventeen years old, loosely holding on to his machine gun, flicked his long brown hair over his bloodshot eyes and offered us a floppy sarcastic salute. Their middle-aged commander lay on a mattress beside them, beset by flies, picking his feet, swatting his face and yawning as he dozed the long afternoon away. It was hardly a compelling advertisement for Benghazi's thirst for victory.

No matter: if you watched the Libyan War on television, you would have seen this gate. Every TV journalist did a piece to camera there, signing it off as the Ajdabiya frontline. But the fighting, if there was any, was forty kilometres away by now. The only visible casualties of war were the stoned teenage volunteers boiling tea on broken ammunition crates and giggling at the sky. Ajdabiya was a very underwhelming face of war. We managed to get a few kilometres beyond the rest of the press before we were turned back, apologetically, by a special forces unit huddled in an abandoned oil village in the desert, their pick-up trucks sprouting weaponry like fearfully aroused hedgehogs. To soften the blow, they gave me a fistful of hash through the car window. It was very good indeed; but then, this was a very static front.

The reason the rebels wouldn't let us through the gate was that every time a convoy went though, it got shelled. They blamed the journalists; they hadn't considered the fact that all reinforcements immediately reported to the only building for a hundred miles, a deserted oil pumping station marked on every map in the country. Every day the government shelled it, and every day the Benghazi rebels took it as a surprising new affront. They blamed journalists for giving away their position. It was only months after the war that they realised a hastily installed CCTV camera mounted on top of the gate had recorded every single car and truck heading to the front in real time for Gaddafi's hungry artillery. Welcome to Benghazi, the erratically beating heart of Libya's revolution: a city outfought in every battle, whose survival depended on NATO jets, and who presumed to run the war.

With the short-sighted control-freakery of all Arab dictators, Gaddafi had massively restricted journalists' access to Tripoli, so Benghazi happily took up the slack. Misrata was too dangerous of course, at this point, for most television channels, so whatever news came out of Libya came out of Benghazi, generally from the palm-fringed foetid lakeside foreshore of the Hotel Ouzu, where journalists repeated wire stories as if they'd hunted them out themselves and waited desperately for career-advancing movement at the front; but there was no movement, not at this front.

The Benghazi rebels, it quickly transpired, were militarily useless. The only question now was whether they would lose the war before Misrata won it.

Without access to the front, the war, for any journalist sentenced to a Benghazi posting, was a numbing series of press conferences, overly optimistic press releases and long afternoons in the Ouzu's smoke-wreathed lobby, batting away the swarms of fixers who latched upon new white faces, watching Libyans huddle in conspiratorial fugs of smoke and coffee cups full of cigarette butts, plotting their war.

One man, a lushly bearded rebel in his fifties, seemed to stand apart from the Ouzu's revolutionary demi-monde. In his exquisitely pressed American desert fatigues and smartly shaped beret, with a brace of pistols in his belt, he looked like a hard-bitten brigade commander waiting for orders to move his men to the front as he scanned the journalists and politicians around him with serene detachment. One afternoon, woken by the sound of explosions under my bedroom balcony, I saw him lob hand grenades into the shit-brown lake then scoop up the resultant dead fish with a plastic bag on a stick. As he took his spoils of war to the hotel kitchen, I made a mental note to assume nothing about the rebels from their appearance, and to avoid the daily fish course from then on.

———

The problem for the rebels and their foreign backers was that their leadership – the NTC – seemed worryingly inept. If the rebels were to win the war, these were the men, and they were all men, who would have to oversee the transition to democracy, or at the very least stave off anarchy. Mostly minor functionaries under the regime, their internal squabbling and blinking nervousness in front of the world press was woefully apparent. They all wore the nervous sidelong glance of the accidentally over-promoted, as if terrified the cosmic error that had thrust them on to the stage of history would soon be discovered and recti- fied. They would give press conferences claiming that, for example, the Italian government had agreed to send them tanks, only to issue muddled clarifications in the face of the Italians' firm and instant denial that, while the Italians hadn't in fact offered to donate tanks, said tanks (or other heavy weapons) if donated by the Italians (or anyone else) would be very gratefully received.

A note of contempt began to creep into journalists' voices during the nightly press conferences at the Ouzu, where the general theme had evolved into: 'You do realise you guys are fucking this up?' It was beginning to look very much like the West had backed the wrong horse in Libya, particularly after the rebels' chief military commander was abducted and murdered by one of his own brigades in murky circumstances which have never yet been satisfactorily explained. The NTC's pitch to their foreign backers was based on the conceit that they would be able to prevent Libya from sliding into chaos, yet it was now apparent they were unable to provide security even in the capital of their rump statelet. In a city with no effective rule of law, where a Call of Duty-style arsenal of assault rifles and rocket launchers was freely obtainable for anyone with a spare few thousand dinars, the only thing preventing absolute anarchy was the strength of support for the revolution among the civil population. Indeed, the lack of crime was the most remarkable aspect of the entire situation: if Benghazi were London, the city would have been a smouldering ruin by the second week of revolution. True, the situation in Benghazi would darken after the war was won; but by then the world's media would have moved on to other conflicts.

***

One night, a month in, a car bomb exploded on the seafront promenade. When I reached the scene, Libyan journalists were being beaten away from the site with rifle butts by furious rebel fighters. A large crowd had gathered around the wreckage. In any other city in the world, security forces would have established a cordon around the site in case of secondary devices, but this was Benghazi. Instead, a large crowd danced around the mangled car, shouting defiance at the regime. One man placed his toddler on the

ARIS ROUSSINOS

smouldering wreckage and took a photo on his smartphone for posterity. A local ran up and breathlessly informed me that the night before, the dictator's LSE-educated heir apparent, Saif al-Islam, had made a speech on state television promising a nasty surprise for Benghazi. 'And here we are, you see,' the local added, gesturing at the chaos around him. In the narrow side streets leading off the corniche fistfights had broken out between knots of angry locals. Pistol shots cracked worryingly in nearby dark alleyways. I saw a teenage rebel dragged away from a fight with another group of youths by his friends, still shouting at them that he'd just returned from Misrata and they were all fucking cowards who knew nothing about war.

But car bombs aside, Benghazi in the spring was quite a liveable place. The city centre, wrapped around the glittering sea, was largely composed of handsome Italian apartment buildings, long shady colonnades, and derelict municipal buildings. A vast, twin-domed cathedral – once the largest in Africa – loomed over the scene, long-since abandoned. In the general air of revolutionary bonhomie, middle-aged couples strolled up and down the corniche at dusk, haggling over revolutionary tat from the many stalls manned by children selling flags, dummy pistols, and the cap badges of the purportedly elite rebel units. A makeshift open-air museum of captured government helmets and unexploded munitions attracted the curiosity of the city's

92

sightseers. Children clambered over a burned-out tank, its barrel painted in the rebel colours.

Above the idling crowds, the sad-eyed faces of Benghazi's martyrs, Photoshopped into giant posters bright with rebel flags or lurid Alpine backgrounds, peered down from the outside wall of the city's burned-out courthouse, where they hung thickly, like pop stars in a teenager's bedroom. In tents nearby, white-haired men handed out free glasses of bitter tea and discussed the day's news from the front. Every night, while the rebel youth huddled in their desert outposts or, posing with their weapons outside the cafes, tried to catch the eyes of single girls, their fathers would assemble in the main square for the *maghrib*[13] prayer, and the fiery revolutionary speeches given from the pulpit by the local clerics, dressed in their traditional finery of fezzes, embroidered waistcoats and baggy pantaloons. Their wives and daughters clustered like brightly coloured birds in an adjacent plywood enclosure painted with French and British flags, safe from prying eyes. Bright blue fishing caiques bobbed emptily in the fishing port: their Egyptian crews had all fled the war.

———————

To navigate safely in Benghazi, you needed a local expert, a streetwise chancer with access to both the squabbling politicians and the panoply of heavily armed rebel factions

13 Sunset in Arabic

on the ground. But I only had Dawood. He saw me long before I saw him. He was one of the dozens of wannabe fixers who hung around the Ouzu lounge, chain-smoking and eking out a *macchiato* all afternoon, trying to catch a journalist's eye and talk their way into a job. Like an eighteenth-century gentlemen on a Grand Tour of the East, every journalist needed a dragoman to smooth their way through checkpoints, procure permits from the NTC, and translate their fumbling questions into Arabic. The barrier to entering the fixer profession was low: by this stage, a moderate facility with English and a plausible manner were enough.

Dawood needed money; he hadn't worked for weeks after, it transpired, starting a fight with heavily armed rebels at a lonely desert checkpoint, to the distress of the TV crew paying and accompanying him. In many ways Dawood was a sort of anti-fixer, who dangerously escalated the most easily resolved situations, and unerringly irritated the most important rebel military contacts. But when he saw me – pale, unshaven, and mildly shell-shocked from my time in Misrata – wandering around the Ouzu trying to get a WiFi signal, he must have known he'd hit pay dirt.

'Hey, brother,' he rasped, waddling over to my table, 'you are finally here! Jonny told me to look after you, where have you been?' He shook his head in mock concern. 'Jonny and me, we worked together all the time. And now I work with you, yes?' Jonny was my predecessor in Benghazi; Dawood must have seen us together during our brief hand-over, before I went to Misrata. Jonny pointedly didn't hire Dawood, I later discovered. No matter: Dawood sat down, shouted at the barman to bring me a coffee and offered me a cigarette in one fluid motion. Two heads shorter than me, crop-haired and unshaven, Dawood looked like a seedy cherub. He poured his sizeable pot belly into a colourful array of tight, flammable-looking tracksuits; when he grinned, as he did often, he revealed teeth black and warped from a diet of sugary coffee and endless borrowed cigarettes. He'd just turned eighteen, I later learned; he'd been a hotel bellhop before the war offered brief but rapid social advancement. And now he'd made himself my fixer.

A few days later, I was talking to some French security contractors – who, in all their expensive tactical finery, couldn't look more like mercenaries if they tried – in the Ouzu lobby when Dawood waddled over, helped himself to one of my cigarettes and grabbed my laptop to update his Facebook profile. The French looked at him with unalloyed disgust. He was wearing a tight Brazil tracksuit, his paunch straining eagerly to escape its polyester grasp, and they jeered at him openly, asking him if he played much sport, if he considered himself a fit kind of guy. Dawood looked like he was about to cry. 'I hate these fucking French,' he said once they'd left. 'You know they have their own villa in the town? They think it makes them more safe than the hotel.' He shook his head dismissively. 'The town is not more safe.' He had a point.

The French contractors were waiting for their boss, Pierre Marziali, to arrive before trying to secure a military training contract with the NTC. But Marziali was only in Benghazi a couple of hours before the rebels killed him. The forty-seven-year-old Frenchman had served a full twenty-five-year career as a paratrooper before setting up his own private security company, SECOPEX. Like many contractors, he must have seen the Libyan War as a glittering business opportunity. France was the NTC's most active military ally, and the *tricoleur* fluttered gaily, it seemed, from almost every lamppost in the centre of Benghazi in a show of rebel gratitude. He must have felt he knew the risks; his men had already rented an anonymous villa in the city's suburbs for their base, believing it offered greater security than the handful of hotels where all the other Western journalists, spies and hangers-on clustered together. Marziali had been gunned down in his car at a rebel checkpoint. It was an accident; he'd tried to run the barrier and reached for his gun, the rebel spokesmen variously briefed. The rumour amongst Libyans was that he'd been found dead, face down, in a disused cement factory a few miles outside town. Welcome to Benghazi.

In the lobby of the Ouzu Hotel, at his luridly gilded desk, the NTC's spokesman of the day gave me the official version of events. 'It was very sad,' he briefed, 'a terrible accident. The guy who shot him was just a kid manning the checkpoint, he was scared. He saw the guy reaching for his gun – why did he even have a gun here? He didn't have permission for that. A terrible accident, but this is war.' He watched me put away my notepad and pen, then asked me if I wanted the true story. Off the record. Of course, I nodded, and he leaned forward with conspiratorial glee. 'He was a spy. We know he was working for Gaddafi. You know how we know? The French told us, the French security services. They told us to eliminate him for them, so we did. People need to know not to play games with us.' We both knew this was nonsense, but it didn't matter. This was Benghazi, a chaotic wonderland of spies and conspiracy theories, where automatic weapons and hashish were traded openly in the *suq* and everyone had their price.

I suppose all revolutionary strongholds must veer schizo-phrenically between hope and fear: the people of Benghazi had thrown off their hated dictator, and every wall in the city had been daubed with graffiti in the rebel colours of red, black and green; the long seafront corniche was now home to a sort of village fete of brightly coloured tents and stalls selling gimcrack revolutionary tat, all manufactured in Egypt. Men fired celebratory bursts of gunfire into the air constantly, for seemingly little reason. The war was elsewhere, with one hundred and fifty miles of desert between the city and Gaddafi's troops, and NATO patrolling the skies overhead; teenage boys strutted around town at dusk with heavy machine guns dangling from their shoulders, slurping *macchiato* and smoking, checking their heroic-looking reflections in plate-glass café windows. But at the same time, the war was far from won; whenever Gaddafi made a speech, issuing rambling threats against the 'rats' who dared defy his rule, everyone sat staring glumly at the TV screen in silence, thinking, chainsmoking, worrying.

Summer had come. The government still held the eastern oil refineries of Brega and Ras Lanuf and every rebel assault on them had been flung back in chaotic retreat. With no access to oil revenues, the NTC had run out of cash. Wages had been unpaid for two months; the banks were all shut, the city's two or three ATMs weren't working and the cost of food was spiralling. The greatest fear was that Misrata would fall, and then a fickle NATO would quietly divide the country in two. The NTC needed a victory, fast, but compared to Misrata, the Benghazi rebels were lacklustre fighters. NTC spokesmen briefed off the record that they needed to win before jihadi fighters filtered in. 'For now, we have no al-Qaeda here, we look to NATO,' one said, 'but the longer this goes on ... We are gentle people here, moderate people. We don't want al-Qaeda here in Libya, but they are watching us and soon they will come. We need to win quickly, but to win we need weapons, heavy weapons, and we need them now.'

At a press conference, blinking in the camera lights, the NTC's spokesman rattled off a long shopping list of heavy weaponry he expected the West to gift the rebels: 'long-range missiles, tanks ... basically, you know, the game-changing weapons, the kind of weapons we need to take the fight to Gaddafi.' Do you honestly think NATO countries have stocks of heavy weapons just lying spare to hand out to you? I asked. And even if they did, do you really think they'd give them to you? And you do realise that these are complex weapons that take trained soldiers months to learn how to use? How long will it take your men, who are essentially untrained civilians, to use them without being a danger to themselves and to civilians in the conflict zone? He gave me a wounded look. 'Well, you know, if you have time to learn, it takes time. But we need them now, so we'll just learn quickly.'

In the meantime, the rebels made do with what they had. Dawood took us out to a barracks on the city's outskirts where engineers were sawing and welding away at mangled weapons, salvaged from the wreckage of NATO airstrikes, trying to return them all to use in a sort of lethal Scrapheap

Challenge. Mechanics in greasy overalls bashed away, clanging at rusty rocket launchers and anti-aircraft guns, ironing out kinks and welding them on to the back of technicals. The most impressive weapons, in a Mad Max way, were the pod-like multiple rocket launchers snaffled from grounded helicopters that they were bolting on to Toyota Land Cruisers: they looked like a child's fantasy of a weapon of war, but they worked, in a wildly inaccurate but terrifying-sounding way. The Land Cruisers were all painted with a sandy leopard-print camouflage to merge with the desert scrub; watching a line of them queueing up for fuel at a civilian petrol station before zooming off to the front, bristling with anti-aircraft and machine guns, was an impressive sight.

Military discipline, such as it was, was markedly less impressive. The barracks looked like a rubbish dump, with tins of spoiled food surrounded by flies piled everywhere, and discarded uniforms scattered in worryingly human poses behind bushes and outhouses as if their occupants had been suddenly vaporised. I saw one rebel furiously puffing away on a cigarette while perched upon a pile of long grey wooden crates. According to the stencilled lettering on their sides, they contained 'Parts of Tractor' and 'Digging Equipment', assembled in North Korea before delivery to Tripoli. What's inside? I asked the rebel. Dunno, he shrugged, and hopped off to open one. As he prised open the creaking lid, he leaned in curiously, spilling hot ash on what turned out to be 107mm rocket warheads. 'Rocket,' he said cheerfully as I slowly backed away.

In an office building within the compound, I was trying to charm a colonel into giving me access to the weapons workshop when a private walked in without saluting, flopped into the armchair next to me and took a cigarette and lighter from the commander's desktop packet. He lit up, tossed the lighter back on the desk and enumerated a long list of demands for the colonel, counting them off one by one on his fingers. The colonel angrily waved him away. As the rebel wandered out, I turned my gaze back to the officer in amazement, and he said, 'It's OK, he is my son.' He sighed. 'So, the weapons workshop. I am colonel here, in the infantry barracks, but not in the workshop next door. For me, I am happy to let you inside, but the officer in charge there says you must come back tomorrow.' For what reason? I asked. 'There is no reason.' Is he a colonel too? I asked. The officer narrowed his eyes and pinched his forefinger and thumb in front of him. 'A colonel? No. He is an insect.'

On the parade ground outside, a company of newly minted soldiers in mismatched uniforms scrunched and scraped smartly on the hot gravel as they practised for their passing out parade the next day. Within hours of the parade's end they'd be at the front a short drive away, using their weapons against the government for the first time. For all their slovenliness and indiscipline, it was impossible not to admire them, and to wish them a swift and overwhelming victory.

The first thing the Benghazi rebels had done at the outbreak of the war was to remove the placards and posters of Gaddafi's face that loomed down from every billboard in the city, instantly replacing them with spray-painted revolutionary graffiti and, ironically, caricatures of Gaddafi's face, only this time as a *kippah*[14]-wearing, sidelocked Jew with blood dripping from his fangs and a Star of David on his forehead. Considering the ubiquity of this image, it was remarkable how infrequently it appeared on the news back in the West, no doubt because it would complicate the story unnecessarily. In the rebels' media centre, a burned-out shell of a building that was once the regime courthouse, where smiling young volunteers smoothed the path of newly arrived journalists, printing them shiny FREE LIBYA press cards and arranging their passage to Misrata, I stole an A4 booklet of media-friendly buzzwords for the volunteers. Don't say *shahids*[15], it said, say martyrs or victims; don't say Jews, say Zionists or Israel, or better yet don't talk about them at all.

14 Jewish skullcap
15 Martyrs

The booklet had been printed by a Qatar-based PR consultancy whose man in Benghazi, Patrick, was often to be seen in the Ouzu coaching NTC figures in how to spin their war in the most unthreatening and reasonable-sounding terms. Benghazi was Qatar's pet project: a tiny pinprick in the Persian Gulf, and the richest country in the world, the island monarchy was funding the NTC, training rebel fighters, paying for twenty-four-hour rebel TV news channels and doing all it could to unseat Gaddafi. Its Al Jazeera satellite channel stoked the flames of Arab revolution abroad, while remaining silent on the feudal autocracy at home whose petrodollars funded it all; its zigzag flag, along with the French *tricoleur* and, very occasionally, the Union Jack, hung everywhere. France and Britain were slowly ramping up their involvement, and Cameron dispatched a few dozen British Army officers, specialists in logistics and communications, to Benghazi on a semi-secret mission. Secret except to everyone in Benghazi, that is. Every taxi driver in the city talked about 'the British hotel', El Fadeel, that had been taken over for the course of the war by UK PLC; from time to time, you'd see British officers jogging along the seashore in their army-issue green PT shirts and blue shorts, sweat dripping from their Oakleys, or milling around the corniche in polo shirts and cargo shorts, buying rebel tat, surrounded by a score of plain-clothes Libyan heavies.

A security contractor for a wire service I met in another city later on told me a story: he was wandering around Benghazi when he met a colleague, still serving in the SAS. After the customary pleasantries, he asked what his old buddy was up to in Benghazi. It's a funny story, his mate said. Every night we have to mask up and go on raids in the suburbs looking for Gaddafi loyalists. And what happens when you find them? asked the contractor. A shrug. We hand them to the rebels, and it's not our problem after that.

Mere rumours, of course, but this was Benghazi. The entire city lived on rumours, cigarettes and the sound of gunfire.

———————

One day, Benghazi's hazy afternoon slumber was shattered by the thump and crack of rockets and heavy machine-gun fire from downtown. Dawood rushed to my room and banged on my door. 'Brother, let's go into town – the Agouri are here!' The Agouri, it transpired, were the dominant tribe in suburban Benghazi, and the night before Gaddafi had made a speech on state television claiming that they supported him and would soon retake the city on his behalf. In their quixotic Libyan way, the Agouri now flooded the town en masse in their gun trucks in a show of force and loyalty to the revolution. Warriors on horseback cantered along the seafront boulevard, waving their rifles in the air and whooping, while others of their tribe fired long bursts into the middle distance from the machine guns mounted on their pick-up trucks. Some waved French *tricoleurs* or revolutionary flags, others home-made placards saying GAME OVER and SAVE MISRATA; most just waved their Kalashnikovs or fired them in the air in a constant deafening fusillade of defiance. One man standing on the roof of a moving minibus emptied his AK magazine without aiming, peppering the stucco façade of an Italian-era apartment block with bullets and showering me in plaster dust. All the while, uniformed traffic cops watched the wild parade of whooping tooled-up warriors with utter helplessness, shaking their heads. It was clearly going to be difficult to put this genie back in the bottle once the war was over.

It's an impressive sight, I told Dawood. 'Yeah, sure,' he shrugged, 'but Benghazi is built on the Agouri land. What happens when they want it back?' Seeing our camera, a tribal elder in a turban and camouflage fatigues corralled his braves into a Bedu war dance in front of us, rhythmically clapping and chanting in a circle, while he fired his AK into the air over their heads. 'Gaddafi says the Agouri are with him,' one told me in French. 'But look! I am Agouri, he is Agouri, all these men are Agouri. One hundred per cent.' He beamed at me, exultant at the deafening roar of automatic fire all around us, at the sheer heart-stopping thrill of war and revolution. I grinned back, my heart pounding with joy. One man stepped close and fired his rifle in the air above my head, emptying his magazine in one long burst and scattering hot brass over my face and shirt while I laughed manically under this warlike Libyan cumshot.

It was easy to mock the eastern Libyans for their celebratory waste of precious ammunition, and with Misratans I often did. But for the first time I felt the power of such a joyous fusillade, the magical ability of gunfire to lift a fighter's spirit. It's difficult, perhaps impossible, to explain, unless you've seen it. But in the middle of a war they were losing, this show of tribal firepower had revived their spirits, rebooting their self-esteem as warriors and as men. If morale can be bought so efficiently at the cost of just a few crates of ammunition, then however unsoldierly it all looks to Western eyes, such extravagant displays are a perfectly valid tool of war.

For all Dawood's many faults as a fixer and as a person, he had an encyclopaedic knowledge of the tangled tribal hierarchies that made up Cyrenaica's social system. He could rattle off without thinking the long lists of tribes that were feuding with each other, or which had buried feuds for the sake of the revolution, which sub-tribe claimed descent from whom, and which had treacherously switched alliance in some dim ancestral desert past. In a country with no effective government, and whose pre-Gaddafi political system was based entirely on tribal affiliation, it seemed likely that the tribal system would receive a sudden boost from the revolution. Gaddafi had threatened to unleash tribal warriors on Misrata after his troops pulled out from the city centre, to the clucking concern of instant experts back in London, and after the sudden sprouting of a vast billboard on a central Benghazi roundabout, which showed a photo of a turbaned Bedu wielding an axe and shotgun above the unconvincing slogan 'There is no tribalism in free Libya!', the tribal system clearly deserved further study, so the day after the Agouri demonstration, we took a car east into the Jebel Akhdar – the Green Mountain – the long lush range of hills overlooking the sea to the north and the desert to the south, in search of Dawood's uncle, a tribal chief.

The Jebel Akhdar is, in fact, a high plateau rather than a craggy mountain range, and its gentle, European-looking landscape, lush with poppies and tall grass and buttercups, is the heartland of Libya's Bedu tribal system. When the Italians invaded Libya, they turfed the local tribes out of the Jebel and established model farms and Puglian-looking villages for their army of peasant colonists. Their abandoned farmhouses, sturdy and handsome-looking, could still be seen, surrounded by apple orchards on the Jebel's slopes, fenced off by crumbling drystone walls and lowing herds of alpine cattle. Turning into the gentle fold of the Marj plain, in a landscape of young wheat and oak trees that looked impossibly like Dorset, we arrived at the uncle's compound.

I'd half hoped, despite myself, for a fearsome desert prince in a camelhair tent, and was instead greeted by a perfect country squire, surrounded by grandchildren, sitting in the shade of his apple tree. It wouldn't have been odd to see him wrestling with the *Telegraph* crossword, I thought. He shook our hands with a firm grip and offered to kill a sheep to welcome us; I demurred Englishly, assuming I was meant to, saying oh, really, there's no need. He looked hurt. We were ushered into his *majlis*, a long cool room lined with divans, where we sat cross-legged and drank Turkish coffee as I asked him if the revival of Libya's tribal system wouldn't destabilise the country.

He spread his hands in an expansive, dismissive shrug. 'How was Libya before Gaddafi? It was a very fertile land, with people of high morals. There was no civil war, no tribal conflict. We had a very stable independent country, with democratic government.' He shrugged again, gesturing at a tired-looking man in his fifties sitting on the banquette opposite. 'Look at this man here. He is from a different tribe, but we are friends. He and his family have been staying here since the beginning of the war as my guests. My house is his. This is the true Libya.'

The other man nodded sadly. 'I am from Brega, I am an oil engineer. But my home is taken by Gaddafi now.' He looked like he was about to cry.

'You will be home soon,' I said. 'And until then, look around you,' I added, gesturing at the trees outside and the gentle trill of birdsong. 'There are worse places to be.' He smiled sadly, and I felt a terrible dick.

We ate a hearty lunch of spicy mutton pasta from a communal bowl and then Dawood and I followed the chief's grandson to the pastures outside, to graze the family's flock of sheep in a wildflower meadow shaded by tall pine trees. His grandson was about ten years old, and shepherded his flock this way and that with shrill cries and jabs of his crook. Fat bumblebees ambled from flower to flower across the meadow as we basked in the cool upland sun.

A tall African ran towards us waving his stick until Dawood shooed him away with an angry shout. 'Stupid Sudanese,' Dawood rasped. 'He tells the boy not to scare the sheep but his grandfather *owns* all the sheep, and the Sudanese. Blacks are not intelligent people. Here in Libya we say they have a quarter of a mind. This sounds racist, but I'm not a racist. All my friends are blacks. But they are not intelligent people like us. They just pretend they are gangsters and robbers. And when they make money, they spend it all on good clothes and expensive cars.' He sighed exasperatedly. 'Give me a cigarette, brother, I am angry now.'

We left Dawood's uncle, stuffed with good food and sated with sunlight and strong coffee, after shaking hands firmly and promising we'd be back, and that next time we'd stay for a few days and accept the offer of a roasted sheep. Our car dawdled down winding country lanes shaded by poplars and tall hedgerows, to the flatlands of the coast. We had an appointment in the village of Tocra with the sheikh of the Al Arafa tribe, a pensioner promoted by the revolution from a position of rural obscurity to one of military command.

When Gaddafi's troops fled the east, harried by Bedu insurgents all the way, the regime's network of rural guard-posts and barrack blocks swiftly found themselves converted into the headquarters of rural militias like that of the Al Arafa. The blockhouse at which we had arranged to meet was empty when we arrived, and I killed time at the ancient Greek seaport of Tocris a few hundred metres away, examining shards of ceramic wine cups and amphora handles from the unguarded site as blue waves lapped lazily under the fierce sun. Greece seemed so close, a bare day's sail north of this quiet village.

Eventually the emissary found us and told us to hurry up, because the sheikh was waiting. He had been at home, instructing his womenfolk to cook us up a feast. The emissary, a late-middle-aged farmer, stroked his long white beard nervously when he saw our camera and earnestly told us to ignore his facial hair. 'You Europeans, when you see our beards,' he said, 'you think we are all al-Qaeda, all Hezbollah. But there are good men with beards and good men without, and bad men who wear beards also. It is an Arab thing, not a religious thing.' I assured him I generally wore a beard, when I wasn't onscreen. He shook his head, smiling, as if I was a silly child trying to impress. The sheikh was waiting on a chair outside the blockhouse, wearing his Ottoman-looking tribal finery and cradling an olivewood staff.

After the customary enquiries into each other's health, he began to assure us of his unimportance in the scheme of things. 'Sure, all thanks be to God, I am the head of the revolutionary committee in this area. But it was the young men who appointed me. When the regime fled, things were unstable and we needed order here. Because I am the elder, and the leader of my tribe, I command things here now.' Is your loyalty to your tribe, or to the revolution? I asked.

'What is a tribe? It is simply a matter of shared ancestry, of kinship. It is a social institution, not a political grouping. And that is all.' He shrugged regally.

———————

On the way back to Benghazi, we stopped at the country town of Marj, where tractors from across the surrounding plain lurched around the dusty streets. The town is the site of Libya's largest mosque, a vast pseudo-Mameluke structure that then featured on the country's banknotes. When was it built? I asked the sheikh's emissary. 'It was finished in the nineteen seventies, I think.' So Gaddafi did some good things then? He fixed me with an angry stare. 'But the idea was the king's.'

There was a modest undertow of monarchist feeling in Cyrenaica, most notably stoked by a wealthy businessman of Cretan origin, who possessed his own TV channel on which to expound his political ideas. In a few villages north of Benghazi, communities of Cretan Muslims, refugees from the revolution of the 1860s, lived quiet lives producing olive oil, intermarrying, and preserving their traditional dances and blond beards along this alien coast. Monarchist sentiment was as much a minority endeavour as Greekness, however; for the most part, a spirit of revolutionary communalism was the order of the day in Benghazi, with the rarely expressed understanding that in the new Libya, Cyrenaica would be an autonomous, tribally organised, Bedu statelet once again.

Until then, everyone pulled together for the revolution. Boy scouts with gleaming whistles marshalled cars at the infuriatingly slow digital-countdown traffic lights of Gaddafi's devising, or picked up litter from the city's dusty roadside verges. Women volunteers in bright hijabs swept the streets, and any foreign journalist walking the city's streets would suddenly find a cluster of local cars swerve to the side of the road beside them, their drivers clamouring to give them a free ride.

In the Qala restauarant at the edge of town, a local businessman had organised a platoon of volunteers to cook food for the fighters at the front, delivering the foil cartons of couscous and meat to the lonely desert checkpoints twice a day. He proudly took me to the courtyard where, under gaily coloured Bedu awnings, a handful of black women stirred vast cauldrons of mutton sauce and couscous. 'We make fourteen thousand five hundred meals a day,' he said proudly, 'lunch and dinner, twice a day, at a daily cost of twelve and a half thousand dinars. We are all volunteers here, and all the money comes from donations from local businessmen.' The city's notables were clubbing together for the revolution, to provide the troops with the necessary sustenance the NTC couldn't afford to give them, and the taste of home that proved their city cared for them. Inside the air-conditioned restaurant, beneath a plasma screen blaring out Al Jazeera Arabic's updates on the war, a dozen men in their twenties packaged the food in an efficient assembly line, singing the Benghazi FC song that had become a revolutionary anthem.

We followed the lunchtime food delivery to the Ajdabiya gate a hundred and fifty miles away in the desert, stopping every few miles to drop off food and radioactive-looking bottles of fizzy drink at the checkpoints dotted along the only road. At one roadblock, marked by a ram's skull on a stick, the bored rebels manning the anti-aircraft gun asked where my newly arrived cameraman and I were from. England, I said, and France. They shook my cameraman's hand eagerly, giving him a thumbs up, saying, 'Franzia number one! Sarkozy very good.' And England? I asked. They shrugged. 'England OK.' But one wandered off into the cinderblock guardhouse behind, returning with a Second World War vintage Lee Enfield No. 4 rifle. 'English *bundiga*, very good,' he said, 'very long shoot this gun.' Perhaps some forebear had looted it from the battles that had raged back and forth across Cyrenaica seventy years before and stored it for just such an eventuality. I'd seen other rebels promenading up and down the Benghazi seafront with such ancient relics of war, Webley revolvers and German Lugers tucked showily into their belts, even a Sten gun whose owner tried to convince me it was a brand new Beretta sub-machine gun. No doubt in seventy or a hundred years' time, the revolution's lovingly stored Kalashnikovs will be dug out for some future period of Libyan instability.

At the Ajdabiya gate, as we dished out the food, a bearded rebel in a cowboy hat again prevented us from heading down the heat-hazed road towards the front. He took the lid off his carton and sniffed the tepid couscous suspiciously. Can you eat some, for the camera? I asked. 'I've already had lunch,' he said, 'I'm not hungry. And it's too hot now.' Well, I need you to, for my film, I said, for the revolution. He ate a few spoonfuls of dry couscous with visible distaste before washing it down with long glugs of fizzy orange drink. It was a poor sort of revenge.

One night a week later, after I'd sent my package off to Tehran and spent the next few hours smoking hash with Dawood and the Egyptian satellite engineers, listening to 1990s hip-hop in their hotel suite, I went back to my room to chill. I lay on my bed, listening to the nightly chorus of rifle fire across the lake from downtown. Tonight it seemed more intense, I thought, blaming the hash. It sounded like every rifle and machine gun in Benghazi was being fired all at once. The loud crump of RPG fire sent me to the balcony where I could see, across the black shimmering water, a sky lit up by tracer fire and the flashes of explosions. The guards in the car park below were crouching behind low walls, filling AK magazines and scanning the horizon. One saw me and shouted at me to get back inside. This was something different. Shit was going down in Benghazi.

An urgent hammering on my door announced the arrival of Dawood, white-faced and red-eyed. 'Brother, this is not good,' he mumbled, still stoned, 'I think now he has come back to Benghazi.' I sent Dawood to work out what was going on while I woke up my cameraman. Journalists from other networks were wandering around the hallways in full body armour, calling their bases and making plans. Dawood grabbed me and told me he had a car ready to take us downtown. 'It's OK, brother,' he smiled sheepishly, 'it is only happy shooting. The devil's son is dead, killed by NATO.' By now, the rolling news channels were reporting that a NATO airstrike on Gaddafi's fortified Bab al-Azizia complex in Tripoli had killed the dictator's sixth son Saif al-Arab, along with a handful of his young nieces and nephews.

Saif al-Arab was no great asset to the regime, and had no real military or political function in the prosecution of the war. The louchest of Gaddafi's many louche playboy princelings, Saif al-Arab was notorious for his run-ins with the police in Germany, with a long charge sheet of arrests for domestic abuse, drugs and weapons possession during his time at Munich University. But if he was low-hanging fruit for NATO, his obliteration in his sleep marked a new phase of the war for the Western alliance. The campaign of airstrikes against military targets was proceeding less effectively than NATO had hoped; now, clearly, it had begun to target regime figures directly, in a decapitation strategy that went well beyond the UN resolution authorising the war, and which seemed to indicate a sense of growing desperation back in Brussels.

But for Benghazi it was time to celebrate, and celebrate they did. The streets of the city were filled with a throng of revellers, almost all of them armed, and almost all of them blatting dangerous quantities of lead into the air. Men wandered around firing their AKs one-handed into the air in long bursts, huddling together in circles, clapping hands in furious Bedu war dances, and generally celebrating the dictator's loss. Infants waved pistols in the air from their perches on their fathers' shoulders; revellers unnervingly thrust hand grenades or bayonets into our car window as we drove slowly past the throng; one idiot pointed his pistol at my head at point-blank range to illustrate what he intended to do to Gaddafi. Processions of cars honked past with teenagers sitting on the roofs and bonnets, waving pistols and huge French flags and firing AKs into the air, like a dystopian Marseilles celebrating a French World Cup win. Benghazi was partying as only Benghazi could.

I spoke to one ordinary-looking family milling around enjoying the festivities with their small children as if at a fairground, except the men all dangled Kalashnikovs at their side like umbrellas. The father, a jovial-looking man with a grey moustache, explained the mood for me. 'We are very happy, very happy to see his family die one by one, and after that we would like to see him.' His wife, a cheery-faced woman in a hijab, leaned in to enumerate her personal hit list. 'But the last one Gaddafi. First one Aisha,

after Aisha Saif, then Saadi, and the last one Gaddafi.'
She smiled winningly, pretty much the first Libyan woman
I'd spoken to in a month in the country. I wondered if
Gaddafi was watching all this, if he now realised how much
his people hated him and his entire family and wished the
whole Gaddafi clan a sudden violent death.

One skinny young guy in jeans standing beside me fired
a long burst from a machine gun that had clearly been
wrenched off a tank but was now hanging from his neck
by a thick webbing belt. The gun wasn't designed to be
fired like this, and the recoil threw him on to his back still
firing a long dangerous burst of tracer all around him, like
he was wrestling a giant fiery snake and losing. A grinning
guy in a beanie hat came up to me, saying, 'I'm very happy,
very happy one son Gaddafi today – this night! – die, for
God. Thank you, God,' he added, looking heavenward
and saluting. *Thank you, God or Thank you, NATO?* 'Thank
you, NATO. Thank you, God. Thank you, people Libya!'

Only the night before, Gaddafi had made a typically
rambling speech on state television, alternately conciliatory
and threatening. But he had held out the prospect of a
truce, a sign of his growing desperation. With the front-
lines mired in stalemate, and the NATO air campaign less
effective than any of the rebels had hoped, it had looked
as if a negotiated settlement could be reached. But this
one air strike at the heart of the regime had revived the

rebels' will to fight and win. I asked the crowds around me how long the war would last now. One day, two days, they said, three weeks at most. One man, a gentle-voiced poet I knew from the Ouzu, approached me through the bustle. With his white hair and tweed jacket, he looked a world apart from the hundreds of youths shooting recklessly into the air around us. Is this a victory, I asked him, or is it revenge? He smiled sadly. 'It's a victory, let's call it a victory.' A burst of nearby machine-gun fire made us both duck. For now, this meagre jab at inflicting pain on their hated dictator was all Benghazi's people had to celebrate. It would have to do.

DAFNIYA

July 2011

It was still dark when the Islamists arrested us as spies. After a day-long drive across the desert from Cairo, we were only an hour from Benghazi and sleep when we hit their checkpoint. At the entrance to Tubruq, their pick-up trucks mounted with heavy machine guns sprawled across the road, their yellow beacons blinking on and off in the black night. Straggly-bearded men in Afghan-style *shalwar kameez*[16] and camouflage webbing waved us on to the sand beside the road with their rifles, then took our passports and car keys. They were distinctly unfriendly, and I began to regret my Israeli passport stamp and the bottle of whisky secreted in the boot.

The cells were full in the small jail they controlled, so they gave me a white plastic chair and plonked me in

---

16 Afghan/Pakistani-style men's dress

front of their curious captives. The other detainees stared sadly out from behind bars, one giggling coquettishly and blowing kisses at me. Who are these people, I asked the commander who'd arrested me, Gaddafi loyalists? 'No, no,' he said, 'drunks, men who make sex with other men, just ordinary criminals. We keep the spies in a special place.' The interrogation, such as it was, was perfectly amicable, circling over and over again around the Israeli passport stamp. The commander told me he'd captured over a dozen Egyptian and Israeli spies in the past two weeks. I nodded with faux-conviction, emphasising this was all a mix up, that no one was at fault, we were both reasonable men, and that I was sure we'd soon straighten it all out. After a couple of hours my driver managed to rouse the NTC's press spokesman and handed his mobile phone to the commander, who flinched as he received a shouted torrent of London-accented abuse down the earpiece.

When the call was over he handed the phone back to my driver. 'He says you're a journalist, so I'll have to let you go,' he said in a sad quiet voice. 'But no spying, OK?' Hand on heart, I gave him my word, and he sighed, and ordered a wild-looking minion to hand me some hot soup and a chunk of crusty bread. The other detainees stared enviously as we ate together in awkward silence. It was a typically eccentric welcome back to Free Libya.

In my month away from here, sitting in London avidly watching the war continue on TV, the war had sputtered on unconvincingly, the eastern rebels still beaten back at every faltering advance, the western rebels making slow gains in the countryside, and Gaddafi firmly ensconced in Tripoli and the central desert belt around his hometown of Sirte. Ramadan was coming soon and the rebels had hoped to celebrate Eid in Tripoli. It seemed an unlikely prospect. By now, the talk in Western capitals was of a negotiated settlement, and partition of the country. To convince NATO to continue its air campaign, the rebels needed a sudden military success, and my guess was the push would come from Misrata. Sources within the NTC had told me that Benghazi was sending droves of volunteers and stockpiles of heavy equipment there on civilian ferries, in an attempt to effect a sudden Blitzkrieg on the coastal road to Tripoli. I wanted to be a witness when it happened, and I wanted to discover what control – if any – the politicians in Benghazi still had over the fragile rebel alliance.

———

In Benghazi, I arranged an interview with the rebels' military spokesman, Colonel Ahmed Bani, at the NTC's secret military headquarters in a deserted holiday village on the coast. Bani's minutely detailed directions were superfluous, as – like every taxi driver in Benghazi – our driver knew precisely where the secret headquarters were located. After promising not to film the building, the car park or the local area, we were escorted into an air-conditioned office where Bani sat at a gigantic desk with a plastic photo album placed squarely in front of him. He asked for my business card; I apologised for not having one; his face crumpled. Opening the photo album, he began to leaf through his collection of business cards donated by previous visiting journalists. He extracted his favourites and showed them to me. 'CNN have interviewed me, see? And Al Jazeera, and the BBC and the *Wall Street Journal*.' I assured Bani he was a very important man and he slammed the album shut purposefully. 'Let us begin,' he said.

Bani was something of a cult figure amongst Benghazi-based journalists. We all called him Bunny or Bunnykins, with ironic affection, and traded stories of some of his more self-important quotes. A fighter pilot who had defected to the rebel cause at the very beginning of the revolution, Bani's collection of exquisitely pressed camouflage uniforms, invariably topped with an RAF-style side cap, belied the fact that he commanded an entirely non-existent rebel air force. The Benghazi rebels had shot down their only fighter jet by mistake a few months earlier on its first mission, killing his best friend. So instead of leading thrilling aerial duels against government jets, Bani's role in the revolution was to provide updates on the progress of the war to the foreign press, in his trademark elaborate oratory that never quite crystallised into a confirmed fact or a usable quote.

I asked him why the NTC had banned journalists from the desert Brega front. 'I cannot take you to the frontline in case they shoot us or shell us with Grad missiles,' he said, pointing at me. 'You will lose your life and I will feel ashamed, you know?' But the rebels in Misrata and the Western Mountains let journalists see the fighting, I said. He shrugged dismissively. It was hard to escape the conclusion that the eastern rebels were ashamed of their utter lack of progress. More than ever, the supposed rebel capital of Benghazi seemed an irrelevance in this war, with little or no leadership role at all in the bitter conflict being waged hundreds of miles away to the west.

I asked Bani about the level of co-ordination between the western rebels and Benghazi. 'We have excellent co-ordination, but strategically, you know, if you are fighting in the Nafusa Mountains you don't need to wait for my orders here in Benghazi as a leader. You have the right to make the decision in that moment and then inform me.' Are the advances in the west being co-ordinated with NATO? 'No, I don't think so,' he said, shaking his head. 'No. They do their job and we do our job.' Where will the advance on Tripoli come from then – from the Western Mountains, or from Misrata, or from Benghazi? 'We will attack him from the mountains and from the sea, and from the air and from under the ground,' he said. 'From everywhere we will attack him.' Yes, but from where precisely? He looked startled. 'But I have just answered that question.' Well, what will happen when Gaddafi falls or is killed? Who will establish security in Tripoli – the NTC or the fighters in the west? Bani shrugged, waving his hand dismissively. 'Let him die first, then we'll see.'

I'd lost patience with Benghazi. The NTC leadership appeared utterly inept, had no apparent control over the progress of the war, and seemed to exist only as an endless series of balding men in Italian suits giving dull press conferences to a dwindling and increasingly sarcastic press corps. With the eastern front firmly locked away, many journalists had already fled to the Western Mountains or Misrata in search of stories, and I went to join them.

The days of free boat trips were long gone; now Misrata's survival seemed certain, the revolution had been monetised, and it took hours of haggling with the representative of Huddud Logistics at Benghazi port to secure exorbitantly priced floor space on the next ferry to Misrata, crammed in with returning refugees and young Benghazi volunteers with a thirst for decent action. Rebels loaded trucks covered with tarpaulins on to the ship's rear ramp, shouting at us not to film. Ethically – and legally – transporting weapons on a ship crammed with civilians and journalists was a highly dubious enterprise, but this was Benghazi after all. As soon as their munitions haul was safely onboard they started waving at us to film again, the need for operational security vying with the Libyan compulsion to be helpful to foreign guests. The journalists clustered together in what was once the restaurant, swapping gossip about colleagues and comparing pay rates; teenage fighters in Chelsea shirts and combats milled about smoking, or compelling passing cameramen to film their V for Victory signs, or re-enacted Leonardo di Caprio's splayed arms from *Titanic* on the prow as we sliced through the lapis-blue sea. In the café I got chatting to Ahmed, a young Misratan footballer, over bad coffee. His best friend, a professional footballer for Misrata FC, had been killed a few days before, and had appeared to him in a dream at the moment of death, he said. 'His face was white and his eyes were shining,' Ahmed said with a blissful smile, 'so I know he is in heaven with the other martyrs. Now I hope to join him soon.'

As we neared Misrata, a plummy English voice squawked instructions over the bridge radio as NATO warships guided us in. A school of dolphins joined us, leaping in turn through the ship's wash as the rebels on the deck sang and clapped them on, cheering as each dolphin broke through the surf. The men were young and free and happy that they were going to war. Children on board waved rebel flags at the armed technicals along the dockside and the rebels onshore honked their horns in response. It felt like coming home.

The carefree days of the siege seemed long ago. Now journalists were scrutinised carefully by the Misrata Media Committee on arrival, who used the city's sole internet connection to Google their work before deciding whether or not to allow them to stay. Now the city was relatively safe, Misrata had become a playground for freelancers and the odd human flotsam that collects in any war zone. One American freelancer who styled himself a medical expert had won the Misrata rebels' enmity by shinning up a front-line telegraph pole with a GoPro camera attached to his helmet, drawing government artillery fire that wounded a number of rebels and saw journalists temporarily banned from the front. He later acquired a sniper rifle and joined in the action, to the universal disgust of every other journalist. The only way to see combat now was to attach yourself to a powerful commander with enough clout to face down the soldiers manning the checkpoints.

Like everywhere else in rebel Libya, any businessman with enough cash could set himself up as a commander, buying cars and weapons and paying men to join his own personal brigade. With one hundred and twenty odd *katibas* at the front, Misrata was fielding 30,000 fighters against Gaddafi, a force three times the size of Britain's commitment to the Afghan War drawn from a city the size of Norwich. Any male of fighting age was at the front, it seemed. A few months earlier, these men had been civilians with weapons; now they were an army, disciplined and committed to the fight, their rifle sights uniformly set – like those of Western armies in warfare like this – to three hundred metres, their weapons carefully oiled and maintained, their individual sectors in the trenches delineated with military precision.

I joined up with the al-Ghabra brigade, a tiny unit of eighty men, mostly mechanics, funded and commanded by Sadiq al-Fitouri, a bear-like businessman in his fifties. By Misrata standards, al-Ghabra was small fry. The largest brigades, al-Marsa 1 and al-Marsa 2, were owned by a dairy magnate who kept his men at the front well supplied with ammunition and ice cream and whose units straddled the strategic highway to Tripoli. Each brigade had its own unique character: the notoriously combative fighters of the al-Shahid or Martyrs battalion were mostly English students from Misrata University, who wrote poetry in the trenches and published their own newspaper – written in markedly Dickensian English – in their downtime. But al-Ghabra were working-class kids, mostly drawn from the Fitouri tribe, who liked a joke, did the best they could with their meagre supplies, and had been allotted a dangerous stretch of the trench lines a few hundred metres south of the Tripoli highway. They welcomed us straight away, emphasising that journalists had so far ignored their struggle and high casualty rate. After a lunch of mutton pasta and hot green peppers, Commander Sadiq outlined the progress of his personal war as he drove us to the front in his SUV, the seats still wrapped in clear plastic.

'We began in the first days of the revolution,' he said, stroking his grey beard, 'fighting in Tripoli Street. I swear by God, we had nothing, just a few rifles and shotguns, but God gave us victory. We had no name at first, but then we called ourselves after this guy – he was one of my group, his name was Mohammed Shaush, and his nickname was al-Ghabra.' Sadiq tapped the photo sticker of al-Ghabra's face on the windscreen as he drove. 'He was the best guy. Once I was telling him to shoot and he replied that there were lots of women, lots of children, so he didn't want to shoot. A tank shot him into two pieces, completely into two pieces,' Sadiq said, shaking his head slowly. 'He was the first one of my men to be killed. It is a very bad situation. We started fighting in central Misrata all the way up to this place, and we will continue up to Tripoli and Bab al-Azizia, and for sure we will capture Gaddafi. And then we will put him in a rope, by his neck. Yeah, for sure.'

Sadiq's car careered down the dusty track, shaded on both sides by long lines of poplars. All around us, vast olive groves spread out to the horizon, songbirds burbling from their branches. This stunning countryside was once the personal fiefdom of Count Balbo, Italy's richest man, who had laid out this vast estate for his tenant farmers in a simulacrum of Sicily, here in Libya. For forty long kilometres, Misrata's fighters had pushed uphill with only these thinly spaced trees for cover, taking on tanks and armoured personnel carriers with rifles and light machine guns, and winning. The burned-out husk of a radar station stood on an escarpment to our right. 'NATO bombed this,' said Sadiq. 'It's a very old design, nineteen fifties or sixties, completely useless, but NATO bombed it. They don't bomb Gaddafi's soldiers when we ask them, but they bomb this junk. I don't understand NATO.'

He drove the car directly over an unexploded mortar bomb wedged in the middle of the road, which fortunately didn't explode, and turned down a narrow lane up to an unfinished concrete villa, the sort you'd see in the Corfu countryside, surrounded by a shady garden of fig and lemon trees. A rebel was washing his face and neck at an outdoor tap; others were tinkering with anti-aircraft guns, clanking them with spanners, or curled up sleeping on the marble-tiled veranda. The sound of Arabic pop music warbled out from the shady kitchen where a bearded cook fussed around crates of fresh tomatoes, rice, onions and parsley. Next to the food were stacked rifles, an RPG launcher and a few meagre crates of ammunition, dated older than me.

'This is our back base, close to the front,' said Sadiq proudly. 'This house belongs to one of my family members. It's a nice place, very green. It's good to come here in summer.' A few bees drifted around us lazily. High above, the distant rumble of an invisible NATO jet merged with the crump of incoming artillery rounds and the occasional burst of anti-aircraft fire. 'Yeah, it's a nice place,' I said.

A few minutes down the road, we reached al-Ghabra's frontline positions. A long, shallow berm of red soil stretched as far as the horizon, dotted every few metres with gun-mounted pick-up trucks shaded by olive and eucalyptus trees. Long convoys of armed trucks manoeuvred over the rutted track past us as more and more reinforcements came to shore up this section of the line. On each of Misrata's three landward perimeters, thousands of men had set up shallow fortifications like this, ringing the city in a vast hedgehog of weapons and men like a medieval fortress. 'Where are my guys?' muttered Sadiq as we reached his command post. He beeped his horn impatiently. A baseball-capped head popped out of a concrete drainage pipe and then a couple of rebels scrambled to meet us. They greeted him with warm handshakes then began to offload crates of ammo from the back of our SUV, dragging them to a tent full of coolboxes of bottled water and fizzy drinks. A couple of the men began to grumble to Sadiq and he beckoned me over.

'They say that NATO have been flying since four o'clock this morning, but Gaddafi has been shelling this area all day and NATO are not taking any action. We hear the planes on top but there is no action.' Why? I asked. Sadiq shrugged expansively. 'I don't know! You should be more active! One of my guys is in hospital, he was injured today, but we don't see any action from NATO.' Do you think the jets can't find Gaddafi's soldiers? I asked. Sadiq gestured angrily at the trench with his car keys. 'But we can actually *see* them. They are only a couple of hundred metres far from here! Come and look.'

He led me into the trench line where a couple of dozen rebels, some just schoolboys, milled around with their rifles, peering over the lip towards the enemy or sheltering from the sun under trees. 'Don't film them,' said Sadiq, gesturing at a couple of fighters masking their faces with *keffiyehs*, 'their families are still in Zliten.' If they were shown on TV, their families in a regime-held town might suffer dearly.

A few sporadic rifle shots whistled past us from Gaddafi's lines. I crouched down but Sadiq stood upright, indifferent, forcing me to stand up again out of shame. 'We captured these trenches ten days ago,' he said. 'It was a very difficult battle, but *hamdullilah* we resisted them, and we pushed them back from this place. Now this is my trench, and soon we will move forward again.' Because government troops had dug these trenches as a line of defence facing Misrata, they were the wrong way round for al-Ghabra, their tall sand berm useless at the rear and a pointlessly shallow sand lip buttressed with sandbags facing the enemy. I lay down on a bed of dry pine needles next to some fighters and handed out cigarettes, shaking hands and making nice. Aside from the rasping of cicadas and the crack of rifle shots, it was quiet here. I peered over the sandbags towards the enemy and saw nothing but a small herd of brown Swiss cows, utterly unfazed by the war around them.

Crouching down, a rebel in his thirties wearing a cowboy hat and sandals shuffled towards me, introducing himself in broken English as the field commander. He pointed at the sky above him, and said, 'NATO! France, Britannia, good. Turkey ...' He shook his head dismissively. 'But Amreeka good good good! NATO Amreeka very good, every day bomb Gaddafi. But Turkey *mafeesh*.[17] No good Turk.'

We ducked as a couple of anti-aircraft rounds from the other side whistled through the trees above us, scattering leaves. 'NATO must kill Gaddafi. Kill Gaddafi! But not bomb! Go to Bab al-Azizia and take Gaddafi – ' he mimed grabbing my shirt collar '– then kill Gaddafi and Libya free. Gaddafi is a problem for all the world, an international problem. He must be killed, same as Dracula.'

Sprawled under the trees guzzling water and smoking cigarettes, we chatted about the war for an hour or so as

---

17 Nothing

government rifle shots whizzed over us and rebels answered back with short machine-gun bursts. It was all quite chilled, until the mortars started.

You heard them whistling as they came in, looping down in a long slow whine until they fell on top of your position. The rebels didn't move for the first few, just pointed in the air saying, '*Hown*[18] Gaddafi – boom!' The first couple landed in the open field just behind us with a sharp crack and a cloud of dust. 'You know,' said Sadiq, 'you are safe if you can hear them. If you can hear the bomb it won't hit you.' Yeah, that's not actually true, I said apologetically. Another landed closer to Sadiq's SUV in a loud crump, kicking up dust, and then there was a tinkling sound as it speckled the concrete drainage pipe with shrapnel. 'Maybe we go inside for a while,' said Sadiq. Crouching, we ran into the pipe, which was now crammed with rebels.

The crump of mortar rounds landing closer and closer to us punctuated our conversation as we huddled together. 'So I bring these pipes from the port and put them here like a shelter,' Sadiq said, 'we have nothing so we have to impro-vise.' He pointed to Arabic calligraphy scrawled along the curving wall. 'These are the names of our martyrs. I had two men wounded today by mortars, this morning, right here. One in the head and one in the back.' I see, I said, nodding uncertainly. There wasn't much else you could say.

---

18 Mortar

A bearded, earnest-looking rebel in wire-framed glasses ran into the crowded pipe and the men cheered him ironically, shouting 'Ya Doktor' and laughing. We made room for him and he crowded in next to me, shaking my hand. Are you the medic? I asked. 'No, no, no, they are joking. I was a practising intern at Misrata Hospital, in paediatric medicine. But now I am a fighter.' He flinched as a mortar landed just outside with a loud boom, making our flimsy shelter shudder. 'Yeah, since one week ago I have been fighting here. This is my place now.' Do you think you can win? I shouted over the incessant thud of explosions. The intern scratched his thin beard before answering. 'It is a strange thing now to say soon these men will be in Tripoli, but when you look at them, I think so. They are strong in here,' he said, pounding his chest. '*Takbeer!*' shouted Sadiq in his booming voice, and the men shouted *Allahu Akbar, Allahu Akbar* in response, raising their rifles in their fists and beaming happily. It was a good thing for morale, having foreign journalists in your dugout.

After half an hour or so, the bombardment began to wind down and we crawled back outside. Gaddafi's mortar crews were overshooting now, and the bombs were landing harmlessly in the field beyond us. A handful of rebels were eating lunch under a tree, utterly indifferent to the explosions just behind them. A civilian SUV had come to the lines, and a short middle-aged man began handing out slices of hot pizza wrapped in tin foil. 'We have a kitchen just behind us, in a farmhouse, so my men get hot food every day. Sometimes I try to bring them ice cream, when it gets too hot.' The pizza was delicious, essentially a Vegetarian Hot, and Sadiq thrust another half-dozen slices into my hands, saying, 'Eat, eat! You are my guest!' as the odd mortar still whistled overhead. 'And now it is time to feed Gaddafi,' he added, and led me back towards the trench. We curled down behind the sandbank as rifle shots whizzed just overhead. A couple of Sadiq's men sniped back with FN rifles, giving covering fire as a technical reversed up to the line right next to us. A worried-looking kid in the back struggled with its jammed anti-aircraft gun as bullets cracked past him. He was completely exposed.

'He is new,' said Sadiq, 'so we are teaching him how to use this gun.' It looked to be a steep learning curve. The older rebel next to him bashed at the gun with a spanner and they finally managed to clear the jam, an empty 14.5 shell clattering on to the flatbed. Leaves fluttered slowly on to our heads as bullets scythed through the treeline around us and I chainsmoked cigarettes. The gun finally boomed into action with a short burst, then a series of longer thudding bursts, each time ending in a shout of *Allahu Akbar!* from the rebels as they raked the government positions opposite. 'Now those bastards will be quiet,' said Sadiq grimly.

I spent the next few weeks getting to know Commander Sadiq, sometimes at the front but more often at his barracks, a converted car workshop in a suburb of Misrata. We'd spend long afternoons lounging around on mattresses, sharing spicy macaroni and tea and cigarettes with his men as they dozed or watched Al Jazeera on the granny-loud flat-screen TV, reporting on the battles they'd just fought in or were about to join. Whenever one particular reporter came on they'd jeer and throw paper cups at the screen; they thought he was a spy for Gaddafi, who'd given away their positions during live broadcasts. The rebels had thrown him out of Misrata and now he was reporting from the static Brega front. In the unsettling way of modern war, they'd switch the channel to Press TV to watch themselves on my reports, then tell me where I was going wrong or what I'd neglected to say.

Sadiq was a charming character, a self-made man who'd sacrificed everything for the revolution. A former communications engineer at Misrata port, he now owned a marble warehouse and a couple of downtown jewellery shops, and was frittering away his wealth on the revolution. Willingly or not, his wife and daughters had handed back to him their extensive collections of gold jewellery, which he sold to buy weapons on the Benghazi black market. 'The NTC in Benghazi give me rifles and bullets for free, but everything else I pay for,' he said. 'I have eighty soldiers. I pay for their food, their shoes and clothes and cigarettes, and then the four-wheel drives and heavy weapons I also pay for. My youngest son is in Kufra, deep in the desert, buying four-wheel drives for me. Each one costs me fifteen or twenty thousand dinars. Then I pay three hundred dinars each to bring them from Benghazi to here, all from my own pocket. An anti-aircraft gun costs me two or three thousand dollars on the black market in Benghazi, where they don't even need them. We need more help from Europe. We ask for help and they give us nothing.' Sadiq looked furious. 'Because Gaddafi tells them we are al-Qaeda. We have no Qaeda here in Misrata, this is just Gaddafi's lies for Europe. Misrata people are fighting because they hungry – hungry for freedom. We are fed up with Gaddafi, fed up to here,' he said, placing his hand on top of his head.

A young fighter with long curly hair and a long beard ambled in and everyone cheered, shouting, 'Osama!' One tousled his hair. He smiled shyly and sat down cross-legged in front of the TV, leaning his rifle against the wall. 'He is my son Osama,' beamed Sadiq. 'My guys all call him bin Laden, just as a joke, because of his beard. We're not really terrorists. I tell you, if we see Qaeda here, we will fight Qaeda before we fight Gaddafi. We don't want to fight a criminal and put another one in his place. We are Muslim, we pray. But we don't want to hurt the other side, we don't *want* to kill them. They are Libyans like us. We just want to kill Gaddafi, and they are standing in our way.' He shook his head angrily, knitting his grey brows together. 'They know they are going to die. This is the difference between our people and Gaddafi's people. Gaddafi's people refuse to go to Misrata because they know they will die here. Our people *want* to fight – this is the difference.'

Misrata was quite a conservative place compared to Benghazi. I never once saw a woman in the street there, for instance. When I asked my translator Hashem why, he informed me it was all due to the chivalrous nature of Misratans. Hashem had been assigned to us by the rebel media centre, to translate for us and keep an eye on what we reported. We were paying him twice my daily rate, in a simultaneous victory for the rebel PR effort and Misrata's entrepreneurial spirit. 'I mean, we men make all the shopping for our wives and sisters, so they never have to leave the house. All they have to do is cook our food. You see, they are more free here than in the West.'

But for some women the war was a kind of liberation. With the men all at the front, a space had opened up for women to organise themselves, and many grasped their new civic role eagerly. Hashem took me to a charity where Misratan women had set up a kind of group therapy-cum-primary school for children unsettled by the war. The therapy hardly skirted the war – every wall was plastered with lurid childish paintings of tanks and rockets blowing up houses and men with machine guns standing over bloodied corpses – and the women lined the children up for us, to sing rebel anthems in front of the camera.

Is this helping? I asked one woman. 'Yes, of course,' she said in perfect English, 'many of these children are orphans now, it is important for them to understand why their parents have been martyred.' Kids with wide intense eyes scribbled horrific doodles as we moved around the classroom. And you, the women of Misrata, I asked, do you think after the war you'll be able to play a greater role in society? 'Yes,' she said, smiling, 'we hope so. When the men come home they will see how we have kept the city running and how brave and strong we are. We hope after the war, in the new Libya, we will play a greater role.'

There was a high-pitched shriek and a Grad rocket slammed into a nearby street, shaking the classroom and making the children start wailing in fear. Some hid under their desks, others ran to the helpers for hugs and comfort. 'You see how we live here,' said one woman, as more rockets pounded the streets around us, 'even our children at home must learn to be brave like fighters. They have no rest from war.' I looked at the cowering children.

'You see,' said Hashem proudly, 'we are raising a generation of warriors.'

We left the school and drove to the impact site a few hundred metres away. A plume of black smoke billowed up from a building at the end of the street and wailing ambulances screeched past knots of armed men towards the inferno. Grads had hit a rebel barracks in what was either an incredibly lucky or exceedingly well-aimed salvo. Rebels aimed a high-pressure hose at a giant ball of flame in the car park, where a rocket had hit a row of technicals. The vehicles emitted loud bangs as their fuel tanks exploded or sudden popping cracks as the ammunition inside burst like fireworks in the heat. As some of the drivers and their comrades tried to douse the flames, others stood around waving their rifles in the air, shouting *Allahu Akbar* and making threats against Tawergha. 'It is another city near here,' explained Hashem, 'where the blacks live. They all support Gaddafi, and that devil's rockets bomb us from there. I promise you, when we win the war we will destroy Tawergha. There will be no Tawergha, just New Misrata.'

For all the rebel spin about a country united in struggle against an evil dictator, in Misrata the local divisions that underpinned the war were clearly apparent. Until the Italian invasion in 1911, the port city of Misrata had lived on the slave trade, with the nearby oasis of Tawergha used as a dusty desert holding area for African slaves. The Italians had freed the slaves, and Misrata had never forgiven the Tawerghans for it. The Tawerghans had been

142

cosseted by Gaddafi, who gave them generous handouts and, for the first time, a standard of living comparable to the rest of Libya. When Misrata rebelled, the Misratans believed, Gaddafi promised the Tawerghans the city if they could take it. Certainly many Tawerghans joined the government forces for the assault on Misrata, releasing YouTube videos of black soldiers swathed in the emerald green turbans of the loyalist cause, chanting how they would destroy the city from the turrets of their tanks. Misrata would never forgive them for that. Many Misratans claimed to have seen videos on captured mobile phones showing Tawerghan men raping Misratan women, but when you asked for evidence, they always said the videos had been deleted to preserve Misratan honour. 'They are not human beings like us,' Misratans said. 'When we win the war Tawergha will pay.'

It wasn't just Tawergha. Despite ostensibly being on the same side, Misratans frequently griped about the rebel capital of Benghazi, accusing them – with some justice – of being feckless, militarily useless braggarts. 'You know there's a special forces unit from Benghazi here in Misrata?' said Hashem. 'But they never fight, they just stay in a five-star hotel so Benghazi can pretend we're all fighting together. They just go on Facebook saying, "Yeah, we're in Misrata, we're all so brave," but they are no use to us.' He shook his head. 'Sometimes I feel bad we're fighting Tripoli and not Benghazi. Man, I hate those guys.' What's the point of sending reinforcements who don't fight? I asked. Hashem shrugged. 'It's a bit more complicated than that, they're for when we take Zliten. Maybe eighty per cent of Zliten people support Gaddafi, so they keep Benghazi soldiers here to take charge of Zliten after we capture it. They know we hate Zliten and Zliten hates Misrata. Otherwise, it'll just be a massacre.'

In Misrata, the war against Gaddafi often felt like a war against the entire rest of Libya.

———

Over the next few weeks, the fighting sputtered on unconvincingly, with Sadiq's *katiba* losing men here and there to mortar and rocket fire as they huddled in their trench line, waiting for the order to advance. An offensive was being planned for Ramadan, and until it came the men had no choice but to hold their positions under shellfire, taking casualties and firing back the odd wildly inaccurate helicopter rocket welded on to a makeshift trestle stand, shouting *Allahu Akbar* as it whooshed off in a crazy spiral in the general direction of the enemy.

The casualty rate was increasingly distressing to Sadiq, not least because he'd spent thousands of dollars buying his men body armour from the UK, only to have the shipment impounded by customs at Malta. 'You know,' he lectured me angrily, 'Europe needs to decide, are they gonna be on our side or not?' He was angered by the return of one his best fighters, Omar, to the Misrata base from hospital, hobbling weakly into the room to loud cheers, hugs and kisses from the other men. Omar was mildly famous in Misrata as the city's best diver, and his eyes shone as he remembered spearfishing for octopus in better times. 'No more diving for me.' He smiled sadly as he lifted up his t-shirt, displaying a long line of stitches across his torso. He'd been shot twice through the chest, and wheezed weakly as he spoke, coughing throughout as he chainsmoked the cigarettes the other men tossed to him. Omar was heading back to the front that day. He was in a poor state, but he was fit enough to sit in a trench and man a machine gun, just.

In an effort to preserve his manpower, Sadiq had ordered a job lot of cumbersome, medieval-looking armour from a local workshop. I helped him lift the heavy vests, clanging dully, on to the bed of his pick-up truck. 'It's quite heavy, but it does the job,' he said. 'We have to do something to protect our people. They are made of steel, sheet steel, with ropes to hold them on.' They're quite heavy, I said. 'Yeah, they're about twelve kilos each. I get the metal from my shop and then a local guy, he welds them together for me, nicely. We have already tested them and they do the job. They do the job. Come, you will see.'

In the car, heading towards the front, I asked Sadiq if the armour wouldn't be too heavy to wear during Ramadan, when Muslims were forbidden to eat or drink during the hours of daylight. 'If you cannot fast at this season, if you are travelling or fighting, then you can fast later, you can make it up after Ramadan. But I prefer my men to fast.' And the enemy, I asked, do they fast? Sadiq looked horrified. 'I hope so! They should be fasting, they are Muslims too. As far as I know.'

As we neared the front and heard the first thump and crack of mortar fire I crossed myself and Sadiq smiled contentedly, saying *bismillah* and stroking his beard reflexively. A pious man, he respected faith in others. 'You know, Islam is a beautiful religion, very peaceful, we are not terrorists like you say in the West. You know,' he said, indicating the olive groves to his left with a sweep of his hand, 'we are even forbidden from cutting down trees in war, *even trees*. It is a sin to kill a tree that gives fruit. But Gaddafi's men, they kill anything, even women and children, even cutting down trees. Islam is the best way for us to live. Let me ask you,' he added, 'what would you do in the West to a thief, someone who steals a thousand dinars?' I don't know, I said, put him in prison. He nodded, as if this confirmed something, then asked, 'And what if he stole one dinar?' Give him a caution, I ventured. Sadiq shook his head, smiling indulgently at me. 'No, no, no. You must cut off their hand. One thousand dinars, one dinar ... both are the same, you must cut off their hand. This is the law sent by God. This is how we must live in future.' The sound of artillery, both incoming and outgoing, was far louder now, and we both raised our voices as we spoke. 'But when this war is over I will go to Europe for a holiday, to London. I will go to Harrods.'

We parked up at the trench line and Sadiq shouted for some fighters to crawl out of their dugout and take the armour. One fighter tried on a vest and waddled around under its weight in his sandals like a Roman legionary diver, thumping his steel-armoured chest with his fist. Sadiq kneeled down by a small depression in the dirt and picked up shiny silver mortar fragments to show me. 'One of my men was wounded here this morning by this, in the head.' Another fighter pointed out the crumpled remnants of a plastic Portaloo and Sadiq laughed bitterly. 'They even hit our only toilet, look. Imagine if you were killed in there ...' He ordered his men to loose off a few S-4 rockets at the enemy lines, then began to distribute pieces of paper to the fighters clustering around. 'So you see,' he said, 'now we have the capability to restore the mobile telephone network, but we are waiting to see if the men want us to or not. For security reasons, because the enemy might listen to them at the front and learn what we are doing. But then, the families may want to talk to their husbands and sons fighting up here, so we will take their vote and decide.'

The high whine of enemy mortars began to whistle through the air and Sadiq sighed. 'Every day it is like this, but today is more heavy, more posh. And still NATO does nothing, I wish I knew why. They are playing a game with us, I am sure of it. As you see my men are not fighting, it is Gaddafi's people who are fighting us, we are only on standby.'

It must have been dispiriting to wage a war like this, static, outgunned, sitting ducks for the regime's artillery, but the fighters seemed to take it well enough. Some sat under an olive tree eating their lunch as mortars fell all around them with sharp cracks and clouds of dust, munching away utterly unconcerned and taking turns on their *shisha* pipe. We are waiting for orders.' Sadiq sighed. 'And so we wait.'

At the rebel headquarters in Misrata earlier, I'd been turned away from a planned interview with the military council, who were locked in discussion about the way forward. I'd waited an hour or two for the meeting that never came, chatting to the young sentry stationed outside who showed off his newly camouflaged SUV, completely repainted in dull brown leopard spots apart from the gleaming chrome roll bar, the glint of which would be spotted hundreds of metres away. Yeah, I know, he said when I remarked upon it, but it looks so nice it would be a shame to paint it. Inside the building, the military council was wrestling with the Zliten problem, the city blocking the route to the capital still doggedly resisting the rebels' advance: some wanted to bypass it and head straight for Tripoli, it was rumoured; others wanted to take Zliten to secure their supply lines for the assault on the capital. The result, for now, was stasis.

At the height of the siege, months earlier, I'd interviewed Salaheddin Badi, an air force fighter pilot turned guerrilla leader, who'd commanded my sector of the city centre during the bitter house-to-house fighting. Now Badi had been assigned the quietest sector of the front after, it was rumoured, a personality clash with the rest of the military council.

Abd el Rauf was a grim oasis settlement on the far south-eastern edge of Misrata, where the olive groves and wheat fields sputtered out into the wrinkled desert sands. To the east, Grad rockets were launched from Tawergha at Misrata daily, further justifying, to Misratan eyes, its future eradication. To the south, somewhere in the desert, was Bani Walid, a city populated by the Warfala tribe, still fiercely loyal to the regime. Every few days, Bani Walid would send a handful of technicals towards Abd el Rauf to scout out and shoot up the rebel positions, and rebel patrols would roam the desert to intercept and ambush them. But for the most part, nothing happened here. The fighters of the Al-Jibal brigade I met in Abd el Rauf looked less convincing than those on the Dafniya frontline, just greybeards and teenagers with giggly untested confidence. They were nice enough – handing out sweet *basbousa*[19] dripping with honey, cooked by their sisters, insisting I fire an FN into a berm, showing off their unsafe-looking home-made bazooka, insisting we take group photos beaming at the camera together – but a look at these fighters, so clearly a second-line force, made it apparent how vital the western, Dafniya front was to the military leadership. An offensive on Tripoli was coming, it was just a question of whether we'd capture the start, and whether it would succeed. Misrata wanted to be the first rebel force into Tripoli.

We were near Misrata's Hekma hospital when the first dead came in. Pick-up trucks full of fighters came roaring into the city from Dafniya, and the men shouted *The holy warrior is beloved of God* in straining voices as they picked up the corpses of their friends and carried them through the bustling car park into the hospital. Some fighters milled around the car park in a daze; others sat on breezeblocks weeping. Old men in traditional dress scanned the printed lists pasted to the hospital walls for news of their sons. Every so often the list was replaced with a longer one. A couple of men, their heads completely swathed in bloody bandages, had mortar fragments embedded in their skulls. I saw one of them, drenched in blood all over his body and face, wandering dazed across the car park until fighters stopped him and dragged him back to the bed he'd escaped

---

19 Semolina cake

from in the chaos. He was trying to get back to the front. The offensive had started, and it was bloody.

We filmed a group of fighters carrying a cheap pine coffin on their shoulders out of the hospital doors, their faces crumpled, red and wet with tears as they slid it on to their pick-up truck and crowded around it, before we realised these were our guys, from al-Ghabra. Their field commander had been shot three times in the chest, and was fighting for survival inside the emergency room. Two other fighters I'd hung out with just days earlier, Bel'aid and Breka, had been killed. Bel'aid had died almost instantly, bled white from a severed artery. They didn't look us in the face, but drove off to deliver the body to the family before returning to the front.

A mile or so behind the frontline, wounded and dead fighters were being transported to a field clinic in a former country villa hidden down a long straight dusty road shaded by tall poplars. Volunteer doctors bustled around the car park as the pick-up trucks and ambulances screeched in, rushing patients into surgery or wrapping the dead in plastic sheets and writing their names in felt tip across their chests. The air was filled with the rasping buzz of cicadas and the crack and thump of mortars, bursting in the air over our heads, and littering the clinic roof with sharp steel fragments.

'We've saved so many lives, especially those with head wounds and abdominal trauma,' said one English-speaking surgeon in blue scrubs, a refugee from Tripoli, 'but those with head trauma, by the time we take them to Misrata Hospital, already have permanent brain injury.' He didn't flinch at the sound of the mortars bursting overhead, the primary cause of such frequent head trauma among the rebels in their trenches. Aside from the war and death, it was a typically bucolic Dafniya scene, like a village in southern France somewhere: lowing cows and shady avenues of trees, with ambulances screaming down them, raising clouds of dust.

One young fighter with a big grin, dressed in a Real Madrid shirt, hopped out of a technical, limping on one leg and using his rifle for balance. 'They tried to shoot me but I ran away. My friend, he shot one here,' he said, chuckling and patting his stomach, 'and the other in the leg, but when we tried to capture them they shoot at us, so we left them and go back.' He hopped into the hospital giving a V for Victory sign, and his friends drove back to the front. When we followed them, we drove down a long, eerily empty stretch of road the Misratans had just captured, lined by dense olive groves on either side. A berm of sand had been dumped here across the road to consolidate the new position. A handful of fighters manned this new rebel checkpoint, who turned out to be the much-heard-of reinforcements from Benghazi, in high spirits.

'Today we have pushed forward eight kilometres,' announced their smirking commander with typical Benghazi bravado, 'we will not surrender, we win or we die.' One of his men peered through a rangefinder on a tripod at the minarets of Zliten, shimmering like a mirage in the distance, still tantalisingly out of reach. They didn't look like the elite troops of rumour, just kids in jeans and sandals giving V for Victory signs to the camera, the odd helmet perched on top of a hipster outfit or machine gun draped around a neck looking more like props than tools of war. One kid leaned back in a wheeled office chair, his FN rifle jutting phallically from his lap as he observed the bombardment. The sound of outgoing rocket salvoes ripped through the air around us. It took the explosions of enemy RPGs bursting in the air above us to illustrate how fragile this victory was; the rebels had pushed forward along the road but their flanks had been ignored, and the thick hedgerows and olive groves for some miles on either side of us were still full of regime troops preparing to counterattack. This was a bad place, and we left in a hurry. An hour or so afterwards, the regime attacked this checkpoint in force, and the Benghazi reinforcements fled, abandoning the day's hard-won gains. When they reached Misrata, the local fighters packed them on to the first ship home in disgrace. Misrata would never accept reinforcements from a foreign city again.

In a city loud with the chants of funeral processions and prayers for the dead from every mosque, I learned that my mother had been diagnosed with a brain tumour, and was about to die. I spoke to her when she briefly escaped her coma, and tried to explain where I was and that I was trying to come home as soon as possible. Dying, confused, she couldn't understand. I spent days at the port waiting for ships to Benghazi, but Gaddafi was bombarding it with missiles and no ships could dock. Dazed with shock, I spent days trying to find a route back home. By chance, I met Jawad, the rebel fighter and my companion from the worst days of the siege, in the street, and he tried to find me a place in a fishing boat out of the city. He had shaved his head now, and looked drawn and old, though he wasn't even forty.

'I've nearly been killed twice by snipers now, these last weeks,' he said, 'I know the next time will be my end.' I told him about my mother. He shrugged. 'My aunt was killed last month, by a rocket, sitting on her doorstep. To bury her, we had to pick her up like this,' he said, miming scooping handfuls of flesh into a bucket, 'so why be sad? This is God's will.'

During daylight, a sandstorm filled the city with a hazy fug that made me feel like my brain was about to explode. At night, violent summer storms merged with the flash of missiles landing on the port and across the city. I finally

A typical revolutionary demonstration in Benghazi.

Almost every building in Benghazi was covered in revolutionary graffiti.

The rebels needed little excuse to celebrate, whether or not celebration was justified.

The Libyan rebels generally wore a mish-mash of uniforms and football shirts.

Taking a helicopter ride to the Bor frontline, South Sudan.

Malian army armoured personnel carrier smashes down the exterior wall of Gao's courthouse to clear a path for an infantry assault.

Malian troops retreat from Gao's courthouse under heavy fire from MUJAO rebels inside.

Taking cover during the ambush outside Bor, South Sudan.

Below: SPLA soldiers escort me around the site of a recent massacre, Juba, South Sudan.

Doing a piece to camera in the middle of a bloody ambush outside Bor, South Sudan.

YPG fighters sleeping in a farmhouse
on the Ras al-Ayn frontline, Syria.

A Kurdish farmer-turned-YPG fighter
on the Ras al-Ayn frontline, Syria.

Kurdish civilians cross the river border between Northern Iraq and Syria.

Left and above: YPG martyr's funeral cortege, Qamishli, Syria.

Grieving mothers at the funeral of their YPG fighter sons, Qamishli, Syria.

A YPG checkpoint guarding the Ras al-Ayn frontline, Syria.

Tea and cigarettes at a YPG frontline checkpoint, Syria.

aving breakfast with rdish fighters on the Ras al-Ayn frontline.

A Hezbollah-aligned arms dealer tempts me with a captured Israeli M4 rifle, Beirut, Lebanon.

A Sunni fighter and arms dealer shows me his illegal weapons stash, Tripoli, Lebanon.

Chilling out with an armed Sunni child during clashes, Syria Street, Tripoli, Lebanon.

found a fishing boat to Malta, a day's sail away, and flew home from there to peaceful, alien, hateful Europe. I sat by my mother's bed for three months, distracting myself with the TV next to her, watching the fall of Zliten, the storming of Tripoli, the downfall of the regime and the capture and murder of Gaddafi, consoling myself with the sound of gunfire as she slept, wishing I was there. Within two weeks of my mother's funeral I was back in Libya.

TRIPOLI

October/November 2011

You know an interview's gone wrong when your interviewee cocks his rifle and jabs it in your chest, threatening to shoot you. While I'm all for a right to reply, I'd generally prefer it to take the form of a snarky online comment underneath the finished piece, but that's Libya for you. When the interviewee in question claims – with pretty convincing circumstantial evidence – that he's the guy who murdered Gaddafi in cold blood, then, well, you've got a problem. Making my most hey-I'm-a-reasonable-guy face, I looked him in the eyes and tried to calm the situation down.

'How about we all sit down and have a cup of tea?'

But let's rewind a bit. Libya in November 2011 was a strange place. After months of gruelling attritional warfare, the rebel militias had stormed the capital and asserted a shaky sort of control over the country. Only weeks before, the fugitive dictator Muammar al-Gaddafi had been cornered in a storm drain outside his besieged home town of Sirte and shot like a mad dog in disputed circumstances. The rebels' political leadership, the NTC, claimed to have no idea who'd killed the country's former tyrant, and promised the West that as soon as they found a suspect, they'd send him straight to the Hague. No one was holding their breath.

But even with Gaddafi gone, the country was still far from secure. Lethal clashes between different rebel militia groups were killing a handful of people every day as the squabbling bands of victors marked out their territory. At night, I'd stopped getting out of bed to try and film the heavy machine-gun and rifle battles that raged across the loyalist district of Abu Salim. It just wasn't newsworthy any more.

The day I met Ahmed Muhammad al-Swayib had already been a total headfuck. Two tribes, the Zawiya and the Wershefana, had been contesting the strategic village of Imaya, a half-hour's drive west of Tripoli. The Zawiya claimed the Wershefana were secret Gaddafi loyalists, without any real proof. The Wershefana claimed the Zawiya had stolen huge tracts of their tribal lands. So both sides started shelling the fuck out of each other with Grad rockets.

The handful of government soldiers at the Imaya check-point denied there'd been any fighting at all, even as the odd desultory rifle shot cracked over our heads. They urged us to check out Zawiya a few miles down the road and see how calm the situation was. In Zawiya we filmed a hospital ward full of dead and dying fighters, heard outlandish rumours of loyalist snipers picking off fighters at checkpoints, and saw a terrified African refugee kicked off the back of a pick-up truck and bundled into jail as a suspected spy, blood streaming from his mouth. Calm for Libya. It was about to get worse.

On the way back to Tripoli, the road suddenly emptied of all life, the classic warning signal of fighting ahead. Ours was the only car on the road. As we slowed down, a burst of rifle fire cracked right over our roof from an unseen position a couple of hundred metres away. We slid to a halt to show how harmless we were and waited to die. My trembling driver snatched off his rebel-flag baseball cap and hid it under his seat, just in case. Nothing happened. Slowly, we started the car up again and trundled off, then sped down the road to the Imaya checkpoint. The government soldiers who'd sent us off to Zawiya peered over the walls they were hiding behind and looked at us like we were crazy. 'What are you doing?' they shouted. 'There's a war going on down there.' Cheers, guys.

Back at the hotel in Tripoli, I went straight to the fridge to grab an ice-cold bottle of Libya's vile alcohol-free beer. 'Hey,' shouted a bald rebel, sprawled cockily across the sofa in the lobby, like a North African Danny Dyer, 'remember me? I know you from Sirte.' Sorry, I wasn't at Sirte, I told him, truthfully. He looked pissed off. 'I know you from Sirte,' he said. 'We were friends. You know me. I killed Gaddafi.' I looked back at him, at his two armed mates and at the pistol he'd plonked on the coffee table next to his crossed feet. Oh, yeah, of course I do, I said. Silly me. I'm Aris. What's your name again?

Ahmed Muhammad al-Swayib was thirty-five, born in Benghazi to parents from Misrata. Like many volunteers from Benghazi, Ahmed had travelled west to fight in Misrata – unlike most, he didn't then immediately flee back to the relative peace of Benghazi. Instead, he stayed and fought all the way through the war to its bloody climax in Gaddafi's home town, as a rifleman in one of Misrata's most hardcore militia units, the Lions of the Valley.

I had seen his face before, I realised. Bald, wild-looking, with one wonky eye, he was the starring character in a video taken moments after Gaddafi's murder. In the clip, a group of rebels are surrounding Ahmed, kissing him on the head and proclaiming him Gaddafi's killer. 'I saw him do it,' one says. 'I saw him kill Gaddafi with his own hands, just now.' Ahmed smiles bashfully then raises two pistols in the air – the instruments of summary Libyan justice. I looked at the pistol on the table and the pistol in Ahmed's waistband. The same two pistols: FN Five Sevens. Even in a country awash with guns, these pistols were very rare. Manufactured by Belgium's FN Herstal, only three hundred and sixty were delivered to Libya, all destined for the elite 32nd Brigade, commanded by Gaddafi's son Khamis, or for the dictator's personal bodyguard. The only place they would be found in Libya is surrounding Gaddafi. Things were looking good, so I sat down to talk.

However, there was a problem. Ahmed didn't want to do an interview. His situation was complex. He was staying in a three-star hotel in Tripoli that he couldn't afford – someone else was paying his bills – and we both knew going public as Gaddafi's killer would be a one-way ticket to the Hague. Sure, I said, no interview. So I switched on my BlackBerry voice recorder and slipped it on the table next to him as I chatted to his friend.

His mate, Muhammad Juma al-Shoshni, was twenty-five, and from the western coastal town of al-Khoms. Dressed in double denim, with a Kalashnikov by his side, he claimed to have killed Gaddafi's son Mutassim. Unlike Ahmed, Muhammad spoke very good English, and even more unlike Ahmed, Muhammed wanted to raise his media profile. He thought he knew what the story was worth

– $5,000 – so while I made vague noises about raising the money, he ran me through Mutassim's last minutes.

'There were four of us, including another man from Benghazi, watching the yard of a house. Some of Gaddafi's people came forward, and started shooting at us. We killed two, and I was injured by Mutassim's bodyguard. We caught three of them. The third one said, "Let me live and I'll tell you a secret. The first one in the yard is Mutassim."

'When we searched the yard, Mutassim started shooting with a pistol. We wounded him – just a small wound – in the throat and he surrendered. We took him to a barracks and I asked him, "Why are you killing the Libyan people? Look at your father now. There used to be hundreds of cars full of people, following behind him, saying how great he was. Now there are hundreds of cars taking him away to die."

'He started arguing with us and pissing me off, so I told him to say the *shahada* – the Muslim declaration of belief. I said, "The Libyan people will never forgive you, but maybe God will give you some mercy." But he just smiled and touched this magic necklace on his neck, one like the Africans have. I even put my hands on his head and said, "This is the Qu'ran, the last thing and the first thing," and he just smiled and touched this evil thing on his neck, so we shot him. And then we took his necklace and burned it.

'Then I just lay down on the ground and cried, and my friends poured water over me and said *Allahu Akbar, Allahu Akbar*. After a few minutes I came back to normal. When we were in Sirte I would wake up and pray to God every day to make my heart strong, and God listened to me and gave me this blessing.'

This was all good stuff, but I wanted Ahmed, and I wanted him on camera. My driver was chatting away to him in Arabic, saying 'God is great' at choice moments and translating tidbits of his story for me. 'You know what Gaddafi's last words were? He said, "This is forbidden, I am your father." So Ahmed shot him!' Muhammad guffawed appreciatively. But whenever I asked Ahmed whether he'd let us film his story, he shook his head angrily. Muhammad winked at me and whispered that he'd be able to arrange it. 'Ahmed's a good guy,' he said, 'but he's a bit crazy. Don't worry, I'll fix it. But tell me – how much is an iPad in your country?'

The next day, Muhammad beckoned me over to a corner of the hotel lobby. 'Don't worry,' he said, 'I'll fix it now. You'll get your story.' He went upstairs to convince Ahmed while my cameraman set up his tripod in a corner of the room. A few minutes later, the lift doors pinged open and Ahmed came out, brandishing his Kalashnikov like a boss-eyed Libyan Scarface. He came towards me, cocking the rifle, and jabbed it in my chest. The hotel receptionists crouched down behind their desk for cover. Muhammad sidled out of the lift behind him, white-faced, staring at the ground. The next few seconds passed very slowly.

'I did not kill that devil for money,' said Ahmed quietly, 'I killed him for God and Libya. Do you understand?' I said I understood. His voice quavered. 'I will kill the first person who tries to give me money for this. I will kill him with this –' he shoved the barrel into my chest again '– like I killed Gaddafi. Do you understand?' Again, I said I understood. Very slowly, I apologised for the apparent misunderstanding. It's all a mistake, I coaxed soothingly. Ask Muhammad. His friend stared sheepishly at the ground. Ahmed lowered his rifle. The hotel staff stood back up. We all sat down and had tea and sugary fruit juice and too many cigarettes. When they left an hour later, I went to my room and vomited.

Over tea, Ahmed started crying and apologised for threatening me. 'I get too emotional at times,' he said. 'It's all been very difficult. Sometimes I can't control myself.' I assured him I understood and that there was nothing to apologise for. I was in London when Gaddafi was killed, and whenever commentators threw their hands up in horror at the brutality of his murder, I'd shrugged it off. Whoever did it, I'd figured, was probably some heavily PTSD-ed eighteen-year-old kid from Misrata who'd gone off to war without any training, seen his city destroyed, his family huddling for shelter under rocket fire and his best mates killed in front of him. It was a Libyan end to a Libyan story, with a brutal, not undeserved, sort of justice.

But the truth, if Ahmed's story was the truth, turned out to be slightly different. He was twice as old as most of the Misratan fighters, had been a drifter before the war and had a reputation even among his comrades for wild, dangerous mood swings. Maybe he killed Gaddafi and maybe he didn't. But the people on the scene were certain that he did and he was at the right place at the right time, with the rare bodyguard-issue pistols to prove it. Perhaps even more convincingly, I'd experienced for myself his sudden outburst of rage and immediate bout of tearful remorse. If ever someone was likely to suddenly shoot an unarmed captive, it was Ahmed.

The day he checked out of the hotel, he beckoned me aside and whispered in my ear. 'Don't trust Muhammad,' he said. 'He is a liar. He did not kill Mutassim, he just wants the money. Only I am the killer.' He seemed to say it with as much sadness as pride. A few days later, in a bombed-out hotel café, I chatted about Ahmed with Hashem, my old fixer from Misrata. He shrugged it off. 'Who cares? Everyone wants to say they killed him, but it was a group effort. All of us did it – all of us Libyans. It was the perfect end. They fucked him and then they killed him.' He smiled winningly.

165

With the war now over and Gaddafi dead, Libya was still its usual chaotic self, if not more so. At times, it felt as if the country was less in the grip of a revolution than a mass outbreak of psychosis. Now armed teenagers from across Libya strutted across Tripoli's grand colonial boulevards, some dressed in the captured braided panoply of regime generals. Every night saw loud gun battles between rival rebel militias or between militias and remnants of the loyalist guerrillas. But insane and volatile though it was, it was better than home.

I'd been sent to Libya without a press visa then turned back with apologies by black Berber soldiers at the Ras Jdir border post with Tunisia. Now the war was won, and the rebels didn't need our rolling news PR effort, journalists were the focus of suspicion once again. On the Tunisian side of the frontier, border guards in ironed steel-grey uniforms dripping with silver braid urged me in impeccable French not to go back inside. 'They're all crazy there,' they said, as rifle fire popped pointlessly through the air from the Libyan side, 'they were always like this, even under *him*. But now they're even worse.'

I had to go back to Tunis to sort out my visa and on the flight there I was seated next to Rami, a young Tunisian air traffic control officer, who expounded for the entire course of the journey on the inherent backwardness and mental instability of the Libyan people. When he took the inevitable Arab Facebook selfie of us grinning and hugging each other, an elderly Libyan eight rows behind strode up and demanded to flick through his phone, to ensure it wasn't an elaborate ploy to capture images of his equally decrepit fully *niqab*-ed wife. 'You see,' said Rami, tapping his head like Asterix calling the Romans crazy. 'You see what these people are like? Just you wait, now is when they begin the real war, every town against its neighbour. Maybe these people needed Gaddafi, to stop them all killing each other.'

———

When I finally got to Tripoli, for all the rebel flags fluttering from the stucco-ed apartment blocks and rebel kitsch for sale on every street corner, it was hard to avoid the feeling that I'd reached a conquered city. Aside from a couple of districts that had fought hard against Gaddafi throughout the war, the Tripolitans had, by and large, remained loyal to the regime until the very end. When they formed their first *katibas* in the very last days of the revolution, it was more to safeguard their property from provincial liberators than to fight the regime. And of all the city's supposed liberators it was the Zintanis, Bedouin rebels from the arid, impoverished Western Mountains, who had the worst reputation as looters.

'The Zintanis, *wallahi*, we joke that they even stole the elephants from the zoo,' said our new fixer, Mohammed, a middle-aged petroleum engineer and raconteur, 'and they stole jet skis and brought them back to their mountains. We threw them out of Suq Juma, you know – if they ever come back they will be killed. If they come like guests, we will place them here,' he added, resting his palm flat on his head, 'but if they come back like Rambo again we will eliminate them. Now, the Misratans, they are the opposite – this is why they are popular here. Even when Tripolitans tell stories about them, they add more salt and spice, you know?'

Like much of Libya and almost all of Tripoli, Mohammed was a survivor rather than a revolutionary. During the war, he'd felt the regime's warm breath on his neck throughout and survived; as soon as the rebels reached the capital, he made sure he and his sons were seen at the centre of the fight for Gaddafi's central Bab al-Azizia citadel. 'We didn't want the Misratans and Zintanis to say, "We are the ones who liberated you," he explained, "that way we'd never get rid of them."' His revolutionary credentials secured, aided by a baseball cap in rebel colours which he donned to pass through the dodgier checkpoints, Mohammed was now on the precious shortlist of rebel-approved media workers, meaning he was trusted to escort Western journalists around the chaotic city without going too off-message.

My memories of the city are almost all of Mohammed driving me around the endless boulevards and flyovers, laid out with all the user-unfriendly grandeur of any Arab dictatorship's road network. As he drove he would expound his wisdom, light new cigarettes from old, and swear elaborately at other drivers. He'd shout *Allahu Akbar* out of the window as he sped away from every checkpoint to prove his revolutionary fervour to the bearded kids manning them. A born raconteur, Mohammed answered any question with a dazzling supply of anecdotes which never quite found resolution, each one opening into a new anecdote and so on and on, like Scheherezade bamboozling her husband with her 1,001 tales. But somewhere within the storytelling was revealed, intentionally or not, wider truths about the general insanity of post-liberation Tripoli, and the callous brutality of life under the regime.

Like post-war Berlin, Tripoli had been carved into rival fiefdoms by the various victorious militias, and every local's journey around his own city now took account of this mental map of proliferating checkpoints and potential flashpoints. Misratan rebels held the suburban coast road to the east, and their fearsome-looking black-painted technicals and armoured vehicles studded the capital's western roads, heavy weapons aimed at oncoming traffic as young fighters checked all drivers' documents. The Zintanis had set up camp in Tripoli airport and occupied the more luxurious coastal villas in the city's affluent western suburbs; they were loath to return home without a fight. The Tripoli Brigade, a Qatari-trained Islamist unit that had led the final push on the city from the west, had made Mitiga Airbase – formerly America's Wheelus Airbase – their armed camp, and crowds of civilians could be found outside, waiting to petition Tripoli's new kingmaker, Abdulhakim Belhaj, like medieval peasants waiting for an audience with their sultan.

Belhaj was a controversial, and largely unpopular, figure in the new Libya, a former Islamist militant who'd been delivered like a gift to Gaddafi by MI6 when Blair was courting the Libyan dictator, then released in uncertain circumstances and reinstalled by Qatar, many Libyans claimed, as the Gulf nation's new puppet ruler. Here and there, black al-Qaeda flags fluttered from small barracks we always drove past quickly; the ineffective NTC government had removed itself from Benghazi to the Corinthia, Tripoli's best hotel, insulated from the city's anarchy by armed guards and a wall of bomb detectors.

With so many competing factions in the capital, clashes were inevitable and came frequently, usually at dusk or in the early hours. During these outbreaks, I'd lie in my room listening to the sound of rocket and heavy machine-gun fire, trying to work out whether or not they were heavy enough to get out of bed for. Gaddafi's supporters hadn't gone away, and rebel patrols were frequently ambushed by loyalist fighters from the slum district of Abu Salim, home of the regime's most notorious jail, and site of a famous 1990s massacre of political prisoners. 'It's nothing,'

Mohammed would always say, 'they just don't accept they've lost yet, but they're not strong enough to fight. It's quiet now. If they even raise their voice, not a gun, just their voice, we will kill them all immediately.'

One day, driving through town, I asked him what life was like under the regime. 'Every night during Ramadan they'd show executions of people on TV. A time for prayer and contemplation, and we have to watch this.' The car swerved in traffic as he lit a new cigarette from the butt of his last, angry drivers behind us honking their horns. The traffic police were too afraid of the rebel victors to come back on to the streets. 'I told you about the time I was on regime TV?' No, I said. Mohammed laughed. 'So, my neighbour was killed in a NATO airstrike, cut in half. Not near me, thank God, he was at work. But I went to his funeral, of course, and the regime cameraman came up to me and asked me to condemn the imperialist invaders. *Wallah*, what can you do? I'm a rebel, I live in a rebel district, the army were too frightened even to drive through my neighbourhood. If I go on TV, the rebels will kill me. if I refuse, the regime will arrest me.' So what did you do? I asked. 'I'll tell you, but first let me tell you the story of the Ministry of Anti-corruption … '

He pointed at the burned-out building to our left. 'This held the records of every minister suspected of taking bribes, every businessman who stole from the country.'

And NATO bombed it? 'No, this was the first building destroyed on the first day the *thuwwar* liberated the city, after the regime fled.' I asked him if he was telling me the NTC politicians in Benghazi wanted to cover the tracks of previous crimes. 'I didn't say that,' he said, 'I'm just telling you a story. What you do with it is up to you, you're the journalist.' I never did find out how Mohammed resolved his TV interview dilemma.

The car screeched to a halt in Suq Juma, outside a fucked-up ruin of a house, shorn in two by NATO airstrikes. We got out, and Mohammed summoned up the owner, a middle-aged black Libyan in a white *dishdash*, whose wife and daughter had been killed in the bombing. The intended target, a minuscule regime barracks, lay untouched a few metres down the road, now flying a rebel flag. A few shoes and oddments of clothing lay scattered about the grey concrete rubble. 'What happened here?' the man said. 'This is a rebel neighbourhood, we all support the revolution here. With all the technology they had, they killed my family and for what?' NATO denied this incident ever happened, as it did the vast majority of the death toll from collateral damage in Libya.

Mohammed wandered about the ruins, bored. 'It's war, people die,' he said afterwards. 'We're very grateful to NATO. But tell people in Europe and America this: if you ever send one soldier to put his boots on the ground in Libya, all of us will turn our weapons away from each other to fight them. We are Libyans.'

The sheer scale of NATO's ability to destroy made me never want to work on the wrong end of an airstrike. At Tripoli's 77th Brigade barracks, huge hangars once filled with weapons had been blasted open by precision munitions, scattering charred and warped assault rifles everywhere like matchsticks in an ashtray. At Gaddafi's Bab al-Azizia compound, a vast complex in the middle of Tripoli, block after block of offices and warehouses had been pummelled into rubble, with oddments of uniform and leaves of paperwork fluttering in the breeze. 'Until a few weeks ago,' said Mohammed, 'you wouldn't even look at this place when you drove past, in case they brought you in for questioning. Look at it now.'

Civilians drove around hauling away cables and steel rods from the wreckage as loot, one heavily bearded man and his ten-year-old son threatening me as a CIA spy until Mohammed told them to fuck off. We wandered through the ruins to Gaddafi's villa, once a sort of modernist chalet, about the size and design of a successful dentist's house in Elstree. Until a few weeks earlier, this had been the heart of the dictator's regime. Now it was a burned-out shell, with one word prominently scrawled in English all over it: MISRATA.

There'd been talk of clashes between the western town of Zawiya, long a revolutionary stronghold, and the Wershefana tribe, considered a pro-regime fifth column, whose lands straddled the highway to Tripoli. When Mohammed and I reached the flashpoint village of Imaya, a knot of fighters and heavy anti-aircraft gun trucks from the Tripoli Brigade had set up a roadblock along the highway, waving away traffic and assuring us, the only journalists there, that everything was fine. Rifle shots rang out every few minutes from the fields to our right. A Wershefana fighter began shouting at the camera that the Zawiya had advanced twenty-five kilometres into tribal lands, and fired rockets at them, until hustled away by their commander. 'There was a problem earlier, just a small disagreement, but no one was hurt and now it is all over,' said the commander. 'Everything is fine, thank God.' If it's fine, I said, are we OK to go to Zawiya and have a look around? 'Erm ... yes,' he said, uncertainly. 'Why not? Everything is fine now.'

We drove west along the storm-flooded road through date palm groves, past Base 27, the disputed barracks. The Wershefana had drawn up armoured vehicles alongside the road, and set up machine-gun posts facing Zawiya. Traffic thinned out until we reached the town, and entered the hospital grounds. As we drove into the car park, we heard the boom of outgoing rockets from somewhere nearby. The hospital director greeted us with surprise, and took us into the intensive care ward where dying fighters lay swaddled in bandages beside drips and beeping machines. 'You can see there are casualties, one of them is my relative. There are dead people from both sides. This is the truth. If we want to build a democratic country, we must show the truth. There are four dead here, and I hear about three on their side.' He looked exhausted and on edge with stress. 'What is the surprising thing,' he added, 'is on both sides they will shout *Allahu Akbar, Allahu Akbar*. On both sides!'

As we left the hospital, it was clear the situation had deteriorated. The Zawiya forces had called up around a dozen light tanks to their last checkpoint, all arranged with their heavy-calibre barrels pointing down the road towards the Wershefana. At the barracks beside the road, the Zawiya commander agreed to an interview. While we were setting up his microphone, a truck drove through with some of his fighters surrounding a terrified African, bleeding from his mouth. They pushed him off the flatbed into the dust and kicked him into a Portacabin, shouting all the while. I asked who he was, and the commander said, 'Maybe a spy.' I asked if we could film. He said no.

The interview over, we drove back towards Tripoli, the road now unnervingly empty. One fighter, crouching down as he scuttled along the side of the road behind a wall, motioned at us to take cover. I told Mohammed we should slow down, and he replied breezily, 'No, why? He was just waving at us.

That's how Libyans wave.' Within seconds, rifle fire whistled over the roof of the car and we screeched to a halt as we argued whether it was safer to stop and show our peaceful intentions or drive on faster. Terrifyingly, Mohammed slowly took off his revolutionary-flag baseball cap and hid it beneath his car seat as surreptitiously as possible. Another few rounds whistled over us as we sat still, which we took as an order to drive on, and we did, hurtling down the empty road until we reached the Wershefana checkpoint. The Wershefana fighters and Tripoli Brigade troops there were all hiding behind concrete walls and sandbanks for cover as they waved us through, and ordered us to park behind a building for our own safety while they checked our papers.

'Why did you drive down there?' asked the commander who'd waved us through earlier, shaking his head at our irresponsibility. 'It's dangerous! Are you crazy?'

———

I only had a few days left in Libya and wanted to go back to Misrata to see how victory had affected the rebels. First, I needed to get permission to travel there, so we drove to the former women's police barracks in central Tripoli, now the headquarters of the capital's Misratan contingent. We were ushered into the office from where a young Islamist commander ran his new fiefdom.

Saadoun Swehli, thirty-three, ran a construction company before the war. Now he was one of the most powerful men in Libya. A servile black minion gave us Turkish coffee and baklava, with bows and scrapes, while we waited for the interview. A middle-aged Libyan in a grey suit sat beside Swehli, trying to convince him that Misrata needed to buy a fleet of Mirage jets from France, emphasising that their utility had been proved in the war. When I introduced myself, the man whispered in Swehli's ear that I shouldn't be trusted. Swehli glared at me as I dropped names of commanders I'd met and battles I'd witnessed at the height of Misrata's siege. It worked, finally, and he softened, giving me the stamped paperwork I needed. A week later he arrested my replacement and kept him in the dungeon beneath his office for weeks, accusing him of being a spy.

On the edge of the city, a new black-painted archway had been constructed as the formal entrance to Misrata, surrounded by tanks and armoured vehicles painted black, in the new Misratan colour scheme seemingly designed to look as sinister as possible. Misratan fighters checked the paperwork of every driver who turned up, turning away non-Misratans or taking them off for questioning. The rebel stronghold had become a paranoid Spartan city state, a place apart from the rest of Libya.

After a while, the guards at the checkpoint let us into the city, and we drove to the Goz al-Teek Hotel, a bleak 1970s building ravaged by the war. The foyer had been wrecked by tank shells, and the top floor had been made unusable after rockets and mortars had shorn their way through the roof. The long orange and brown corridors looked like a more sinister version of the hotel from *The Shining*, given the occasional bloodstains on the carpets. Regime snipers had used it as a base, until they'd all been killed. Stained, abandoned boots and uniforms still littered the roof, surrounded by empty cartridges. But it was cheap, it had internet and the food, brought in on a TV dinner tray from a nearby rotisserie, was good. In the stadium beneath my window, a military helicopter looped around doing aerobatic tricks for an adoring crowd. A long convoy of beeping cars fluttering Syrian and Libyan flags drove slowly past cheering bystanders, raising men and money to send to the latest Arab war.

For all the time I'd spent in Misrata, the regime had used the black Libyan former slave colony of Tawergha as a base for the missiles that pummelled the city daily for months. The rebels had always vowed vengeance against Tawergha, and when the town fell in August, they took it. I'd secured permission to visit Tawergha with a Misratan guide, and the next day we drove through the desert to the bleak settlement of Soviet-style apartment blocks looming from the sands.

Tawergha was entirely deserted, apart from a few Misratan fighters busily looting the abandoned homes. We crunched over broken glass through emptied shops, with graffiti scrawled on the walls saying 'Tawergha out, Tawergha is no more, Misrata lives for ever'. Dead camels lay in the street, black with fat flies. More flies buzzed around large patches of disturbed earth beside the road. Some fighters saw us, and after checking our paperwork took us on the grand tour of the town. They shot open the lock to a grand villa and took us around its abandoned rooms, carefully smashing every piece of china in the display cabinets, then the display cabinets themselves, and finally ripping up family portraits they'd broken from the frames. 'No good Tawergha,' one young rebel said, showing me a photo he'd found of a young black guy in military uniform before throwing it on the ground and treading it into the broken glass with his boot, 'Tawergha finished.'

We went through other homes, up concrete stairwells into abandoned apartments filled with piles of clothes and school certificates or wedding albums, a child's tricycle still standing in the corner of a kitchen beside the open stinking fridge, as the fighters mooched around, looking appraisingly at photos of young women with braided hair and beaming smiles beneath their college graduation mortarboards, or clowning around with the fragments of uniform still dotted about. They shot open the locked door of a schoolroom and we walked into a scene eerily untouched since the town fell, except for a pall of dust on all the desks. The writing on the blackboard, in a looping English hand, praised Gaddafi as the protector of all Libya. They tore down the green flags from the wall and burned them. They took us on to the roof and showed us the view of the town as the sun set, smoke rising all around us from the looted homes their colleagues were burning to the ground. A shot rang out, the signal that curfew was beginning and Tawergha was to be evacuated for the night as a closed military zone. 'No more Tawergha,' said the fighter, twiddling his pistol in his hand, 'now maybe new Misrata airport here. *Allahu Akbar.*'

Misrata had fought the hardest of all the revolutionary enclaves, but its fighters now made bad victors. When Zliten fell, the Misratans captured dozens of tanks and armoured vehicles from government stocks and quickly assembled an armoured brigade, painted all in black, to assert their city's power wherever necessary. They saw themselves as Libya's only true revolutionaries, and believed that Misrata now deserved to rule the entire country. It was a hard thing to see the noble rebels I'd fallen in love with transformed into hateful looters and swaggering bullies. The worst thing was the natural charm and easygoing good humour they now applied to their conquest of Tawergha. It was as if this was always how it was meant to be, that this was how all revolutions end: with the total subjugation and displacement of the vanquished. I couldn't blame them, really. It was my own naivety that pained me most.

SUDAN

BLUE NILE
Summer 2012

We were drinking coffee when we were bombarded by the Antonov, a Russian cargo plane tricked out as a makeshift bomber by the Sudanese Air Force. When the aircraft's slow lumbering drone interrupted the morning briefing, the officers of Sudan's SPLA-N guerrilla army paused with their coffee glasses in their hands, scanning the cloudy sky. Then, with shouts of 'Antonov', everyone in the secret barracks deep in the bush scrambled, rushing into shallow foxholes to await the attack. The bombs, eight in total, exploded harmlessly in the undergrowth a few hundred metres to either side of the rebel outpost. As the Antonov flew away the men clambered out of their foxholes, laughing nervously and brushing dirt from their uniforms. Only a teenage recruit still hid in his shelter, staring up at the sky, his young face creased with fear.

'The Arabs are too afraid to fight us like men, in the bush, so they bomb us with Antonovs and shell us from miles away,' said Brigadier-General Mohammed Younes. 'I swear by God, if we had just one anti-aircraft missile, just one, the Antonovs would not come again, and we would be in [the provincial capital of] Ed Damezin by now.'

But the SPLA-N guerrillas of Sudan's rebellious Blue Nile state had little hope of obtaining modern weaponry. When South Sudan declared independence in July 2011, the new country withdrew its comparatively elite 10th Division from Blue Nile state, leaving its erstwhile local allies to fight the Sudanese government alone, equipped with just a handful of outdated anti-aircraft machine guns and ageing T-55 tanks. The rebels possessed perhaps a dozen Toyota pick-up trucks to move men and supplies across the war-torn province's few dirt tracks. Their only strengths lay in their ability to live in spartan conditions and their eagerness to fight and die for the unwieldy-sounding goal of 'popular consultation', which in practice meant the installation of their leader, former state governor Malik Agar, as president in Khartoum. The likelihood of this ever happening seemed precisely nil, but still they were willing to fight and die for the cause.

The conflict in Sudan had dragged on, in one form or another, for fifty years, killing over 2 million people and leading to the dispossession of millions more. A peace agreement in 2005 between the mostly Christian, black African SPLA (Sudan People's Liberation Army) rebels of the south and the Arab government in the north was followed in 2011 by the birth of the new, independent nation of South Sudan. But not everyone was celebrating. While South Sudan began its faltering existence as a military dictatorship-meets-UN protectorate, struggling with the worst health, education and development metrics in the entire world, the peace agreement had condemned the SPLA's allies in Darfur, South Kordofan and Blue Nile either to acceptance of Khartoum's rule or the continuation of the liberation struggle, alone. They chose to fight on, in a bloody, sputtering campaign of bush and desert ambushes and village massacres almost entirely ignored by the outside world.

I needed a war to cover, and this looked like the one. For freelancers, covering conflicts involves a series of calculations about the commercial viability of other people's tragedy. You need to be either the first journalist in, before the big networks flood the battlefields with crews, SUVs, and satellite uplinks, or the last in, when it's too dangerous for the big networks to insure their staff. I'd delayed the big war of the day, Syria, for too long, trying to get a commission in advance, and now everyone I knew was in Aleppo, bussed in and escorted around by the FSA (Free Syrian Army) rebels who still thought the presence of journalists could make some kind of difference, stepping on each other's toes and competing for the fickle attention of the big news organisations. Syria was commercially unviable now, but no one was in the Sudan border zones. I hadn't considered this may have been for a very good reason.

Decades of war and underdevelopment had left South Sudan logistically the most difficult country in the world in which to work. Roads were practically non-existent, and the few pitted dirt tracks across the vast, empty savannah and thorny bush were made impassable for half the year by the summer rains which annexed half the road network to the Sudd, the world's largest swamp. A handful of tribal insurgencies, supported by Khartoum, made road travel inadvisable across much of the country at the best of times; the drunken aggressiveness of the SPLA constabulary made the thousands of lonely bush checkpoints along the road a cumulatively wearying ordeal.

It was May 2012, and after weeks of negotiation and travel, armed with impressively stamped paperwork from the various military and internal security branches of the South Sudanese government and the northern rebels, my friend and colleague Stéphane and I finally reached Doro, a refugee camp on the farthest north-eastern border of South Sudan, which functioned as the Blue Nile rebels' main logistics base.

In Doro, we spent weeks living in the straw hut compound of Sila Musa Kenji, a former District Governor of Blue Nile now living in exile as a refugee, entirely dependent on the UN for food and security. The Blue Nile rebels weren't accustomed to journalists, and kept us with Sila's family for nearly a month of circuitous conversations with barefoot internal security officers about our journalistic intentions and political affiliations until they finally trusted us enough to let us cross the border into the war zone. Perching ourselves on top of a Land Cruiser crammed with rice and aluminium cooking pots distributed by the UN to refugees, which were then promptly commandeered by the rebels to be sold on to adventurous Ethiopian traders inside Blue Nile, we drove for hours along a dusty trail that wove its way through thick palm forests and over lushly wooded hills to the border.

This, it transpired, was a faded piece of red cord strung across the trail, manned by a few bored rebels. Knots of refugees had passed us in each direction along the way: women bringing goats for sale towards Doro; children carrying bales of possessions on their heads; hunters resting spears across their shoulders, their scrawny hounds yapping at their feet. Driving in Blue Nile was always a greater danger than the war itself, the rebels' few Land Cruisers being crammed with up to thirty fighters balanced atop whatever bales of goods they had to sell. Whenever the drivers saw a giant hole in the road, they dealt with it by speeding up and conquering it with brute force rather than negotiating it carefully. On this trip, I flew off the car at a nasty corner and hurtled metres away into the mud, which was fortunately soft enough for me to land unharmed. The soldiers clucked and gasped in concern as, muddied and bleeding, I shouted at the driver in bad Arabic never to speed at corners again. He nodded, chastened, smiling sheepishly. At the very next corner I flew off again.

We drove for hours through an eerie landscape of deserted villages. In one village, Bellatoma, the rebels showed me the grave of eleven civilians killed a couple of months before when government Antonovs bombed the once bustling market. They gathered up sharp fragments of rusty steel to show me, picking the lethal shards out of tree trunks and tossing them on to the dusty ground. The survivors had tipped the mangled bodies into a bomb crater, covering the makeshift grave with thorn branches to deter scavenging animals, before fleeing across the border. Now Bellatoma lay abandoned, its cluster of grass huts collapsing in the summer rain, its trees heavy with unpicked fruit. The rebels gathered long sticks and beat the sour harvest from the trees with happy shouts and beaming grins, filling their pockets with peanuts from an abandoned hut before clambering back onboard the Land Cruisers and heading on. That night, we slept in a rebel compound of grass huts in the abandoned town of Yabus, a constant target for government bombing raids. Now all the farmers had fled across the border, the local wildlife was reasserting control of the area. The rebels gave me an armed escort when I went outside to piss before bed, to guard me from the lions prowling outside. Giant centipedes uncoiled themselves by the hundreds from the straw roof and dropped on to us with heavy thuds while we slept.

Our constant companion in Blue Nile was David Stephen, a young rebel military intelligence officer just back from a training course in Uganda with a pair of shiny black boots to show for it. He took painstaking care not to muddy them in the camp's many puddles, and took a preening pleasure in his appearance.

When he was assigned to us back in Doro, he'd politely answered our questions about conditions at the front with vague deflections before summoning up courage with a deep breath and asking us for the information he most craved from the outside world. 'I need to ask you one thing, as journalists. It is very important to all of us.' Go on, I said. 'It is about Craig David. Is he still alive? We have received information that he has lost his life.' I reassured him this was not the case, and he laughed exultantly. 'I am so happy, so happy. We love Craig here. He is a good man, with wise things to say about women and love. You know, I have named my only son Craig? And because he takes my name as his surname, his name is Craig David too.' I imagined this young Craig David growing up in a refugee camp while his father went back and forth to the front. David scrabbled around for a Craig David tape and put it in the Land Cruiser's cassette deck, singing along loudly as the rebels in the back were jolted over the trail, staring out impassively at the silent forest all around us.

Like many rebels, David had been pressed into the SPLA as a child. 'I was nine when I joined,' he said. 'It was very hard at first. They taught me how to march, and how to roll on the ground, and how to use the gun. It was very heavy. But the government had sent people to burn our village and kill our people and take their cattle. I saw this with my own eyes. It made us very sad, so we joined the SPLA. I was captured by the government when I was twelve, after a battle in a place called Gabela, near Kurmuk. They took us to Khartoum, where I spent sixteen years. They wanted to train us as leaders to rule Blue Nile for the government. Khartoum was good, I learned English and began my studies at Khartoum University's Medical Faculty. But I didn't have enough money to finish my course so when the war began I came back to Kurmuk and rejoined the SPLA.'

As far as David was concerned, this was a purely ethnic conflict resulting from the Khartoum regime's showing favour towards Arab and Arabising nomads over the settled African tribes. 'The government ruled that all our lands belong to them, so when our people cut trees and dug the gold from the ground, they sent men to punish us. They even let the Arabs come to our villages with their cows, and when the cows ate our crops in the fields we would fight them and then the army would punish us. They gave the Arabs guns and let them beat us, and so these things made us run away and join the SPLA. We are fighting for our rights, and our autonomy, that is all. But they refuse. So we will fight them all the way to Sennar[20] and stop there for a while, and then fight all the way to Khartoum and make the whole country a democracy. And tell the people in Britain, it is your responsibility to give us weapons because you gave us to the Arabs long ago when we were still free. You colonised the Arabs and then they came down here with you, and they married our sisters, and when they produced children they told these children you cannot marry these black dogs and instead they take our land for themselves. So that is why we fight.'

We drove on in silence, as Craig David crooned in sugared tones of making love while we made our way through the dark forest.

Yabus was just a rear base, the de facto capital of the Uduk tribe who made up most of the SPLA's younger fighters and junior officers. With a strange precision, the Uduk officers all informed me they had been converted

---

20 Town in northern Blue Nile, once the capital of the powerful Funj kingdom

to Christianity in 1939, which set them apart from their senior officers, Muslims who drew their roots from the once-powerful and long-crushed Funj sultanate in the wild hills further north. The real fighting was in the north, away from Uduk territory, another full day's drive across a few dozen kilometres of dirt tracks and rushing streams. At each of these, at least one of the three or four vehicles in the convoy would get stuck in the torrent and fighters would jump off, setting down their rifles and squawking trussed-up chickens on the muddy banks, to dig out the wheels and push the vehicles free, accompanied by work songs and whoops of exultation. The rebels had captured bull-dozers from government convoys and used them to clear new trails through the forest until the Antonovs latched on, and made them unsafe to use by constant bombing, and the process of trail-clearing began again. But the rainy season was setting in and soon all the trails would become impassable. Once we were at the front, we'd be stuck there until the skies cleared, weeks or months later.

The SPLA-N – the ramshackle northern offshoot of the SPLA, which, south of the border, had become the national army – moved constantly between a succession of impromptu bases, mostly abandoned villages of circular mud huts, hidden away in clearings in the thick forest. It was a bucolic sort of existence, sleeping out beneath tall trees on spread blankets or wooden cots, falling asleep to the croak of frogs in nearby streams and the occasional crash of government artillery firing blindly at the thick bush. At daybreak, the soldiers would rise slowly, shivering in the morning cold, folding their blankets away and spitting their smokers' phlegm into the dust. Brushwood fires would be lit and the officers would huddle in a circle, sipping hot coffee or tea from old plastic brake-fluid containers and discussing the day's strategy as their men were drawn up into ranks for morning parade, smartly wheeling and stamping their way through drill inherited from some long-gone colonial past, here beneath the towering baobab trees.

The strategy was generally one of waiting where we were. Since the government of South Sudan withdrew all meaningful support for the Blue Nile rebels, the SPLA-N were hampered by an almost total absence of supplies, particularly of fuel. A plan had been drawn up to recapture the strategic hill town of Kurmuk straddling the border with Ethiopia, which would open up new supply lines and allow them to press an advance towards the north of the state, but even taking Kurmuk would require stockpiles of diesel for the rebels' dozen or so Land Cruisers and handful of ageing, captured T-55 tanks, which they simply didn't have. There were ongoing, off-the-book negotiations between the rebels and sympathetic generals in the South Sudanese army for a one-off shipment of fuel, but until that arrived, the rebels weren't going anywhere.

'The most important thing is to have very good plans for our forces,' said the officer commanding this sector, Brigadier-General Abdullah Ali, a softly spoken rebel who'd looked after us from the day we arrived, 'how to attack the enemy and how to keep our soldiers safe. I made very, very good plans how to attack, because we have our visions, and we are suffering a lot in the bush, because as you see now we are not in the towns, and we are asking God to support us so we can get our refugees and get our IDPs[21] back home. This is our plan and all our soldiers know that. But the main problem is logistics, especially food and fuel, and then some ammunition. And then, additionally, the rains are too heavy these days, the people cannot move. They are moving and finding problems on the main road, and getting stuck. That is a problem.'

The impossibility of moving across roads that the rains had turned to pools of liquid mud was, in truth, a sort of blessing for the rebels. The impassable bush trails neutralised the government's vast superiority in wheeled transport, making their convoys slow-moving and vulnerable to the ambush parties the rebels sent out trudging through the bush every morning, to shoot up the soft-skinned lorries full of ammunition and terrified government conscripts. But without their own supplies of food, life was getting harder for the rebels. UN food aid for the refugees in the

---

21 Internally Displaced Persons, i.e. internal refugees

camps was often commandeered to feed the fighters at the front to the north, and heavy sacks of USAID sorghum would arrive every week or so for the men to dole out amongst themselves.

General Abdullah complained to us once that the UN weren't airdropping his men food, and asked how they were expected to fight in these circumstances. It was difficult to explain why this was impossible: for these men, this was a total war, waged by the government primarily against the civilian population. All these fighters lived in the camps and commuted to war and back every few weeks, leaving their families behind them. The border between Sudan and South Sudan existed only on paper, and if the government didn't respect the laws of war, then they couldn't see why international organisations were compelled to respect Khartoum's sovereignty within Blue Nile.

We lived between feast and famine. On good days, the officers would order sheep slaughtered and we'd eat five or six meals of chargrilled meat, or bowls of bitter innard stew, livid green with undigested cud, atop *asifa*, a dense and sticky sorghum polenta. In bad weeks, we might have a handful of boiled sorghum grains a day, or even nothing at all for a day or two, and everyone would be too hungry to do anything but lie beneath the trees, dozing or chainsmoking the harsh Supermatch cigarettes rationed out to the men. 'It is not good to keep your men in their positions without food for days,' General Abdullah told me. 'They are hungry and some of them are already beginning to put down their weapons and walk back to the camps to get food.'

And always the government bombers would be overhead, the low whine of their propellers sending us rushing beneath trees for cover, the camps silent as we huddled still, holding our breath, waiting for them to pass overhead. The bombing was constant and ineffective, the unguided bombs always landing with a crash somewhere in the distance in the empty bush, and when the payload landed, seven, eight, nine bombs, and the Antonov flew away, we'd brush ourselves down and wander back out into the sunlight, stretching ourselves and continuing our interrupted conversations where we'd left off.

The Sudanese government uses Antonov cargo planes as makeshift bombers, rolling unguided missiles out of their rear ramps in a sort of steampunk aerial campaign against the rebels – a tactic far more effective against civilian villages than the ever-moving SPLA-N guerrillas. Sometimes I wondered if the sanctions against Khartoum weren't counter-productive; if the regime were given the chance to use guided munitions, perhaps they'd hit the rebel forces and leave the civilians alone. But I'd spent a few days in the Nuba Mountains a few weeks earlier, where the government used their relatively modern MIG jets to drop cluster bombs on civilian villages in the full knowledge that no one in the outside world knew, or cared, or would ever meaningfully protest.

Yet even underequipped, outgunned and under constant aerial bombardment, the rebels were keen to fight and refused to admit the possibility of defeat. 'We will fight with him with the Kalashnikov, this is the rifle we have,' Captain Stephen Tira, a young Protestant chaplain and Moral Operations officer told me. 'We don't have any other weapons. We will fight with him with the Kalashnikov and we will capture them from him. We are fighting for our freedom, we want our freedom, we want our motherland. We want Sudan to become one national democracy for the people of Sudan, all. To become united, to work together. Yeah, we want to rule the Sudan as the negro people, as the human beings. And we have to do that to get our freedom for our motherland. And we will defend our land, we will not move anywhere. We will be around him [Bashir], we will strike all his materials. As he shot our civilians, we will shoot him. We will shoot him.'

In truth, it was unclear what the desired victory would bring. Some officers wanted an independent Blue Nile, others union with South Sudan, others to take the war all the way to Khartoum and overthrow the government there, and then rule all of Sudan. But each of these goals was so far from being achieved it almost didn't matter what they were fighting for. They were fighting because they had to, and because they always had. Almost all these fighters had grown up in refugee camps across the border in Ethiopia, and now their families were living in refugee camps once again, this time in South Sudan. When their sons reached fifteen or sixteen, they too would take up arms and join the struggle, and so it would go on, in an endless war entirely forgotten by the world.

Whatever gross disparity of arms they fought with, the rebels were all buoyed with the invincibility of the magic charms they carried around their necks. Witchdoctors, or *faqirs*, would scrawl Arabic incantations on lined UNICEF paper, wrap them in leather amulets and sell them in the refugee camps for up to $100 a charm, a vast amount for these destitute fighters. All the soldiers would show me their worn necklaces of amulets, saying this one keeps you safe against Kalashnikovs, this one against RPGs, this one against Dushkas,[22] this one against knives. And Antonovs, I asked, is there an amulet against the bombers? They all laughed out loud, shaking their heads, at my ignorance. Of course there isn't, they laughed, no magic can save a man from the Antonovs. Do you know nothing in London?

———————

Colonel Farjallah Hamid was the dashing leader of a commando unit whose men lived closest to the enemy

---

22 Soviet heavy machine gun, designed for use against aircraft

positions and harassed the Sudanese government forces daily. Whenever we visited his men, every week or so, a long drive through the bush in their hilltop eyries overlooking the enemy, they looked content and well fed, though wilder and more piratical than the ordinary infantry, sometimes cooking beef kebabs from a stolen cow, at other times spit roasting guinea fowl the Colonel had detailed snipers to hunt in the bush. Farjallah's men were waiting to lead the assault on the government-held town of Kurmuk, a strategic prize straddling the Ethiopian border, and he kept their spirits high.

A Muslim from the remote and conservative Ingassena Hills, Farjallah nevertheless framed the conflict as a struggle against Bashir's Islamist ideology. 'They want to rule us with what they have in their minds, and this is the system of Shariah law, which cannot take all of us together. Because here you have some of us, they don't even have a religion. How can you deal with them? Yeah, you cannot chase them away from Sudan. So we cannot live together, that is our problem, so we will fight ... even if only one man remains, he will fight.'

In fact, however, those civilians who did remain within the conflict zone were uniformly viewed with suspicion by the rebels as potential spies for the regime. Herdsmen who wandered too close to our encampments would be detained and interrogated then packed away with warnings not to

197

return. The only trustworthy civilians, for the rebels, were those living in the refugee camps or in the few market towns still functioning secretly in the bush. Blue Nile is rich in one resource, gold, flecks of which would glitter in the rushing streams we washed in and drank from. Soldiers would be glimpsed wandering through the bush with metal detectors and spades, searching for nuggets to be gathered together and sold in the secret markets to Ethiopian traders in return for sheep and rice and sugary biscuits and lentils and coffee beans, to keep the army fed and willing to fight.

Long hungry weeks passed, playing endless games of cards, sheltering from storms, swimming in the river, smoking and working our way through endless bouts of dysentery. Whenever a sheep was killed, they'd hang the meat and innards on tree branches to dry in the sun and last us a few more precious days. Within minutes, the meat would turn a writhing bottle green as the flies from the bubbling squat latrine a few metres away clustered on it, gorging themselves. Sometimes, soldiers would break open a termite mound and pan fry the insects in their own oil, winnowing away the weightless wings in the breeze and providing us with a rare treat of nutty-tasting protein. Feral dogs, their patchy coats thick with lice and fat engorged ticks, would snuffle around the embers of the campfire for sheep bones, barely tolerated, kicked away with pained yelps when they came too close.

At night, soldiers with wind-up torches would scour the camp for the scorpions that took a constant toll on the unit's fighting strength. Young rebels would bring their flocks of sheep back to camp from grazing in the bush and corral them in circles of thorn branches, safe from prowling leopards. Soldiers with *rabaaba*[23] made from cooking pans, twigs and bullets would sing long songs about the war in their tribal languages, mournful rhythmic songs that sounded like some ancient African forerunner of the Blues. And always in the background the hiss and crackle of the solar-powered radio, transmitting coded messages in long rhythmic Uduk chants and sudden jarring bursts of English as unseen generals moved their men like chess pieces around the endless silent bush. It was beautiful, in some ways. I was unutterably bored.

The problem was, I'd come here for a war and was living through an interminable low-intensity camping holiday. The brutal truth about television reporting is that without at least a few seconds of thrilling combat to spice it up, it's almost impossible to sell war footage, whatever the actual content of the story. Our Blue Nile footage was exclusive, but consisting as it mostly did of shots of soldiers staring glumly into the middle distance and playing cards, it would be difficult to sell. I began to realise I'd chosen the wrong war – no one in the outside

23 Lyres

world cared about this one, and our footage wasn't about to change their minds. If only I'd gone to Aleppo, I daydreamed, I'd have all the action I wanted and could sell it with a single phone call. Unfairly, I began to despise the rebels for their torpor. No wonder this war had lasted for generations, I told Stephane my cameraman, if this is how they fight it.

Every day we'd wake at dawn and then do precisely nothing but watch the sun slowly traverse the sky until it touched the horizon and the soldiers would get their bedding out and fall asleep again. I'd brought one book, a collection of Graham Greene's travel journalism, which I read from cover to cover seven times, at which point I began to recycle it as toilet paper. One morning, petulantly, I refused to get out of bed at all and slept all day while concerned colonels tried to coax me out of my sulk from the door of my hut. Every couple of days they'd send patrols out to shoot up convoys, but wouldn't tell us until they came back, covered in sweat and wide-eyed from the rush of combat. No matter how much I pleaded, they wouldn't let me film them. In the midst of war, I was going cold turkey from action and I hated them for it. I missed the chaos of Libya and began to hatch plans for Syria, dreaming of war and glory.

Instead, I taught them noughts and crosses and for days we'd play it with twigs in the dust, until I got bored again.

We'd draw long tracks in the dust and race millipedes for cigarettes until that too got boring. I'd walk to the river some days and spend hours washing or panning for tiny flecks of gold which I'd laboriously collect in a cigarette packet – I still have enough for a ring, somewhere. Once, an angry crowd of warriors shouted at us, waving their Kalashnikovs, when we tried to ford a fast-flowing river on a shopping trip for cigarettes. They were from the Mayak tribe, and this was their river, taboo for any non-Mayak to enter. There was a standoff between our escort and the Mayak as they cursed each other, waving rifles in the air for emphasis; the Mayak won. I was half enthralled by this ancient tribal world, half exhausted by all their bullshit. We made a long detour through the forest to find another ford. For all that these men were united in battle against the government, the ancient tribal boundaries still demanded respect.

It felt as if this was an Africa outside time, barely touched by the colonial rule of either London or Khartoum, where hunters still stalked leopards with spears and every move was consulted with witchdoctors. For most of the men, we were the first whites they'd ever spoken to, certainly the first not in a position of authority over them – able to dole out aid or deny it as orders in Nairobi or Geneva or New York decreed. We were anomalies, and they never quite worked out how to view us.

We'd established ourselves after a few days as honorary officers, privileged with a place in the circle of huts that made up the mess, and as all the officers carried a cane wrapped in snakeskin or an iron axe on a long pole as a badge of office, I whittled myself a stick with my local dagger and wedged an anti-aircraft round on to the end for decoration, which I'd carry around as I inspected the troops every day like a First World War general. In a bid to win access to the fighting, I'd shamelessly exaggerated the extent of my TA career, to the extent that I'd confer with the generals as they drew up fantasy plans in the sand for assaults that never happened, debating the best locations to place their non-existent support weapons, or wander around chiding child soldiers like an officious prefect for resting their rifle barrels in the dirt. It was all bullshit but it kept the boredom away, for a time.

On some level, they always suspected we were spies sent by Vauxhall Cross and would feed us false information in a bid to win favour with our imagined superiors or else make long, impassioned pleas for anti-aircraft missiles we were in no position to donate. Once, they sent a military intelligence officer to interrogate us about the war. He'd barely left his village before the conflict, and asked us if it was true that white people couldn't die of natural causes but only by gunshot. I informed him this wasn't the case, that my mother had died of

cancer. He looked at me suspiciously and wrote something – presumably 'NB: Whites CAN die' – in a note-
book he tucked back within the folds of his *jellaba*. With
no signal, we couldn't call home; with no electricity,
we couldn't recharge our camera batteries and thus
even film much; the nightly artillery barrages from the
government side were too sporadic and distant to film
in the dark, and the bombers always flew too high to
make filming them worthwhile. The whole thing was a
massive waste of time and I sometimes wept alone in
my hut from frustration.

One day, I exploded with rage at the logistics officer,
a Brigadier. I demanded to see his superior officer and
state my case to film some action. He told me sadly he'd
love to send me to meet him but he had no vehicles or
fuel. Fine, I said, we'll walk. His general was forty miles
away across the bush. Shrugging to show that this was
a bad idea, he wrote a movement order with a biro in
painstaking military English and his secretary stamped
it repeatedly with all the symbols of his office – for a
guerrilla army of a few thousand men, with a handful of
vehicles and which was reliant on the unwitting charity
of NGOs for sustenance, the SPLA-N were addicted to
all the bureaucracy of a vast Soviet armoured division,
I suppose as a comforting replacement for any ability to
make a difference on the ground.

We trudged off, with no food and far too little water. The tracks had been destroyed by rain and each footstep added another half-kilo of thick clay as we clomped along like Victorian deepsea divers until the mud fell off under its own weight and the process began again. Thick black clouds of flies settled on us for the ride as we trudged through a hellish landscape of charred trees and burned-out villages towards divisional headquarters. Eventually we ran out of water and sat for hours at the side of a stagnant green pool, stinking with rotting animal corpses, boiling water we hoped wouldn't kill us. It was only forty miles but it took us two days: hiding in the scrub at David's insistence from armed and mysterious passersby; all three of us sleeping huddled under my Barbour beneath a thorn tree during a violent storm; making a fire from sodden wood when the sun rose, and trudging on.

We passed streams of refugees on the road, fleeing on their camels from the torching of their villages by government militias, and swapped them sugar and Ugandan tea for water as they showed us the dried roots they'd survived on for weeks on the road. The women looked like crones but carried their squalling malnourished babies slung across their withered chests. They told us the militias had burned down all the huts in their villages, had shot all the men they found and stolen their cattle. There wasn't much to say in response, apart from vague commiseration, so we passed on. Eventually we found some soldiers hunting gazelles in an abandoned village. They nearly shot us by mistake. Reluctantly they took us to their commanders, a few hours' walk ahead, who stared at us with disgust as we drank almost all their supply of fresh water and wolfed down their slender rations of boiled rice.

The meeting achieved little, in the way that meetings in Sudan always achieve little. The general thanked us for visiting, like callers at a Victorian townhouse, and packed us back to our original base by Land Cruiser with empty promises of action, soon. Along the way we stopped at other bases, dropping off crates of ammunition and sacks of sorghum, sitting cross-legged on mats making small talk with the tribal chieftains who commanded each village detachment, sharing cigarettes as they toyed with the long swords by their sides. When we reached the camp again, the officers there treated us like eccentric heroes and stuffed us with stewed red lentils and boiled sugared powdered milk for strength. There was a new sense of purpose at the camp as their overall commander, Brigadier-General Jundis Suleiman, had joined them from his secret base somewhere in the bush, an indication of approaching combat.

His convoy had been bombed twice along the road and he was in a foul mood. Nevertheless, he brought out a sheaf of military paperwork from a distant training course in Uganda and we bonded over the convoluted Sandhurst orders process, a semi-remembered brain-stultifying flow-chart of actions necessary to kill the enemy in the most efficient manner possible. General Jundis was a good man, if perhaps not the most effective officer. The others all rolled their eyes whenever his name was mentioned, and it was hinted that his promotion was more a matter of tribal affiliation than ability. Like all the senior officers, he was a Funj Muslim rather than a Uduk Christian like the majority of his men, but much as they maligned him, he'd brought food with him, which raised morale. We interviewed him for form's sake, pretending we'd switched the camera on. After a polite and circuitous post-dinner chat in broken English and Arabic, I wandered away from the campfire and sat with his drivers to smoke *bango*, the weak wild local cannabis rolled in harsh spliffs of UNICEF notepaper, and to wish I was anywhere else in the world.

The arrival of General Jundis spurred the men into the masquerade of activity that infects any army whose general suddenly shows up. Morning drill was sharper, and the junior officers began beavering away at compiling long lists of those soldiers fit for combat, absent without leave, too sick for action or imprisoned, sucking their pencils thoughtfully as they scrawled in their notebooks in neat English copperplate. The air raids also hit us more frequently – evidence, Jundis claimed, that spies were leaking his location to the regime. He checked we didn't have the satellite phones we couldn't afford. Like all the Sudanese rebels, he was convinced that his data was being sent straight to the regime in Khartoum. After a few days devoted to counting bullets, refuelling tanks, charging radios, doling out shells to the newly arrived artillery battery, and surreptitiously smoking *bango* – which was in theory banned as a breach of military discipline, though self-sown plots of spiky seedlings were carefully guarded even in the centre of the camp – we were sent north-east with a convoy of troops into what days before had been enemy territory.

The soldiers, crammed twenty-five at a time on the back of each Land Cruiser, watched the bush around us carefully. Unusually, they kept their weapons cocked and at the ready, though the officers wouldn't tell us what was happening. Every few kilometres men would jump off the vehicles and patrol the bush before waving us ahead. This was different; this, finally, was war.

———————

At the village of Demasuro, on the edge of Kurmuk, we parked up beneath a stand of giant baobab trees under a craggy cliff face and the soldiers fanned out, setting up machine-gun and rifle positions in a circle around us. We could see government-held Kurmuk on a hillside ahead of us, and our mobile phones all pinged into life as we got a month's worth of missed texts courtesy of the regime network. This was new ground for the rebels. Dust-covered infantry cheered us as we came in, and performed wild war dances, waving their Kalashnikovs and spears in the air and singing songs of victory. These men had captured Demasuro a few hours earlier. There were a few spent ammunition cases on the ground, and no bodies. As war is waged in Sudan, the enemy had fled after a polite show of resistance, with no casualties on either side.

We donned our armour, hoping for action, and waited around for hours for General Jundis' convoy. When he arrived, the men all cheered him as a victor. I just wished they'd get on with the fighting already. His deputy, the wiry and intense engineer officer Colonel Soloman Damdam, gave a rousing speech to his men as they lined up beneath the ancient trees, informing them that two government tanks had fled into the bush and it was their job to find and destroy them. After smartly saluting him and wheeling out of formation, they ran whooping, thirty to a vehicle, and jumped onboard, waving rocket-propelled grenades and rifles above their heads as the jeeps roared off into the silent bush. We had lunch with the generals, waiting for news. There was no news. The assault fizzled out. At dusk, we went back to the base we'd come from, my body aching as the wasted adrenaline ebbed away.

That evening I spent hours discussing tactics with General Jundis, surrounded by nodding officers, and he finally accepted we were capable of filming his men assault the next position, without impeding them. But Stephane, my cameraman, was sick with dysentery. He shat himself repeatedly on the bumpy journey back to base, and General Jundis sadly ordered us to leave for the UK, asking us to return soon with anti-aircraft missiles. I begged him to let us stay, telling him he just needed to ride it out like we had half a dozen times before, but he ordered us back across the border with South Sudan, giving us our own vehicle, the mark of an emergency.

Half an hour into the journey, it ran out of fuel and we were forced to walk for a whole day across parched waterless bush, the evacuation bringing my colleague closer to death than he ever would have been in the frontline. Eventually we reached the border village of Guffa, beside a raging stream. I forced sugary Turkish mango squash and salt down him as he wavered between consciousness and extinction. They set him up a camp bed in the village square and he slept the deep sleep of the dying. Once, when he stopped responding, we placed a mirror over his mouth and decided he'd died when it didn't cloud over. His body was cold and slick with sweat. We said prayers for him and I wondered for hours what to tell his family, and whether they would blame me, as they surely should.

But he finally woke, waking us, vomiting in the dawn, and we started up with shouts when what we thought was his corpse came back to life.

He improved the next day, as we waited for hours for a tractor to take us back across the border. When he'd recovered his strength with coffee and cigarettes, he checked his rucksack and realised his laptop had been stolen by one of our rebel escorts. With finely tuned outrage, I demanded to see the colonel commanding this outpost, and coldly informed him we were his guests, we were the only people in the world willing to witness this war and broadcast it to the outside world, and demanded to know what he would do about the stolen laptop. He assured us he would solve the problem. I assumed he would call a show parade and search his soldiers' knapsacks; instead he took us to the hut of a witchdoctor. I paid the *faqir*[24] $7 and he began to commune with the djinns. He reached into a plastic bag and pulled out a UNICEF notebook filled with Arabic incantations. He extracted a mummified chameleon from the folds of his *jellaba* and broke off its limbs, spitting on each leg in turn and placing it on a corner of the page. When he'd summoned his demons and fallen into a trance, his mobile rang with the old school Nokia ringtone and he checked it quickly before hiding it. We pretended nothing had happened. As he began mumbling his incantations,

---

24 Witchdoctor

the sky turned black and storm winds began to fill the *tukul*[25] with dust. His eyes rolled back in his head as he grasped the air, communing with the other side. After an hour or so of moans and gasps he shook himself out of his trance and informed us he had seen the malefactor. Yes? we asked. It was a soldier, he said, a black man in uniform. Considering we'd barely seen a civilian in a month this was hardly a revelation. He asked us if we wanted to put a curse on the man, to turn his bowels to water and wither his crops for all time. For an extra $5 we said yes and put it down to experience, some superstitious part of me hoping the thief would shit himself to bloody death. We never got the laptop back.

We went to Kenya, tried to sell the footage, failed, smoked lots of weed. The bustling city felt oppressive and threatening after the empty bush. On the flight home from Nairobi, I was seated between a gaggle of nest-haired public schoolgirls, dressed head-to-toe in Jack Wills, braying about how they'd experienced the real Africa on their safari gap year. I wanted to slap their faces. Instead, I drank myself to sleep with BA Bloody Marys and told myself I'd never work in Africa again.

A few months later, I went to Mali.

---

25 Straw-roofed African mud hut

MALI

Spring 2013

It's hard not to look like an all-conquering hero when you're resting your boot on a severed head, but this Malian gendarme wasn't even trying to be magnanimous in victory. Nonchalantly resting his arms on the machine gun hanging from his neck and swathed in a long ribbon of bullets, which glinted in the fierce afternoon sunlight, the young gendarme was grinning triumphantly under his helmet. The severed head's expression was harder to read.

'This jihadist, is he a Malian, do you think?' I asked.

The gendarme gave it a little kick and the head rolled over, staring glassily up at me. A fly crawled out of one nostril and a fresh dribble of dark red blood started to drip slowly from its open mouth into the dust. The gendarme's buddy peered down curiously at the head.

'Him? Nah, maybe from Niger or Algeria.'

He was probably right – after all, by this time northern Mali had been a honeypot for West Africa's most committed Islamists for over a year, since the gendarmes and the rest of the Malian military had run away from the jihadist onslaught almost without a fight. Equally, he could have been a local from one of the Islamist villages a few kilometres up the slow-moving Niger river. Either way, the head was saying nothing.

Nearby, a gaggle of French news crews were filming the chief of police, Colonel Maiga, thrusting branded microphones in his face as he described the Malian army's great victory here the day before. They were pointedly avoiding the head. You'd never get the head on TV, one of the crew told me later, so why bother? What would you be trying to achieve? Around this walled compound in central Gao, a cordon of French soldiers were securing the scene for the media circus and avoiding the cameras. Officially, this was a Malian victory. Why complicate things?

I'd come up to Gao a couple of weeks earlier with the first French convoy since the city was recaptured from the jihadists a few days before. I was freelancing for the Chinese news channel CCTV, happy to have found a war in a fascinating country with little competition from other freelancers. With just one fatality, helicopter pilot Damien Boiteux, the French intervention in Mali had run smoothly up to that point, more like a military exercise than a genuine campaign. This was the kind of war politicians dreamed of, a war without body bags, against an enemy whom everyone agreed were the bad guys. A few days previously, Gao had been home to Western Europe's most feared adversary, one-eyed jihadist commander Mokhtar Belmokhtar, mastermind of the In Amenas hostage crisis.[26] A fearsome constellation of jihadist groups – Ansar Dine (AD), the Movement for Unity and Jihad in West Africa (MUJAO), al-Qaeda in the Islamic Maghreb (AQIM) – had gathered in the dusty Saharan caravan town, to grow fat on the profits from the ransoming of Western hostages and the smuggling of cocaine to Europe, and to plot jihad against the West.

Laden with weapons and explosives smuggled from Libya or confiscated from the inept Malian army, Belmokhtar and his fellow jihadist leaders had turned Gao into the greatest single strategic threat to Western Europe. France had no choice but to act, its politicians said, and its fast-paced Mali campaign seemed a model display of Western military might. The French desert blitzkrieg, supported by air strikes, had recaptured the Islamist-held cities of northern Mali in a matter of days. The enemy had melted away from Gao without a fight. Mission accomplished, everyone said with dark irony. We'd all be home again in a few weeks,

---

26 When AQIM militants seized Algeria's desert In Amenas oil field, leading to the deaths of several Western and local staff

the French officers briefed us, as long as we prevented an insurgency developing, that is. No one wanted an African Afghanistan. Except the jihadists.

Black billboards emblazoned with al-Qaeda's flag greeted our convoy as it entered northern Mali's largest city. *Welcome to the Islamic State of Gao*, the billboards read in jaunty white-lettered French. The Emir of Gao and spiritual leader of MUJAO (Movement for Unity and Jihad in West Africa), Abdelhakim al-Sahrawi, was big on signs. *Don hijab*, they implored from every roundabout, *obey Shariah, fight the* kuffar.[27] But there had been little fighting at this point. A wave of French airstrikes had pummelled the rebels in their bases, incinerated them in their pick-up trucks and dislodged them from their capital days before these supply troops had reached here. The French seemed bored; they fidgeted with their machine guns, guzzled water and tossed their cigarette butts and empty sardine cans into the sand. The other journos in this convoy, mostly Africa hands with an emphasis on development rather than conflict, shared their disappointment. Where had the war gone? Were we too late? But it was OK, the war hadn't gone anywhere. The rebels were waiting for us. They're good like that.

We'd slept in a desert base the night before, in a mud-brick Foreign Legion fort beneath a star-shot sky, lulled to

---

27 Unbelievers

sleep by the purr of the engines of the armoured vehicles. It was an unplanned halt for the convoy: the French had found two newly laid IEDs on the road a few metres ahead of us, and we had to wait for them to be made safe in the morning light. A young Foreign Legion cavalry officer came to chat to us around our campfire. His men had just driven a captured insurgent into the fort, bundled into the back of a Land Cruiser like a trussed sheep, and he was feeling happy. 'They are cowards, these jihadists,' he said, 'when we catch them they cry like children. They're not warriors, like the Taliban. When we catch one, my men hold him down and I piss on him.' They're not too concerned about winning hearts and minds, the Foreign Legion. But then neither are the Islamists.

———————

'The problem with MUJAO isn't that they implemented Shariah,' said Ibrahim outside Gao's Kuwait Mosque as black-turbaned men filtered in for evening prayers. (Ibrahim isn't his real name. A businessman who supported MUJAO's rule, revealing his identity would put him at risk of government reprisals.) 'We are Muslims, of course we should obey God's law. The problem was that they didn't tell us they'd cut off people's hands and feet before they started doing it, to give everyone a warning. They were very bad at communication.' He shrugged. 'That was their problem.'

In fact, many people in the city expressed a degree of sympathy for MUJAO. Gao is very conservative, the kind of place where six-month-old babies wear the hijab. Unlike in Mali's other ancient desert city of Timbuktu, the Islamists of Gao didn't have to clamp down hard on music and dancing: there wasn't much here to begin with. But they still did it anyway.

In the Place de Shariah, a dusty parade ground that passes for Gao's main square, a group of bystanders took me to see the mounds of grey-black ash dotted around the sand. This is where they burned the CDs and SIM cards, they said, here they burned televisions, and here they burned all the cigarettes. They took me to a concrete pillar gouged deeply with machete blows and stained with blood. And this is where they cut off the hands, they said, we saw it all ourselves. A small boy was pushed into a squatting position and his arms stretched behind him around the pillar as they re-enacted the sharp blows with their hands. The right hand first, they said, chop, and then the left foot, chop, like this. How did you feel seeing this? I asked. They shrugged. 'They weren't good kids, the victims,' one said, 'they were just thieves. They were all bad boys.'

MUJAO had taken Gao over by turning on their former allies in the MNLA,[28] the secular Tuareg nationalist group

---

28 Mouvement National de Libération de l'Azawad

who had seized the whole of northern Mali last April, scattering the poorly trained Malian army in a matter of days. The MNLA had made bad victors: they drank the city's bars dry, raped women and children, and looted the city's shops and houses. When the locals gathered in the streets to protest against Tuareg rule, the MNLA had fired into the demonstration. In July 2012 MUJAO launched a putsch against their erstwhile Tuareg allies, capturing the city in a day and restoring order, though of the most uncompromising kind. At least they were better than the MNLA, people said. There were no more rapes, no more thefts. Business was good. If you got flogged for smoking cigarettes in the street, well, hey, cigarettes are bad for you, right?

In their own brutal way, MUJAO tried to be as humane about their amputation spree as possible. 'We're not cruel,' Abdelhakim, MUJAO's leader, had told the town's only surgeon Dr Abdelaziz Maiga in an awkward meeting in his hospital office, 'we don't want to *kill* anyone, God forbid. We just have to carry out God's law.' So he had come up with a solution: how about you cut off their hands, with anaesthetic, in as clean and surgical an environment as possible? Maiga had thought about it, and politely declined. Abdelhakim shrugged as he stood up and left the office. He had rung Maiga a few days later from a nearby village, his voice swelling with pride. 'It's OK,' he said, 'we don't need you any more, we've found a solution. As soon as we cut their hands off, we dip their stumps in boiling oil to cauterise the wound. It works really well, we've just tried it on three thieves.'

————————

I'd met a group of local vigilantes, the Gao Patrollers, while filming in the street. They took me to a nursery school filled with munitions they'd found hidden in safe houses. They opened dusty crates of Russian Grad missiles for me to inspect as kids lolled on the swings outside. 'We found these just this morning in a terrorist safe house around the corner,' their commander said. 'Every day we find something new: rifles, ammunition, explosives.' Clearly, the jihadists were laying up supplies for an insurgency. The Malian army and their Nigerien allies had set up a ring of steel around the city, with checkpoints at every entrance to shake down the locals, search their cars and check their papers. It would be impossible for the insurgents to smuggle weapons into Gao: but the beauty of their strategy was that they didn't need to. The high-walled compounds and abandoned villas of Gao were a warren of arms caches just waiting for infiltrators – or locals – to pick up the weapons and use them against the French. And so they did.

The insurgency began slowly. A few mines here and there, some IEDs placed along the road at night. Then the rebels fired rockets into town, a sign they could operate freely in the surrounding desert. One night, a helicopter hovered noisily above the city's outskirts, hunting down rebels trying to infiltrate the city while we sat in the hotel courtyard, chatting, smoking weed. There was heavy fighting overnight in the nearby village of Bourem, the Malian army told us, a jihadist stronghold. And then the suicide bomber struck: fortunately he wasn't very good at it. Aside from mildly wounding a local soldier, his sole contribution to the Malian jihad was scattering his own head and limbs across a dusty roundabout. But he sent a signal to the French, and to the citizens of Gao. We haven't gone away, you know, it said. We're coming back.

The day after I left Gao, a week after I'd arrived, the rebels struck in force. Black-clad mujahidin attacked the city centre, occupying the police station and firing from rooftops at the Malian soldiers in the streets below. French helicopters circled overhead, firing rockets at the rebels in the police station, until the fighting died down, hours later. No casualty figures were ever released.

———————

Gao's ruined customs house exemplifies France's Malian dilemma. Just two weeks before we arrived, it was a base for MUJAO and their al-Qaeda in the Islamic Maghreb allies – until the French air force intervened like a giant angry finger crushing a particularly annoying ant. It was now a wreck, its courtyard pitted with huge bomb craters, and abandoned boots and uniforms pathetically scattered about the dust. Sheets of aluminium roofing swung lazily from a bombed-out warehouse, creaking eerily in the evening breeze. France's overwhelming military superiority enabled the French to dislodge the jihadists in just a week of desert blitzkrieg. It all looked too easy. It was. You can't defeat an insurgency from 30,000 feet above.

From their vast base at the airport, the nerve centre of France's Mali campaign, the French controlled central Gao. They controlled the lone road south – or whatever stretch they happened to be driving along at the time. But the countryside and empty desert surrounding Gao, and the rest of northern Mali outside the major cities, were in insurgent hands. The rebels were locals, they knew the country. At night, they came and placed new IEDs along the road. By day, they watched the French convoys move up and down, studying how they were manned, where they stopped, analysing their strengths and weaknesses. French soldiers expressed little excitement at their Malian adventure. 'This place is just like Afghanistan,' a sergeant had said to me on the long convoy north, gesturing wearily at the empty desert with his cigarette, 'the only difference is here there are fewer mountains.' A Malian journalist in communication with the rebels told me the same thing, slightly differently. 'You, the French, the journalists, when you drive around Gao and through the villages, you don't see MUJAO. But MUJAO sees you.' He smiled. 'MUJAO sees you. *Tu comprends?*'

With the French huddled in Gao airport, the responsibility for breaking up MUJAO sleeper cells devolved to the Malian army. The idea worked well, in theory: putting a Malian face on the war allowed the ramshackle local forces to gain the vital counter-insurgency experience they would need when the French eventually withdrew, while making the intervention look less like an Iraq-style occupation. In practice, the concept worked less well. The Malian forces were almost uniformly drawn from tribes from the country's deep south, with kitbags full of magic amulets and juju fetishes to prove it. Their local knowledge was almost precisely nil, and their attempts at providing security seemed to consist primarily of detaining suspicious Tuaregs for walking too close to military installations, or the single functioning hotel.

'At least under MUJAO we didn't have all these checkpoints and searches,' one local businessman sighed to me. 'They'd look for weapons, sure, but they wouldn't check your papers or hold you up for hours for no reason. And business was good.' It didn't sound so bad, I said. 'It wasn't. What can I say? MUJAO were OK.'

But then you didn't have to scratch too deep to find sympathy for MUJAO in Gao. Once I interviewed a victim of a punitive amputation in the Place de Shariah, trying and failing to discover the reason for his mutilation as he ummed and erred, giving me contradictory and unlikely-sounding sob-stories that danced around the fact he was a petty criminal caught in the act of robbing a boutique. Halfway through, a smartly dressed local businessman walked over and started berating my interviewee. 'You motherfucker, you accursed thief!' he shouted. 'If you weren't such a fucking thief they wouldn't have cut your hand off. That's what happens! Don't think just because you only have one hand I won't kick your ass, you son of filth.' Tough town, Gao. But it was about to get a great deal tougher.

———————

Over the course of a week, accredited to an NGO trying to track weapons proliferation, I worked closely with Malian neighbourhood patrols, finding and photographing bomb factories in abandoned houses in the city centre. The scale of each day's haul was terrifying: sealed packets of Russian-made propellant charges; huge IEDs made from gas cylinders filled with military-grade explosive, each one of which could send a lightly armoured French armoured vehicle spinning into the air. But more worrying was the fact that the Malian army, informed of the location of these bomb caches, hadn't informed the French army, and that the French, when eventually alerted, didn't have the bomb-disposal capacity to clear them. The French EOD teams were all in the mountains of the far north, trying to clear a path for the infantry to capture AQIM's last Malian stronghold. The French attempt to leave a light footprint in Gao had left the city open to the insurgents. All MUJAO needed to do now was show the inhabitants that they could strike at will. And in the early hours of 21 February, they did.

A few kilometres upstream of Gao along the banks of the slow-moving Niger lay the villages of Kadji and Bourem, both Islamist strongholds, and both completely unsecured by the French army. Moving silently in traditional *pirogue* fishing canoes, a jihadist commando unit slid downriver from Kadji under cover of darkness, evading the checkpoints that studded every land entrance to Gao, and slipped undetected into the city centre. Loud explosions heralded MUJAO's return, as suicide bombers blasted their way into the city's principal buildings, the town hall and the courthouse, and their surviving comrades rushed in and fortified fire positions for the day to come. The Malian forces set up a cordon around the city centre and awaited daylight and the onset of battle. It was to be the heaviest fighting so far in the war for Gao.

After a rushed hotel breakfast of Nescafe and cigarettes, I hopped into a Malian pick-up truck crammed with anxious soldiers and headed to the city centre and the roar of gunfire. The situation was confused: the Malians knew MUJAO were in town, but didn't know where they were holed up or how many they were. Deliberate aimed shots whizzed past us from all directions as hidden jihadist snipers harassed the Malian soldiers. Eventually the colonel in charge deployed an ancient armoured vehicle to batter down the courthouse gates, with soldiers and gendarmes ambling behind it for cover. As the metal gates crumpled beneath it, the 14.5mm machine gun mounted on the back of the armoured vehicle raked the courtyard with fire to provoke a response. It did. We came under accurate fire from the courthouse and scuttled for cover. This was going to be a long day.

The colonel ordered a fire team into the post office opposite, to clear the building of suspected snipers and set up a fire position overlooking the courthouse. I followed five soldiers into the building as they manoeuvred up the stairwells, rifles at the ready, sweat dripping down their anxious faces. They shot doors open and sprayed the rooms with fire one by one, realising with a mixture of relief and disappointment that the building was empty. 'Up on the roof!' said a soldier, and we rushed up the stairwell. We burst on to the flat roof and waved at the Malian soldiers below to show we were friendly, and received a burst of machine-gun fire in response from the jihadists.

Crawling into position, bullets cracking overhead from the courthouse a narrow street's width opposite, the Malians began to spray wild unaimed bursts of Kalashnikov fire in the general direction of the jihadists, hoping to suppress them before the main assault went in. For a half hour or so, the soldiers pummelled the courthouse with rocket-propelled grenades, rifles and machine guns in a display of firepower more notable for its enthusiasm than its accuracy. The jihadists responded with carefully aimed shots. Outnumbered, outgunned, they were nevertheless far better disciplined than France's Malian allies.

An overweight corporal joined us after a few minutes, his arse hanging out of his trousers, and took charge. The Malians didn't have radios, it seemed. Instead, he chatted amicably to his commanding officer on his cell phone while firing wild Kalashnikov bursts into the courthouse with his free hand. After a brief cigarette break punctuated by the constant rat-a-tat-tat of urban combat and the joyful shrieks of the Tuareg machine-gun crew, high on war, we clattered down the stairwell back to the street to assault the courthouse. The corporal had a plan, and the colonel was going to listen to it, whether he wanted to or not. 'Where's the colonel?' shouted the corporal, almost in tears with adrenaline and frustration. 'Where the hell has he gone now?' When he found his boss, the corporal grabbed him by the arm and shouted that they needed to break down the courthouse compound walls with the armoured vehicles before rushing in en masse. 'I need to get permission first,' explained the colonel apologetically, and received an anguished wail and a violent torrent of curses from the corporal in response. But the colonel didn't need to make a decision about the wall: seconds later, a jihadist shot him in the leg, and as he lay in the dust screaming the corporal ordered everyone else to fire with everything they had.

I ran to the low wall that separated the Malian army in the street from the jihadists in the courthouse garden. A dozen men took turns to empty their magazines over it repeatedly: they may not have hit anything, but it looked good, and they were having fun. As an armoured vehicle trundled up towards the jihadist position, we darted fifty metres back down the street to reload and wait for the breach. Jihadist bullets whizzed overhead as the soldiers laid down a storm of inaccurate rifle and machine-gun fire, sometimes standing exposed in the street with the bravado conferred by a chestful of magic amulets as they loosed off bursts, gangster-style, from their sideways-tilted rifles, while being filmed by their buddies on smartphones. The armoured vehicle smashed down the wall and retreated, machine-gun bullets clattering off its thin armour. The hail of fire abated suddenly, from our side at least: the jihadists were still keeping their heads down as the Malians threw each other cigarettes and searched their pockets for spare cartridges, bickering about what to do next. The plan was to storm the courtyard, but they abandoned the mission after faltering under the jihadists' gunfire a couple of times. After four hours of fighting the Malian army had run out of ammunition, and achieved nothing. It was time for the French to ride to the rescue.

Armoured fighting vehicles of the French 92nd Infantry rumbled up to our position in an awesome display of firepower. Hiding behind them for shelter, we inched our way down the street to the wall of the courthouse adjoining Gao's once-picturesque marketplace. The vehicles' rear doors opened up with the insistent beep-beep-beep warning of European health-and-safety legislation and French infantry leaped out from their air-conditioned steel bellies, raking the Islamist positions with short aimed rifle bursts and cannon fire and rockets as the Malians relaxed behind a low wall to watch the show.

I'd come to Gao with these guys, stocky country lads from south-west France who talked about food constantly and tucked rugby balls into the recesses of their armoured vehicles. Now I followed the first fire team as they deployed into the crowded alleys of the marketplace to finish the job for the Malians. Peering around the colonnades, firing bursts into the open windows overlooking us, they crept through the deserted market. A huge Polynesian corporal scanned the alleyway through the infrared sight of his rifle as I peered over his shoulder. A jihadist jumped out of a market stall, maybe ten metres away, and aimed his grenade launcher at us. The corporal dropped him with a single shot. For ten minutes we watched him die, gurgling in the dust and burning sun, before the corporal finished him off with a second mercy shot. The dead jihadist was a kid, perhaps fifteen years old, too young to grow a beard. But it was him or us. He knew the risks. Perhaps he wanted a martyr's death. He got it.

The next day, with the jihadists defeated, the Malian army laid on their victory tour for the assembled press as the French kept a discreet distance, their radios hissing and squawking as they made sarcastic jokes about the Malians. Gendarmes festooned with ammo belts led me round the courthouse, pointing out dismembered limbs and dead jihadists crumpled in uncomfortable-looking positions all around the courtyard. Inside the wrecked building, after stepping over the dusty body of an Arab-looking foreign fighter, a soldier proudly displayed the charred corpse of a teenage jihadist, his wispily bearded head awkwardly folded underneath his shoulders. 'He's all burned, this one,' the soldier pointed out needlessly. A French helicopter's rockets had cooked him yesterday, once their patience had run out. He's young, I said. 'Huh?' He's young, I repeated. '*Bon*,' said the soldier. Good.

In the town hall, next to a body hunched on a stairwell over its machine gun, the Malians pointed out a huge streak of blood that had burst up the wall and all across the ceiling. 'Suicide bomber,' they said, 'look, here's his head.' It was more of a face than a head, a puzzled face, sheared off its skull by the blast, lying wrinkled on the floor in a dusty frown. His torso had been vaporised and his leg was in the street outside, where a hungry dog had taken it.

I went off on my own to find the kid I'd seen killed in the marketplace the day before. His face was young and innocent, contentedly staring into the desert sun. Dark red dried blood streamed from his open dusty lips. Birdsong twittered peacefully from the nearby trees, their leaves rustling in the gentle breeze. Iridescent flies glittered like green-gold jewels as they crawled across his face. I sat on the ground next to him, staring at his face for a long time. I don't know how long. Eventually the chief of police strode over with his retinue. A tall man in a Chelsea FC tracksuit snapped the kid with a cheap camera and said, 'That makes three in the market now, thirteen in total.' The chief of police grunted non-committally. A dozen jihadists, some of them children, had held off hundreds of Malian soldiers for a full day's fighting, until the French were forced to intervene. The city centre was a smouldering ruin. MUJAO had made its point. 'There's more back there, in the ruins,' a gendarme offered helpfully.

'*Non, merci,*' I said. 'I think I've had enough for now.'

SOUTH SUDAN

January 2014

The day had begun well for the forces of the South Sudanese government. Two battalions of fresh infantry had been sent up the Nile by barge to the forward base, some twenty kilometres south of the heavily contested town of Bor. They'd jogged there in formation, singing war chants, before eventually gathering in the centre of the camp to listen to a rousing speech from the general in command.

When he'd finished speaking, they waved their Kalashnikovs in the air and gave battle cries before jogging back to the barges waiting to send them upstream to war. 'We'll have dinner in Bor,' the general in command assured us. 'You will see, then we will send you back to Juba by helicopter to show the world what we have done.'

Mark, the driver the SPLA had just assigned to us, was less keen for the onslaught to begin. He'd spent the morning swigging from a litre bottle of gin, and when the signal came to move forward, it was with reluctance that he turned the key in the ignition. 'I've only been a soldier two weeks, you know,' he said as we trundled off to join the convoy. 'In real life, I'm a journalist. But when the war started they gave me a uniform and made me join the army. These rebels are killing all my people, we have to fight them. But it's not so bad. My uncle there, two cars ahead of us, he is a general, the most popular general in the whole army. He is the only general who leads from the front.' His uncle wasn't the general in command. Between us, a Land Cruiser packed with his retinue jostled its away along the pitted road, his personal plastic garden chair and washing tub clattering against its bumper.

You could smell the frontline before you saw it. The closer we drove to Bor, the more bodies lay dotted about the verges, bloated and stinking in the fierce sun. 'These are the rebels we killed two days ago, when they attacked us at the base. But we beat them,' Mark said with pride. 'And there, look – a woman.' Her legs lay splayed wide beneath the remnants of her brightly coloured dress, her head and torso charred beyond recognition. The soldiers grimaced as they held their breath against the stench. 'It is terrible, these things the rebels are doing,' Mark murmured.

We were driving in the HQ convoy, a long line of air-conditioned SUVs for the generals interspersed with a motley assortment of Land Cruisers for their bodyguards, infantry, artillery and supply troops, as well as a ramshackle militia force of Dinka tribesmen given uniforms and rifles and packed off to war. Ahead of us, the Commando Division had taken up positions surrounding the city, and the first wave of infantry had swept through the dense bush, clearing the way for the slow, vulnerable convoy behind. At least, that was the plan.

A year and a half after I promised myself I'd never return to South Sudan, I was back on the ground with SPLA forces, this time trying to suppress an insurgency on their own home territory. The dysfunctional military government had begun to fall apart. Just three weeks earlier, a mutiny had broken out in murky and still-disputed circumstances in the capital Juba's main military base. While soldiers from the dominant Dinka tribe had their weapons returned to them, those from their historic rivals the Nuer tribe remained disarmed. What happened next threatened to rip the country apart less than three years after its painful birth.

Nuer and Dinka soldiers took their dispute into the streets of Juba, battling each other across the city's compounds and wide boulevards with mortars and heavy machine guns. An attempt by loyalist troops to arrest the Nuer Vice-President, Dr Riek Machar, on the charge of attempting a coup failed as his bodyguard spirited him away somewhere into the bush. Dr Machar denied the charges and claimed that this was an attempt to shore up the Dinka president Salva Kiir's increasingly dictatorial rule after Machar had announced his candidacy for the forthcoming presidential elections, a claim with the ring of truth. But whatever the political machinations behind the fighting, the situation swiftly descended into inter-tribal slaughter as Dinka security forces loyal to President Kiir rampaged across Nuer districts of Juba, slaughtering hundreds of civilians and disarmed soldiers and sending hundreds of thousands more fleeing to the vast UN compound in the city centre for safety.

Further north, whole divisions of the SPLA – those drawn from Nuer tribesmen – defected to the rebellion and took control of the vital cities of Bor, Bentiu and Malakal, cutting off the government's access to the oil revenues that make up almost all the country's income. But any chance of their gaining the sympathy of the outside world was quickly squandered by an attack on a UN base outside Bor that killed three Indian peacekeepers and dozens of civilians, and an orgy of violence that saw Nuer warriors rampaging through Dinka villages, massacring civilians and forcing hundreds of thousands to flee to the safety of squalid impromptu refugee camps on the other side of the Nile.

Long before British colonial rule, the Nuer and the Dinka tribes, both nomadic cattle herders, had fought and raided each other for pasture, cows and glory. During the decades of rebellion against Khartoum, the Sudanese regime found it easy to set the two tribes against each other, sowing discord and pitting rebel against rebel. With independence, the Dinka had become the dominant tribe in South Sudan, and ruled the country with a winner-takes-all arrogance. It wouldn't take much to pit Dinka against Nueronce more. Within less than a month, up to 10,000 people had been killed, hundreds of thousands more had fled their homes and the country looked ungovernable.

Juba was awash with rumours that a vast army of rebel tribesmen – the Nuer White Army, supposedly named for the coating of wood ash they use to protect themselves from insect bites – was on the march through the dense bush to overthrow the government. Almost all the city's vast cohort of foreign NGO workers had fled, and the airport was crowded with government officials and SPLA officers packing their families off to safe exile in Kenya and Uganda. Juba was in a state of high alert, judging by the increased numbers of heavily armed troops visible sleeping under trees at every street corner and roundabout, and everyone swapped wild rumours of sightings of the White Army on the city's outskirts.

It was in an effort to restore public confidence that the SPLA allowed us to embed with their forces on the road to Bor, calculating that footage of victorious government soldiers in the city centre would calm the civil population's nerves and provide a boost to Kiir's bargaining position at the stuttering peace talks in Ethiopia. But it didn't work out like that.

———

The first ambush was just a pinprick, a short burst of rifle fire cracking over our heads from the lush undergrowth to our right. Mark, our driver, froze and my cameraman Phil shoved him out of the door, away from the fire. A bullet thunked into the vehicle. Soldiers leaped from the beds of their pick-up trucks, aiming their weapons into the dense treeline in a vain attempt to find a target. After a few minutes of confusion, a colonel ordered them all back into the vehicles and on we went, passing burned-out tanks that had been abandoned by the government forces fleeing Bor a few days ago.

'They are not even real soldiers,' shouted Mark across the roar of engines, 'just Nuer youths with guns and uniforms they looted from us. I tell you, man, it makes me so angry to think what they did to my town. They looted all of Bor and set the shops and houses on fire. I tell you, they won't even fight us now, they just took everything they could carry from Bor and went back to the bush.'

Bor had already changed hands three times since the war began just over two weeks earlier. The capital of restive Jonglei state, the city lies between the Nile and the long and unpaved road to the capital Juba two hundred kilometres south, making it a strategic prize for both the rebels and the government. The theory was that whoever possessed Bor when the elusive ceasefire was finally called would hold the upper hand in the peace negotiations to follow, and both sides were ready to fight for it. But while the government had the strategic advantage of air support and superior logistics, the predominantly Nuer rebels still controlled the bush.

More than 30,000 Dinka refugees had fled their villages to the relative safety of a Médecins Sans Frontières clinic just across the Nile, and our convoy slowly weaved its way through abandoned mud-hut villages, watched by flocks of scavenging birds and contented-looking dogs. One village lay in flames, half an hour's drive south of the river village of Pariak, the last major settlement before Bor. A burning church emitted a thick plume of white smoke. Abandoned tatters of uniforms, shoes and cooking pots filled with freshly cooked rice lay scattered all around the place. The eerie silence prompted a lull in our small talk, until the machine guns opened up.

Again, the rebels hit us from the bush on the right side of the road, but this time in greater strength. Long bursts of automatic fire punctuated by aimed rifle shots stopped the convoy in its tracks. Mark froze, and once again we pushed him through the door into the ditch beside us, the only cover. The soldiers and policemen we were travelling with loosed off their rifles in long bursts, and the trucks carrying the support weapons careered up and down the track, firing point blank into the bush with anti-aircraft guns and salvoes of rockets, to the accompaniment of dull thuds and jarring booms. It was a confusing and terrifying experience.

After a few minutes the scene fell silent. We joined the soldiers walking in the ditch to Pariak, our rest stop, trudging along with vehicles between us and the hostile bush to our right. It was hot now, and the smell of sweat hung heavy in the air as the soldiers filed along with loose-limbed strides, ammunition belts draped around their necks, swinging their rifles jauntily by their sides. We lit cigarettes from each other, returning the thumbs-up signal to soldiers driving past us, shouted back to soldiers' cries of '*Quays? Tamam?*' that all was fine, everything was good, *alhamdulillah*. We could see Pariak a short walk ahead of us now and we quickened our stride to reach the shade of its mango trees. The general's car revved up and overtook the slow-moving truck ahead of him, heading off to the village in a plume of dust. He'd nearly reached Pariak when the first burst of machine-gun fire hit him.

This time, the rebels hit us from the front as well as the right flank. Machine-gun teams and marksmen strafed the convoy, scything through the soft-skinned vehicles from positions in the bush and from behind the thin wall of rushes surrounding Pariak. The general was wounded in his hand, his car immobilised, his driver killed. When his men dragged him into another vehicle, that too was hit, and the general was killed along with two more men. Soldiers ran around a dusty, wide-spaced hamlet of huts in fear and confusion, trying to find a target, the untrained levies firing wild bursts of automatic fire straight into the air, or into the backs of the soldiers ahead. One man sustained a neck wound when a bullet passed through his back and glanced off upwards from his shoulder blade. It was hard to tell if the bullets whistling overhead were from enemy positions or the untrained troops behind us.

An armoured police vehicle roared off towards Pariak and returned to the hamlet a few minutes later, three of its tyres shot to pieces and its thick windscreen cracked by rifle fire. Its driver asked us, ludicrously, if we had any spare tyres for its gigantic wheels. We shrugged him away helplessly and crouched with the soldiers hiding behind mud huts for meagre cover. A thick plume of black smoke rose from Pariak as rocket launchers pounded the enemy positions and AA guns shredded the treeline ahead. To the right flank, the thick crackle of rifle and machine-gun fire reached a crescendo before dying away to the shrill whistle of an officer regrouping his men. The young platoon commander who cleared the rebel positions on the flank later told me six of the enemy had been killed, two by his own hand. 'I got the guy who killed the general, and the guy beside him,' he said. 'I even took his machine gun. It's brand new. Motherfucker.'

When Pariak was cleared a half-hour or so later, we trudged forward into the village, past the smoking ruins of tin shacks and into the shade of the mango trees beside the river. The soldiers loaded the dead and dying on to the flatbed of our truck, their sticky blood coating our equipment. Wounded soldiers lying in the shade gasped for water, while others roamed about cadging cigarettes, some dazed, others laughing in exhilaration.

'Will we reach Bor tonight?' we asked the general in command.

'Tonight? I don't think so. Maybe tomorrow afternoon now, it is already late. But our forces are ahead, and tomorrow we will hear the good news from Bor.'

The barges had reached Pariak now, and the infantry splashed out of them to clear the riverbank while the dead and wounded were loaded on to speedboats to travel down the Nile to Juba. The generals conferred, sitting on plastic garden chairs beneath a tree, while the men milled around the empty village, catching and killing chickens for lunch, or fishing in the river. A sort of order asserted itself as ammunition trucks drove up to Pariak, escorted by a tank clanking along the road. As the soldiers reloaded their magazines and chatted in the shade, or dozed, or argued, or gutted fish, we wandered to the riverbank where a dead rebel lay with his feet dangling in the still blue river. He was about sixteen or so, in camouflage SPLA uniform, a single bullet hole drilled neatly though the tribal scarification on his temple, wet blood pooling under his head. 'You see,' said the junior officer escorting us around, 'they wear the same uniforms as us, how can we tell who is a rebel and who is one of us?' Beside us, naked soldiers washed themselves in the Nile, splashing each other and whooping with glee.

Pariak is divided by the road to Bor, and while the soldiers made themselves at home in the side of the village next to the river, the other half of it lay undisturbed. 'Shouldn't you be clearing the houses over there?' we asked a soldier, who'd just returned home to fight after thirteen years spent living in Iowa. 'I gotta tell you, man, that's a great idea. That's exactly what we gotta do, man, exactly that. Secure this whole place, just like that.' He flopped back into his plastic chair to enjoy the shade. 'That's exactly what we gotta do.' But no one did, busy as they were with their domestic tasks, cooking, boiling tea and loafing idly in the shade. Phil bumped into some soldiers raping a villager. They told him to leave, and he did. Other soldiers fished, and gave us huge chunks of boiled carp. Such is South Sudan. When the sun began to set, the rebels hit us from the uncleared half of the village in a classic platoon assault.

Pariak was now the general headquarters for the entire front, the brain centre for the assault on Bor. The rebels must have known all the generals were concentrated here, and all the ammunition trucks for the infantry slogging through the bush ahead. It was the division's weakest point, and its most important.

When the attack came, a roar of rifle and machine-gun fire thicker and closer than any ambush yet, from only a hundred or so metres away, the entire gaggle of troops froze for a moment in utter dread that was swiftly overtaken by panic. The officers fled first, their SUVs roaring away down the road back to Juba, leaving their men direction-less and terrified. This time, hardly anyone fired back. The whole force disintegrated as soldiers flung their rifles into the dust and ran away or chased after speeding vehicles to hurl themselves aboard, away from the fighting. With the crackle of gunfire all around us, we jumped in our Land Cruiser and hurtled away until a soldier stopped our driver by thrusting his rifle barrel into his throat, demanding a lift in a manner that was difficult to argue with. Other soldiers wrenched open our back door and shoved a soldier in, bleeding from his chest, his eyes wide with shock, then clambered in over him begging us to save them. The rocket launchers hurtled thunderous salvoes into the huts across the road behind us as we drove off, our new passengers shaking with fear, one vomiting out of the window into the dust. I needed a cigarette.

The rebel attack was beaten off after a while, but it was too late to salvage the convoy as a coherent unit. Trucks drove slowly up the road, asking the knots of stragglers on foot whether it was safer to head down the Juba road or back to the village. Swarms of terrified soldiers surrounded every vehicle, begging for escape, Bor visible in the gloom as a dense wall of orange smoke as the city succumbed to flame. During the lull, we'd kicked out the soldiers who'd forced their way into the car. The wounded man flopped out of the rear door when we opened, landing face down in the dust to die. A year ago this would have distressed me. Even now, thinking about it as a type, it leaves me cold.

On our way back to base, we picked up a brigadier and two of his men, as well as the young platoon commander whose men had all driven away from the battle in his vehicle. He shook his head at the uselessness of his platoon, repeating, 'This is ridiculous, absolutely ridiculous,' in plummy tones picked up at Sandhurst. A few hours later, we found the convoy at the rear base we'd left that morning, their vehicles parked in a circular formation in a dusty clearing. They seemed calm when we arrived, asking us for cigarettes and water with beaming smiles, until something – nothing – spooked them and they all revved their engines and drove off, racing each other through the darkness back to Juba.

We drove most of the night, the convoy snaking for miles along the lonely bush road home, blinding headlights shining through the sea of dust as each vehicle tried to overtake the one ahead, an army crawling home in defeat. We parked up, eventually, in Mangalla, a garrison town barely fifty miles from Juba. Checkpoints were set up along the road to prevent deserters escaping even further back. At dawn, shamefaced, the convoy moved back along the long road to Bor.

A few weeks later, fighting side by side with a heavily armed Ugandan intervention force, the government infantry recaptured the burned-out, abandoned ruins of the city centre. We didn't join them this time round. It's a beautiful country, South Sudan, an endless expanse of unspoiled wilderness and broad savannah, a land of tribesmen hunting game with spears and defending their cattle from encroaching rivals. I never want to go back.

SYRIA

September 2013

In the early summer of 2013, I met a Syrian refugee in the street in Whitechapel, late one night. I was buying cigarettes; he was looking for food and work. He told me he was a chef from Homs and said he could prepare the *best* Lebanese food. He was sleeping with the brothers in the Whitechapel mosque – they were very kind – but he wanted money to buy fruit and cigarettes. I tipsily gave him £30 and he was effusively thankful as I left him apparently choosing a ripe melon outside a late-night off-licence. I also gave him my mobile number, and the first few times he rang – always late at night or in the early hours – I gave him what advice I could, on how to claim asylum and benefits (as I suggested) or to find work (as he did). He always wanted money, and after a while I stopped answering his calls. Eventually he stopped calling. In its own small way, this awkward dance sums up something of the West's haplessness with Syria. We got involved, tentatively at first, when it came at little cost and made us feel good about ourselves. When it began to become a nuisance, we cut it all adrift, left Syria to its fate, unwatched, and felt a gnawing guilt about it, from time to time.

We'd been waiting for hours at the roadside business for the right moment to cross before the smuggler ran inside and told us it was time to go. We shouldered our packs and followed him in the darkness towards the crowd of Syrians waiting to cross with us. Turn your phones off, the smuggler said, don't smoke, don't talk. An old man with a thick white moustache stared at us fearfully. Where are you from? he wanted to know. England, we said. But are you friends of the Kurds or friends of the Arabs? he asked, and I realised he thought we were reinforcements for the jihadist cohorts he'd fled from in the first place, many of them from England too.

With a nod, the smuggler led us to the high bank of the main road, and we waited in the shadows for a lull between the screaming lorries before scurrying across. There were around a dozen refugees, all carrying their belongings in tattered suitcases and heavy bales made up of bed sheets. The eldest, a woman, must have been about eighty years old, the youngest a boy of four or five, wide-eyed, gripping his father's hand tightly. They'd crossed into Turkey illegally before, and now, for whatever reason, they were crossing back. We moved as quickly as we could, hunched low across the rocky scrub, thorns ripping at our clothes, until we reached the first fence. The smuggler looked up to check the watchtower, and it was empty. Placing a wooden plank across the sagging barbed wire, he made a bridge for us to run across into no-man's-land. The border was mined, and we followed in his footsteps as closely as we were able.

Before we reached the second fence, a few hundred metres away, we had to dive towards the prickly ground, burying ourselves in the darkness as a Turkish armoured vehicle clanked past, its searchlight picking out the boulders around us. There was a man with us, carrying all his belongings in a flimsy homemade sack and holding his young son's hand in the dark. The boy was about five years old maybe. I'd wondered, when we'd left, if he was young enough for it to feel like a game to him. The man's sack had split just before the Turkish armoured vehicle had come, and some of his belongings had slipped into the thorns. While the Turks were still heartstoppingly close, he argued with one of the smugglers that he had to go back to find them, shouting almost, the young smuggler almost shouting back for him to shut the fuck up as he shoved the protesting man down. He refused to lie on the ground but crouched, and his young soon held his hand and stroked his hair, saying *abo, abo*, daddy, daddy, to comfort him and keep him calm.

Eventually the armoured vehicle trundled off, and we moved quickly to the second fence. The smuggler's colleagues had made a gap in the wire and we crossed as fast as we could, the refugees shoving each other to be first inside. It had taken us a couple of hours to cross. When we saw the lights from the first hamlet across the border and heard the sheepdogs barking at us everyone breathed out audibly, resettled their bundles more comfortably across their shoulders and began to chat amongst themselves. A tall youngish man in a cheap suit turned to me, grinning, and shook my hand. 'Welcome to Syria,' he said.

———————

It had taken me long enough to get here. While I'd frittered away long months in Sudan and Mali, all my journalist friends had been crossing in and out to the rebel-held north from Turkey, hanging out with fighters from the moderate Free Syrian Army (FSA) rebels fighting to overthrow the Assad regime, filing photos and footage from the makeshift rebel media centres that had sprung up. This was where the real war was, and I was missing it. But as the conflict dragged on, with over 100,000 killed and no prospect of journalists stoking a Libya-like Western intervention, the mood towards the foreign visitors began to harden. Al-Qaeda offshoots like Jabhat al-Nusra, and the Islamic State of Iraq and al-Sham, or ISIS, had formed, drawing in jihadist volunteers from across the world to impose their hardline vision of Islam across the rebel north. ISIS, in particular, seemed more concerned with establishing its presence across areas already liberated from the regime than in fighting government forces, and as its black flag began to flutter from more and more checkpoints across the routes into northern cities, fewer and fewer journalists were going in. More than thirty had been kidnapped by now, mostly by ISIS, with no word of their location given and no ransom demands ever made. It was as if they had been swallowed up by the Syrian meat grinder. By September, a couple of weeks before I arrived, journalists had stopped going in. I'd missed my chance, it seemed. Until a new front and a new opportunity opened up.

In the country's far north-east, in Syria's bread-basket province of Hassakeh, Kurdish rebels aligned with the Kurdish Marxist insurgent group the PKK in neighbouring Turkey had launched a blitzkrieg against regime positions, carving out a chunk of Syrian territory in a bid to win autonomy after decades of Arab oppression. The PKK has fought for decades for a Kurdish homeland independent from Turkey, in a struggle that has sucked in many Syrian Kurdish volunteers. Now, on the Syrian side of the border, a fragile truce with the FSA had collapsed after clashes broke out between the Kurdish fighters and jihadist factions within the rebel alliance in the frontier city of Ras al-Ain, quickly blossoming into a full-scale war. After two years of relative peace, the Syrian War had finally reached the Kurdish areas, but few other journalists had made it in. The Turkish government had closed all the border crossings to the Kurdish region – while leaving those to al-Qaeda-dominated areas wide open – so the only way in was illegally, following the ancient smuggling trails. And now we had taken it.

_____

Kovan's eleven-year-old sister Nesrine picked up the Kalashnikov and a heavy armful of magazines from a corner of the room to make space for us as he tossed a packet of Gauloises at us and sat down cross-legged on the divan. It was the early hours of the morning, and Kovan had sat up waiting for us all night. A friend had introduced us on Facebook, and he'd arranged our passage. 'We have a saying that a Kurd without a weapon is a Kurd without honour,' Kovan explained, 'look, even my mum has a rifle.' He grinned, and counted out a wad of greasy Syrian lira to pay off the smuggler. 'All us Kurds are smugglers,' he added. 'You know, we have a story that on Judgment Day, God will judge the living and the dead and send some to heaven and some to hell. But the Kurds will stand on the side, and smuggle the ones who went to hell to heaven. Just give the Kurds their mountains and some tobacco and they will never be defeated.'

But the Syrian Kurds had no mountains to protect them. Hassakeh is a land of flat wheat fields dotted here and there with the low mounds of long-buried Neolithic villages, or *tels*, each one now ringed with sandbags and barbed wire and refurbished as a machine-gun post, guarding the single road from the Iraqi border to the Ras al-Ain frontline. We were in Mesopotamia now, the heart of the Neolithic Fertile Crescent, and Arab, Christian and Kurdish villages lay jostling side by side, the Arab villages distrusted by the Kurds as potential nests of pro-regime or pro-rebel insurgents, surrounded by checkpoints. A dozen kilometres south of Kovan's flat lay the first jihadist positions – during the day, you could see plumes of smoke on the horizon from oil wells they'd set alight. Unlike the Arab-populated desert to the south, the Kurdish region was rich in water, wheat and oil – around sixty per cent of Syria's total oil reserves and a rich prize for whoever captured it. The Hassakeh front was a war for resources, rapidly taking on an ethnic tinge.

Kovan was twenty-five, and a refugee from the fighting in Syria's second city of Aleppo. Handsome and intelligent, he'd had a good lifestyle in Syria's commercial capital, with a well-paid job working for a textile manufacturer, a brand new Range Rover and an enjoyable sideline seducing old Aleppo businessmen's young and lonely wives. In the early days of the revolution, he'd joined the first protests against

President Assad's regime, waving banners and chanting in the streets for democratic change. But as the revolution soured and turned into a bloody civil war, his opinions changed. 'It's the Arabs, man, never trust an Arab. Even my best friend betrayed me when the regime arrested my brother. We had two nice apartments, you know, in Aleppo, and they've both been stolen. One by the regime and one by the rebels. Everything has gone, everything we owned. But we are here in Derik now and safe amongst our people.' The Kurdish language is more closely related to English than Arabic, and like many Syrian Kurds, Kovan often gave the impression of being a secular European somehow marooned in the Arab world.

Derik, or in Arabic al-Malakiya, is a sleepy country market town on the edge of Syria, which must have felt like a painful comedown for a cosmopolitan young Aleppo businessman. It was Kovan's family's ancestral home, and they'd driven here a few months earlier, passing through regime and rebel checkpoints without any of their belongings on the pretence that they were visiting family for the Kurdish New Year feast. Kovan's father had been a PKK fighter back when the Syrian regime still supported the Kurds fighting over the border in Turkey, and his martyr's photo, wreathed with plastic flowers, hung like an icon in the family's apartment in a jerry-built Soviet-style block. On every wall hung framed photographs of the PKK leader Abdullah Ocalan and gaudy photo tributes to recent Kurdish martyrs fighting for the YPG, or People's Protection Units, the nascent Syrian Kurdish army. No doubt the family's sacrifice for the Kurdish cause had helped them secure their new home from the administration.

Kovan pointed out the kitchen tablecloth, a clear plastic sheet carefully annotated in marker pen with trench positions and machine-gun posts, the once top-secret plan for the regime's defence of Derik. 'This whole building was for regime officers and secret service,' Kovan said proudly, 'a colonel lived here. Then they left and the new government gave it to the IDPs.'

The regime didn't just leave, but neither did they put up much of a fight for Hassakeh. The Arab rebels always claim, convincingly, that the regime willingly withdrew from the Kurdish regions, allowing the Kurdish government or PYD to assert a thin veneer of control, in the knowledge that the conflict with the rebels that would inevitably follow would strengthen the Assad regime's bargaining position in any future peace agreement, showing up the Arab rebels as aggressive jihadists and establishing a precedent for the carving up of Syria into ethnic cantons – an outcome that would leave Assad's Alawite minority with at least a slice of Syria to rule.

Certainly, the Kurdish fighters were now fighting harder against the Syrian rebels than they ever had to against the regime; unlike other areas of the rebel north, the regime had never bombed the Kurdish areas, saving the Kurds from the horror of mass civilian casualties; and regime forces still garrisoned the provincial capital of Qamishli in strength. The YPG were twice rebels, in a way; first they'd taken up arms against the regime to win their freedom, and now they found themselves in bloody revolt against the rebellion that had engulfed the rest of northern Syria, in a bid to preserve that freedom. This was a complex front, swirling with conspiracy theories, where the stark black-and-white journalistic morality of noble rebels versus oppressive regime seemed quite irrelevant.

After a breakfast of flatbread, yoghurt, oil and spicy Kurdish *za'atar*, Kovan took us to see the checkpoint beside his house. Young volunteers in the olive drab uniform of the Asayis police militia greeted him cheerily, taking turns to shake our hands, while the others scanned the horizon for approaching cars. Syrian Kurdistan – now called Rojava, or sunset, by the Kurds – was a land of checkpoints, studding the road every kilometre or so now the jihadists had begun driving car bombs, in a sort of giant, lethal game of chess, into the heart of the Kurdish areas.

The volunteers were all teenagers, grinning happily and toting their rifles with a professional confidence. Kovan introduced me to one young fighter, Hayat Derik, a smiling, chubby nineteen-year-old girl whose fair hair escaped her ponytail prettily, partly held in check by girlish pink hair-grips. We chatted briefly, Hayat interrupting the conversation every now and again to check the ID cards of the drivers and passengers who halted at the sandbank road block every few minutes. She'd check the boot, peer inside the car for hidden weapons, then wave them on their way before returning to talk to us. 'We are doing this to keep our country safe,' she said, matter-of-factly, 'we don't get paid, we do this out of love for our nation.' Hayat would be killed on duty here a few weeks later.

'You see,' said Kovan, 'here there is no difference between men and women, and no difference between Kurds and Arabs,' indicating the *keffiyeh*-ed shepherds whose battered truck Hayat was inspecting. 'The rebels tried to make it an ethnic war between us, but they couldn't.' And the Arabs, I asked, how do they feel about Rojava? 'There is a difference between the Arabs. The tribes who always lived here, they have no problem with us, but then there are the 1963 Arabs – the Syrian regime transplanted them here fifty years ago, to the Kurdish lands, to make the "Arab belt" and divide the Kurdish areas so we could never get independence. That village there –' Kovan waved his hand dismissively at a cluster of low mud-brick hovels just outside the checkpoint, overlooked by a machine-gun post '– they are 1963 Arabs, so obviously eventually we will have to remove them. We will give them compensation, of course, they are victims of the regime too, but they cannot stay here, on Kurdish people's land. We will give the land back to the true owners.'

Further down the road inside the town, after our paperwork had been processed in the Asayis barracks by Kovan's uncle, who looked disturbingly like my dad, we drove to another checkpoint, manned by a trio of Christian farmers. Their commander, an avuncular-looking sixty-something in a polo shirt, gave us glasses of sweet tea while he fulminated against 'the black monkey in the White House' who, he claimed, was sending jihadists to Rojava. Kovan nodded along, mortified, as the commander spoke.

'We Assyrian Christians,' he said, 'we have been here six thousand years. You think we will run away from these extremists? I could take my family to Sweden tomorrow, but I will stay here to defend my farm and my land. Don't think we love Assad. We love democracy as much as you. But you think these rebels who eat human hearts will give us democracy?'

The Christian fighter was referencing a video that had done the rounds a year or so earlier of a rebel carving offal from a freshly killed government soldier and chomping down for the camera; an image that, until new brutalities emerged, summed up the depths to which Syria had sunk. None of the Christian farmers wore uniform, and at this point their loyalty to the idea of Rojava was questionable.

While Christians elsewhere in Syria had increasingly thrown their weight behind the regime, here, where there were no regime fighters, they chose to work alongside the Kurds, though with a parallel command structure. Should the regime return to the area, no doubt they'd happily fight for them instead.

Intrigued by the Christians, I asked Kovan to take me to their quarter of Derik, a quiet, bourgeois suburb that reminded me of Greece, where elderly women watered their geraniums with hoses and impossibly hot girls flicked their long blonde-dyed tresses from side to side on the balconies of their parents' villas, watching passersby in the streets below. A huge banner hung from the cathedral demanding the release of two bishops kidnapped by the rebels some months before; shopkeepers flicked their worry beads idly in their hands outside their stores; it was the last redoubt of a tolerant Syria that everywhere else had been destroyed.

In the empty church of the Holy Virgin, the garrulous churchwarden took us around his collection of icons, reeling off an hour-long monologue of prophetic dreams and well-attested miracles, pointing us to the rock that exuded a sacred, healing oil supposedly inexplicable to modern science but which smelled precisely like olive oil. As he daubed some on cotton wool for us to take home, I asked him if he felt safe here. As I asked him, the call to evening prayer began from the minaret next door. 'Here, safe? So much, so much. As Christians, we have never had any problem with the Kurds, and now they are protecting us.'

This was the essence of the Kurdish miracle here in Rojava; their ability to sell the bid for autonomy as a protective blanket for all the region's minorities. A decade earlier, the Christians here in Rojava had taken in Christian refugees from Iraq, once the rise of jihadist violence in the aftermath of the Western-led invasion had made their ancient homeland unliveable for them; now elsewhere in Syria the local Christians had to flee in turn, almost all to Scandinavia. But in Rojava the Christians still felt confident enough to stay in their shops and farmsteads, and tentatively join the Kurdish fighters at the barricades. This sense of co-existence in the midst of Syria's sectarian bloodbath was one of the strongest arguments for Kurdish autonomy. It was hard not to fall in love with their courage, their pride in their culture, and their willingness to fight both rebels and regime. It was impossible, at the same time, to ignore the one-party state they'd set up to wage this war.

When the sun set, we ate a late snack of falafel, sitting on plastic chairs in the street while watching the world go by: women shopping, youths puttering around on scooters. Such normality would be impossible anywhere else in northern Syria; anywhere in the rebel-held areas we'd have been kidnapped within minutes by balaclava-ed extremists. It was hard to argue against the Kurdish project; it was a war, more than anything, to keep away the war and insulate Rojava from the Syrian bloodbath. But then, the Kurds had never had to live with regime artillery and aerial bombing. When we finished eating, we wandered over to the Asayis barracks to join some fighters on their nightly patrol of the city.

The Kurdish rebels are effective propagandists, and my escort in the back of the pick-up truck consisted of two pretty teenage girls and a handsome young Christian, Fadi, who spoke perfect English. An oil engineer in Damascus before the war, he had fled back to the Christian heartland of Syria's north-eastern Hassakeh province instead of taking up a well-paid job in the Persian Gulf. 'I could be earning ten thousand dollars a month,' Fadi said resignedly as we bumped our way along the dark country roads, 'but here I am, working for free, to keep my country safe. They come from everywhere, these extremists, from Chechnya, from Sudan, from Saudi Arabia; they all come here to fight us, I don't know why. This isn't even their land. They think they will fight us and we will run away, but I am not frightened. When they caught my friend, they cut off his head. And when they gave us back the bodies, two of them, they put one head on the other body and the other head on the other body. Why would someone do this?'

He shook his own head, staring glumly at the bed of the truck. I'm sorry about your friend, I said. In a quiet voice, he replied, 'I'm sorry too.'

———————

Derik was all very peaceful and secure and impressed upon us the Kurdish rebels' ability to maintain order and security in Hassakeh, but the real war was elsewhere. The YPG had captured the entire city of Ras al-Ain – in Kurdish, Serikaniye – sitting astride the Turkish border from the rebels a couple of months earlier, but the city was all but surrounded and the jihadist forces were launching constant suicidal counterattacks against it in a bid to recapture the vital border crossing. We needed to be there.

The road from Derik to Ras al-Ain crosses the entire extent of the Kurdish-held region in north-east Syria, a long and dull half-day's drive enlivened by the need to pass through the centre of Qamishli, still held by the regime, to procure permits to travel from the Kurdish rebel headquarters in the city. As far as Assad was concerned, we were in his country illegally, and regime troops had standing orders to arrest any foreign journalists they found and send them to Damascus for interrogation. A long sojourn in a *mukhabarat* dungeon wasn't an enticing prospect, so we all donned *keffiyehs* in the Kurdish yellow, red and green colours for the heart-sinking ten-minute drive through the loyalist territory of Qamishli, a makeshift disguise that surely wouldn't bear a second glance.

It was a terrifying ten minutes, and even Kovan gripped the steering wheel, white-knuckled with nerves. Tubby regime soldiers in civilian clothes and camouflage webbing waved us through the first few sandbagged checkpoints, the regime flag and the Baathist standard still fluttering high above us. In the centre of the city, we crawled in heavy traffic beneath huge posters of Assad past checkpoint after checkpoint, sometimes only a metre away from the nearest rifle-toting conscript. Sitting in the front passenger seat, I tried to exude a sense of boredom coupled with arrogance, as if I was reluctantly putting up with their presence in my city, my heart beating so fast I was sure they could hear it. A couple of times, black SUVs with tinted windows fluttering regime flags would overtake us and Kovan would mutter *fuck fuck fuck* until we passed them, readying the pistol on his lap; these were the *shabiha*, the regime's goons, and all it would take would be for them to brake and demand to see our papers and it would all be over for us. We made it through, despite Kovan cockily insisting we stop to get espresso on the border fringe of Assadland, on the basis he was Kurdish and no one would tell him what to do in his own capital, while we shouted at him to just fucking move and he sat laughing at us, enjoying our terror. Our papers stamped, we headed on to the front.

Along the way, through a dull flat landscape of rippling wheat fields and drab-looking villages, Kovan would speed up when we drove through Arab villages, which all still

263

flew regime flags from every building. I asked him if the Arabs here supported the regime or the revolution. 'Well, man, they're Arabs, you know,' he said, shaking his head. 'I tell you in this village here there was heavy fighting between them until the Kurdish fighters came in to calm them down. Some put up a rebel flag then others got angry and took it down and put up a regime flag then they all started fighting each other.' He laughed. 'Arabs, man, this is what they do. If there are two Arabs anywhere they'll start fighting between themselves. I wish the Kurds were in Europe and had Europeans for neighbours instead of being stuck next to these donkey motherfuckers.'

Whenever we'd passed the boundaries of the Arab villages – marked by rings of precautionary Kurdish checkpoints and machine-gun towers – Kovan would slow the car down and we'd stop for kebabs or *lahmacun* or *falafel* and idle chatter with the Kurdish villagers. The Kurdish checkpoints, composed entirely of local farmers, were unerringly friendly, and they'd insist we drink glasses of sugary tea or wash our faces at the cool clear springs that always bubbled by the side of the road. With our progress slowed by Kurdish hospitality, the sun was already setting by the time we neared Ras al-Ain and we were flagged down at a checkpoint by fighters waving torches in the gathering dusk. The fighters here were younger, tall and fit and all in uniform, a rare occurrence elsewhere. Their commander informed us that jihadists had captured Alouk and Cava, the next two villages along, a few hundred metres down the road, and the route was now unsafe. We parked up next to their home-made tank, named *Baz*, or eagle, which looked like something from a nerdy child's Warhammer game, and was peppered with bullet holes, to ask for details.

'We cleared their first checkpoint,' the commander said, 'and killed thirty of them. There were so many dead they had to bring up tanks to clear away the bodies. There were only three left alive when we took it,' he added. Kovan looked disappointed. 'Why didn't you kill them too?' he asked. 'We didn't, we took them prisoner.' Kovan nodded, seemingly disappointed by the reply. The two captured villages were both Arab-populated, and I asked if the locals were helping the jihadists. 'Of course the Arabs are helping them,' said the commander. 'When we took the checkpoint we found fresh food and medicine. Where else are they getting supplies but from some of the Arabs?'

It was dark now, and we weren't going anywhere, so the commander detailed one of his local auxiliaries to take us to a nearby village for the night. We turned off the road a few hundred metres back to the hamlet of Atila and were ushered to the headman's house. Divan cushions were spread about an uncovered concrete veranda and we sat down, and dusted off our cameras. They gave us tea, and chatted with the village elders under the stars. They told us about the two annexed villages. While Alouk was Arab, Cava was Kurdish and dominated by farmers who were followers of the ancient Yezidi religion, whose mysterious rites involve the veneration of a sacred peacock.

According to one of the elders, a refugee from Cava who refused to let us film his face for fear of reprisals, the jihadists had beheaded two of the villagers a couple of days earlier for refusing to accept Islam. As we made small talk lit by the glare of our camera light, they brought out for us a wide metal dish of tinned frankfurters and yogurt and honey and *za'atar* and jam and fresh goat's cheese exactly like my Greek grandmother makes, with rounds of home-baked flatbread, and we shared out cigarettes to have with the sweet tea.

Before we fell asleep, we were jolted out of our contentment by the loud booms of a howitzer hidden in the poplars somewhere behind us. A farmer took us on to the roof to watch the rounds land on the jihadist-held villages, and he chuckled at each impact. 'More of them are dead now,' he laughed. A few minutes after the end of the barrage, he pointed out the blue flashing lights of an ambulance crossing from the Turkish side of the border to ferry the wounded away to safety. 'The Turks are helping them, you see?' he said. 'But still we are killing them, and no matter how many they send to hospital in Turkey, we will keep killing them and we will stay in our land.'

We slept under the stars, the fighters swaddled beside us curling up next to their rifles. When the sun rose, and the geese and chickens woke us, we sat blearily waiting for the women to boil us coffee before we went to the front. In the daylight, we realised we were only a few hundred metres from the Turkish border, with goods trains trundling through the lush cotton fields just the other side of the wire. In fact, the train line *was* the border: when the great powers carved up the Kurdish regions after the collapse of the Ottoman Empire, they used the tracks as an arbitrary dividing line between the new republic of Turkey and French-ruled Syria, even carving the border town of Serekaniye in two. Now the Syrian side of the border was at war, and the Kurds here blamed the Turks next door more than the regime or the rebels themselves. 'The Turks opened the border for the extremists to cross,' said one grizzled farmer-turned-fighter over a cigarette. 'The Turkish objective is to empty the Kurdish region and send us all to Iraq.'

It was hard not to empathise with these Kurdish soldiers; while rebel propaganda claimed they were all swivel-eyed ultra-nationalists and Communists aiming to set up their own Kurdish nation, they were clearly just farmers, defending the villages their families had always lived in from a rebel assault spearheaded by foreign fighters, though with a strong complement of local Arabs within its ranks. The men strapped on their ammunition pouches and smoked, chatting, while their wives washed the tea glasses under an outside tap and swept the yard clean with brooms, scattering the honking geese before them. One fighter in his sixties wrapped his *keffiyeh* around his head, strapped his rifle across his back and mounted his motorbike, indicating we should follow him to the frontline.

On the way, we stopped at a military position in an abandoned water pumping station to ask the commander there to let us move towards the front. While Kovan negotiated with him, a pick-up truck approached carrying a group of fighters surrounding two hooded jihadist prisoners who were shoved into the compound. Filming was, of course, out of the question, as is generally the way in ugly village wars like this. Perhaps they were sent further down the line, perhaps their jihad ended right there, who knows? But their arrival seemed suddenly to secure us permission to be elsewhere, so we were waved off to the front. We drove there through a landscape of empty fields and abandoned houses, livestock wandering untended across the road, pick-up trucks full of Kurdish fighters overtaking us on the way.

In the abandoned village of Nedas, a few kilometres along the road, a young female fighter greeted us with a firm handshake and took us on a tour of the frontline positions. We scrambled over the rubble of wrecked farmhouses; crouching low to avoid attracting sniper fire from the jihadist positions a few hundred metres away in the flat tilled fields ahead of us. 'They are just over there, behind that well,' she said, 'and they left two bodies in that chicken run over there, the one that's burning.' Another fighter sat crouched on a veranda, scrubbing away at stripped Kalashnikovs with a bucket full of soapy water and a hard brush. 'We captured these from dead jihadists. Look, they're all new,' said the girl, slightly accusingly. Like many Kurdish fighters, she believed the West was arming the Syrian rebels, with weapons that would soon end up here in Hassakeh, used against the Kurds rather than the regime. The guy cleaning them picked up a rifle strap to show us the dark bloodstain on it, then tossed it into the dust dismissively.

We went into a villa to meet the commander here, who was watching a Kurdish news channel on TV with his men in what a few days earlier would have been a prosperous farmer's living room. He ordered a fighter to boil some tea and handed out cigarettes. Sitting cross-legged on the divans spread out along the walls, we chatted about the war. Despite his thick moustache it was clear this man was young, in his mid-twenties. Like all the commanders here, he would have been voted into office by his men. 'We see ourselves as part of Syria, and we don't want to divide Syria. We want to have a democratic Syria where everyone, Kurds, Arabs, Christians and so on, have their rights. Syria is for everyone – Muslims and Christians – to live together in harmony.' I asked him if the jihadists fought well. 'No, they are not well trained, but they are motivated to fight and go to paradise. They all just rush at us together, without any tactics, and when we kill a few they run away again, leaving their dead behind.'

The farmer who had brought us here joined in, saying, 'One of them lost his leg in Serekaniye, and he told his friends it had gone to paradise.'

We were still laughing when we heard the shots. We ran out, quickly donning our armour and shuffling into our boots, following the fighters to the breezeblock wall that marked the end of Kurdish-controlled territory. The fighters took up their positions alongside us, scanning the flat field ahead of them with their rifles before firing single aimed shots, exactly like professional soldiers, at the enemy trying to sneak up on the village. After a short volley, the commander shouted, 'Enough! They're not visible any more. Enough, they've fled!'

The Kurdish fighters tightly restrict foreign media access to the frontline and the commander ordered us to leave, claiming that a jihadist assault was imminent. As we piled into our car, shaking hands and promising to return, the first enemy mortars began to fall in the empty fields around us. We drove at speed to the next checkpoint down the road, the crackle of rifle fire and the thump of mortars fading into the distance.

———————

The checkpoint guarded the intersection of two roads beside a hillock and overlooked a mud-brick Arab village nestled in a hollow just below. Like all the roadblocks here, barriers of heaped sand had been piled zigzagging across the road, to slow down any approaching vehicles and draw them into the killing zone. A howitzer on top of the hillock fired, now and again, at the jihadist positions facing back to Nedas and a plume of black smoke rose from the horizon. A pick-up truck drove towards us from the direction of the Arab village and the fighters grabbed their rifles, staring closely at the vehicle, until they realised it was one of theirs. The fighter standing in the back, a black *keffiyeh* wrapped around his head, jumped off, clutching his machine gun, and wandered over.

'There's movement down there ... two cars,' he said.

The fighters swung their heavy machine-gun truck to face the road, while others, armed with rocket launchers, set up a position in a sand-and-wood bunker on the other side of the road from us. With the introductions made and defences secured, now it was time for tea. We sat on the shaded veranda of an abandoned shop as the fighters plied us with cigarettes and sticky caramels and knobbly cucumbers from the field beside us, one of them playing propaganda songs on his mobile phone to entertain us. Like everywhere else along this front, it seemed these men were local villagers, manning static checkpoints as a first line of defence, with a mobile reserve of elite troops nearby ready to respond to any incursions.

I asked them if they'd ever expected to take up arms. 'No,' said the fighter in the black turban, who turned out to be a local Arab, 'but they didn't come here to fight, they came to steal. Gangs came here and stole from us. They came into houses and took cars, tractors, electronics, anything valuable. They took women and children and asked for ransom. If they caught you,' he said, pointing at me, 'the FSA [Free Syrian Army] would ask for a million dollars to let you go. The others,[29] Nusra, ISIS, would just slit your throat.' He pulled out a serrated combat knife from his webbing and showed it to me, his callused finger indicating the writing engraved on the blade: MADE IN USA. 9/11. WE WILL NEVER FORGET. 'We captured this from Nusra. When I got it, it the blade was covered in blood. They must have used it to cut off someone's head.'

With the road to Ras al-Ain blocked by the rebels, we drove back to the capital Qamishli to meet the Kurdish fighters' spokesman, Redur Xelil. Our first appointment had been postponed when an ISIS car bomb went off

---

29 Jabhat al-Nusra is the official al-Qaeda franchise in Syria. ISIS is a renegade al-Qaeda offshoot

outside a Kurdish barracks just as we pulled into the city centre, which put the Kurds on edge, and we saw alleyways suddenly filled with armed fighters in civilian clothes – presumably Christians of uncertain loyalties – in a startling display of the capital's ability to turn suddenly threatening.

At Redur's office, after the customary cigarette of welcome, he pulled out a thick wodge of passports harvested from dead jihadists. Libya, Tunisia, Bahrain, Egypt, Turkey: it was difficult to argue against the Kurdish political leader's line that the region was fighting international jihadism as much as local Syrian Arabs. 'Any armed group who wants to enter the Kurdish area, we will fight them,' he told me, 'but the main groups are Jabhat al-Nusra and ISIS. Both of these are al-Qaeda groups. There are other radical groups connected to them, as well as groups connected to the Free Syrian Army. Despite the fact there is no regime presence in our area,' he added, not quite truthfully, 'they [the rebels] are still attacking us, and their goal is not to fight the regime but to occupy our Kurdish land.'

I asked him if he could imagine the Kurdish fighters working in the future with the Free Syrian Army, on the face of it natural allies against al-Qaeda-linked groups. 'First of all, we are not enemies of the Free Syrian Army. It has been proved that the greatest enemies of the Syrian revolution are Islamic radical groups like Jabhat al-Nusra and ISIS. But this is Kurdish land. We have lived here for six thousand years and we will never leave, and we will fight any group who tries to enter our area.'

As soon as we left his office, our car drove into a vast funeral cortege for two Kurdish fighters killed fighting the jihadists the day before. Huge streams of minivans and cars fluttering Kurdish flags drove slowly through the city, regime troops saluting the dead from their checkpoints and the bereaved families waving back in response, as loudspeakers blared out deafening patriotic songs. The procession converged at a city park converted into a war cemetery a few months earlier; the sandy plot was already almost full. In the back of a van, a mother sat hunched over her son's coffin, crying that she would sacrifice her life if only it would bring him back. 'Enough, auntie,' said one of the dead fighter's comrades, 'let us take him out so the others can see. Go and join the other grieving mothers.'

As weeping fighters carried their dead comrades to the waiting earth, women ululated and threw rice on them as if celebrating a wedding. Other women, armed fighters in uniform, scanned the scene with stoic dignity. 'Martyrs will never die,' chanted the vast crowd, 'O Martyr, your blood shall not touch the earth.' Women and children, weeping, sat by graves clutching framed photographs of their own martyred husbands and fathers.

By the standards of the conflict elsewhere in northern Syria, the Kurdish fight was a small war, with far lighter casualties; but fighters were dying every day, and in every town and village across Rojava funerals like this were taking place, the growing conflict now touching every close-knit family. With each death, each funeral, each grieving family, the chances of putting the warring fragments of Syria back together again grew ever-more slim.

The women crowded around the dead, streaming tears and kissing the photographs of the dead pinned to the coffins. The last prayers said, a slow and doomy paean to the martyrs booming from the sound system, a bulldozer finally clanked forward and shovelled the sandy earth on to the dead, the fighters standing at the graveside holding back their tears. Kovan's eyes were red, and his face wet with tears. 'My friend's father died,' he said, wiping his face with his arm. 'His mum ... I can't even look her in the face. Just imagine those people, they were farmers, you know? We pay a lot for this freedom. We pay a lot.'

SYRIA

September 2013

'Me and my friends were arrested in Aleppo in 2011, before the revolution,' said Kovan one day in his mum's flat, 'and one of us was just laughing at the secret police, you know? And they said *why are you laughing*, and my friend wouldn't tell them. So eventually he said, look, I'll tell you what's so funny if you promise not to beat my friends any more, OK? So they say *Yeah, sure,* and he says, I'm smiling because you Arabs in Iraq, you oppressed us and made genocide against us and you used chemical weapons against us, and now Saddam is hanged and dead and the Kurds are in charge in northern Iraq. So we all burst out laughing, it was so funny. So they beat us so hard we were in a coma for a week, man, it was a disaster.' Kovan laughed at the memory, shaking his head.

We had days to kill in his flat before heading back to the frontline and the conversation had turned, as all conversations in Syria eventually do, to detention and torture. Kovan had been arrested and tortured twice, once after the abortive 2004 Kurdish uprising and once a few months before the rest of the country rose up in 2011. His brother, now living in Sweden, had been imprisoned for over a year, and only released after the entire family scraped together a $20,000 bribe to give to regime intelligence officers. As a teenager, Kovan had helplessly watched his mother beaten in front of him during interrogation by Syrian state security. Other Syrian rebels may accuse the Kurds of being Assad's puppets, but it was clear that Kovan was no regime stooge.

'Man, they have more than a hundred types of torture,' he added, lighting another cigarette, 'they have one they call the cross, this is from the Romans. They make you naked and put you on a cross on the wall and make you drink a lot of water after they tie up your penis. Then they leave you there for one or two days so you think your kidney will explode, but there is no physical evidence of torture. Or if they beat your leg they put it in iced water so there is no evidence. Or sometimes they crush ten or twenty people in a room with electric cables on the wall and fill the room with water and turn the electricity on and off. Or they would pull out your nails with pliers. Or sometimes in 2004 they would torture Kurds with Coca-Cola bottles. They would put it in your ass and sit on your shoulders until it goes all the way up.'

Kovan's nephew Balen – a toddler with a mop of blond hair, who we'd nicknamed Destroyer of Worlds for his terrifying fascination with our expensive camera equipment – rampaged through the room, picking our things up and dropping them on the hard tiled floor as Kovan reminisced about his time in prison. It was a surreal and depressing experience. 'One thing they do,' he added as an afterthought, 'is they put you in a metal box a few metres square with a rat, and tell you if you kill the rat they will kill you. Every day they give you an olive and a piece of bread and you have to decide whether to eat it yourself or feed the rat. Yeah, so that's the regime. You know, when you get out, you lose your humanity, you feel less than a rat. You can't even go to your wife in bed for months; you are not a man any more. They hurt you physically but they break you psychologically. All regimes are the same. I wished sometimes I was in a Jewish prison, not an Arab one. At least the Jews treat you like a human being.'

Israel actually cropped up a fair amount in conversation in Syrian Kurdistan. Back in the day, Israel used to arm the Kurdish *peshmergas*[30] in Iraq against Saddam's regime. Kovan had a private joke, it took us a while to work out, of

---

30 Kurdish fighters from Iraq

informing fighters we met at checkpoints that we were actually Israelis travelling on false British passports; fortunately
no one gave a shit. While, like all representatives of a state-
less people oppressed by a more powerful neighbour, Kovan
identified with the Palestinian struggle, his dissatisfaction
with Arab rule inevitably won out. Never trust an Arab, he
would always say. When we drove through silent, spreading
mud-hut Arab villages at night, foot on the pedal, Kovan
would say, 'Fucking Arabs, man, never trust them.' When
he talked about his brother, arrested through the duplicity
of Kovan's Arab best friend, he'd say, 'You bring them into
your house, they eat your mother's food, but Arabs will
always betray you. The Arabs, dude, they're like reeds by
the river: they kneel before whoever's powerful at the time.'
The Kurdish rebels were powerful here now, and the Arabs,
divided amongst themselves, swayed before them, for now. If
the Kurds were to assert themselves as the legitimate rulers
of the Jezirah region of north-east Syria they would have
to win the Arab tribes to their cause; but the decades of
bitterness between them would make this a hard-won peace.

We were on the road again, heading to the front, in a new
SUV Kovan had hired from a mate; our taxi driver from
last time around didn't fancy the front again. We'd stopped
at the town of Amuda, about halfway there, when Kurdish
fighters flagged us down at a checkpoint to check our

permits then insisted we refreshed ourselves and washed the dust off our faces at a bubbling spring. 'Man, I hate Amuda,' said Kovan, 'these guys are all donkeys.' For political reasons? I asked. 'No, they're all Kurds, I just think they're stupid donkeys. Fucking assholes. They walk in the middle of the road like fucking donkeys and if you shout at them they start arguing with you, fucking asshole motherfuckers.' I guess nationalism may make you like your people, but it can't make you *like* them.

We left Amuda and an hour or so later hit the last checkpoint before the battlefield. The car was sputtering as the soldiers tried to convince us not to drive further ahead. The jihadists had apparently set up heavy machine guns and sniper rifles to take potshots at any vehicles heading to the front, though they left the streams of Arab refugees, in taxis and trucks overloaded with livestock, mattresses and shrouded women, alone. We insisted we'd be fine, and drove off. Less than a hundred metres along the road our SUV broke down. Laughing at us, the soldiers from the checkpoint drove up in a tractor to drag us back to safety and Kovan slumped at the SUV's wheel, literally overwhelmed by shame. While a mechanic tinkered with our fucked engine, the soldiers brought us into a forward base hidden behind a hillock: a cluster of Portacabins and reed-matting shelters, with a satellite TV blaring combat footage from the front a few kilometres down the road.

They were cool guys, greying local farmers and twenty-something regulars, and they fed us salad and goat's cheese and chips and endless glasses of tea and cigarettes as we watched TV and discussed the war beneath a full moon. They dressed us up in their webbing and wrapped their *keffiyehs* round our faces, thrusting rifles in our hands while they took photos on their phones, laughing, and calling us terrorists. They fell in love with our military-style Cyalume glowsticks and promptly stole them, taking them off on a patrol, their SUVs glowing an eerie blue and green as they drove into the dark.

When the fun was over, one fighter insisted we stay at his farm for the night, down a dirt track through an olive grove. We slept on his roof beneath the stars, and woke up with the dawn. After a breakfast of bread and olives and yoghurt, he led us a few hundred metres to the Turkish border, and indicated the frontier with his rifle. 'Look,' he said, 'the fence here used to be twice as tall as a man, and now there is nothing.' And indeed, for a kilometre or so all the barbed wire had been removed, leaving the frontier completely open beneath the looming gaze of a concrete Turkish fort. 'The Turks did this a few days ago, just before the fighting here, to let the jihadists in. Every night we patrol here and sometimes we capture the jihadists in groups of three or four. They are trying to send them in behind our positions, to attack us from the back.'

We decided to take a chance on the newly repaired SUV and sped off towards the front, flooring the gas as we drove through the sniper zone, Kovan muttering *shit shit shit* at the crackle of rifle fire in the distance. When we reached the relative safety of the next checkpoint, we jumped out and crouched behind the earth berms next to some fighters peering over the lip of their trench with binoculars, trying to make out movement in the jihadist-held villages on the horizon. 'That is Cava,' one said. 'Cava is a Kurdish village, Yezidi like us.'

I asked the fighter how the Yezidi were treated. He shrugged. 'Well, badly of course. The enemy killed a man for refusing to pray like a Muslim and they cut off a man's hand only yesterday.' For all that, these soldiers were in a good mood, and led us, crouching out of sight of the enemy snipers, to a hut behind a stand of trees where they fed us tea and sugary biscuits, and posed with the whimpering puppy they'd adopted as a mascot. Sitting cross-legged on a rug on the frontline, Kovan was in his element and laid on the charm, making the fighters laugh by recounting long anecdotes about his days in the army. I asked about his friends. 'Some are with the rebels, some are fighting for the regime, it's very strange. I still talk to them all on Skype, you know? They ask about each other, on the other side … if they are well. This is Syria.'

Tea drunk, hands shaken, we moved off further down the road to the outskirts of Ras al-Ain, the flashpoint border town this whole offensive was about. Apart from fighters and a few ragged-looking children, the streets were deserted. Ninety per cent of the city's population had fled the months of bitter house-to-house fighting, and almost every building bore the scars of war. Arabic graffiti on every wall – *the bin Laden Brigade, Chechens of Syria, We Wish Blessings on the Taliban* – bore testimony to the jihadist groups from all across Syria and the wider Islamic world who had flocked here to fight the Kurds and been defeated. Now the Kurdish flag and huge billboards of Abdullah Ocalan, leader of the Kurdish rebellion, were raised high over Ras al-Ain, and the Kurdish fighters here were proud to show off their gains. We jumped in a minivan smeared with mud for camouflage and drove off to the frontline, a few hundred metres from the centre of Ras al-Ain.

After a short drive through eerie streets of shuttered shops and wrecked houses, we were dropped off at the border crossing, jumping out of the minivan like schoolkids on a field trip and strapping on our helmets. It was a hot afternoon, and a few Kurdish troops sat around on ripped sofas at the border post, which was still painted with the FSA flag, drinking tea and chainsmoking cigarettes, and stroking their pet goat. 'We rescued her from the FSA,' one said, 'her name's Genjo. Now she follows me around everywhere, she can't even sleep if I'm not there.' He led me to the First World War-style trench positions that marked the frontline, Genjo trotting along beside us as we crouched down from view of the enemy snipers in the village of Tel Halaf, a few hundred metres away.

Crawling up a berm, we peered through a hole in the sandbags at the enemy positions. 'There are a couple of bodies there from the last time they attacked, look,' said the fighter manning the position, 'one's all rotted away, in the ditch, and the other got flattened by a tank when they ran away.' As I was trying to see the bodies, I saw some movement on the other side of the frontline, and remarked upon it. Immediately the fighter peered over the lip of the trench and began shooting at the jihadists, a curious Genjo climbing up beside us to watch the action. We slid back down the sandbank as a sniper took potshots at Tel Halaf from an unfinished, war-battered concrete building beside us. A Turkish armoured vehicle roared past us on the other side of the border, separated by just a single wire fence.

'You see,' said Kovan. 'You see? Whenever those jihadist motherfuckers come through here, the Turks send a tank along the fence to guard them.' We could see Turkish soldiers standing stiffly at their sandbagged emplacements only feet away from us across the barbed wire, the Turkish flag fluttering above. I waved at one; he told me to fuck off. 'You see what these assholes are like?' said Kovan.

'One day soon the Kurdish flag will fly on that side too, then they will learn not to fuck with us.'

We walked over to the sniper position in the ruined building, Genjo the goat trotting alongside us bleating. Ducking through holes in the concrete walls, stepping over abandoned black jihadist webbing and mouldy tins of tuna fish and beans, we entered the snipers' eyrie. Someone – maybe a rebel, maybe a Kurd – had sprayed *Assassin's Creed* on the wall, after the Xbox game. Beneath the graffiti, a teenage fighter with a downy moustache sat sprawled across a mattress behind some sandbags, his machine gun poking through a hole in the battered wall, a cheap plastic alarm clock by his side. From one window, you could see clearly over the border fence to Turkey a few metres away, and the provincial town of Ceylanpinar, bustling in its peacetime normality. Cars drove up and down its main street, and housewives tramped along the pavement laden down with bags of groceries. From the other window the view was of Tel Halaf and the war, a cluster of cottages and grain stores on the other side of the trenches with the turret of a tank poking over the sandbags.

I peered through the hole in the wall with binoculars as a fighter talked me through the last battle. 'They run at us all in black shouting *Allahu Akbar, Allahu Akbar*, then we throw grenades on their heads and mow the front ones down, and then they all run away again. The ones we hit die after ten or fifteen minutes … we watch them die from this window here. I think they must all be on drugs, you can't fight like that otherwise. You can't fight a war that way.'

I bade a reluctant farewell to Genjo, stroking her soft ears as she licked my wrists. We climbed back in the minibus for the next stop on the tour, a village that marked the narrowest section of the frontline between the Kurds and ISIS, the al-Qaeda offshoot spearheading the fight against the YPG. We puttered along past drab flat fields to a cluster of battered mud-brick houses, arriving after a few minutes to a not especially enthusiastic reception. The Kurdish troops here were divided between the YPG Kurdish infantry, and the YPJ, the Kurdish forces' female infantry arm, and a line of teenage and twenty-something women sullenly shook our hands and gave us tea in delicate china cups. There's something exotic, to Western eyes, about women on the frontline, but the Kurds were all quite blasé about it; if anything, they seem to find the Western focus on their female fighters tiresomely patronising. The male fighters sat around the compound, cleaning their weapons and grinning as we badgered their female comrades for quotes.

'At first it was hard for us, as women,' the female officer of the YPJ told me, 'but now it's normal. We work side by side and can take on the same tasks as the men. Now

we are up to the same tasks, we are equal with no differ-
ences.' Indeed, the female fighters are particularly highly
regarded by the Kurds – and feared by the jihadists – as
snipers; the Kurds believe they have more patience than
the men by their side.

I asked a markedly pretty teenage fighter what life would
be like if the jihadists took control. 'Now we are free, but
if they come here they will impose Islamic rules, and make
us cover our hair and faces.' In fact, I'd been told, many of
the female fighters had run away from domineering families, and were rehomed in women's refuges before being
trained up as fighters. For all the other consequences of
the Syrian War, it had given these girls a taste of freedom.

We left Ras al-Ain towards the end of the afternoon,
the Kurdish intelligence forces at the entrance checkpoint
crossing our names off their list of visiting outsiders in biro.
When we reached the checkpoint we'd had tea at earlier,
we could hear the crackle of rifles and machine guns as
the Kurdish fighters in the newly recaptured village of
Alouk traded fire with the jihadists in Cava. 'We're about
to take Cava,' said the officer in command, 'would you
like to see?' Yes, very much so.

He packed us into an incongruously civilian-looking
Smart car together with a fighter and sent us down an
unpaved track, all squeezed in together, to Alouk, the

sound of gunfire growing louder as we jerked our way across the ruts. There was an eerie feel to the place, with no people visible, just wrecked cottages and abandoned livestock wandering around. Some homes were burned out, others had had walls smashed by jihadist tanks whose huge tracks had torn up the muddy ground in deep ruts. The only evidence of human activity was the sound of gunfire. Finally we found a Kurdish fighter, wandering around with a box of shotgun shells under his arm and a cigarette dangling from his mouth. He waved us down, saying, 'Get out here and walk, it's too dangerous to drive down here.' We asked him where the enemy were, still standing in the middle of the track. 'Well, their positions are there,' he said, pointing with his Kalashnikov, 'and there, and over there.' Everywhere, in fact. Some bullets whizzed right past us and we jumped into an orchard for cover. After a long few seconds, the sound of the anti-aircraft gun that had fired at us echoed from Cava a few hundred metres away. 'You see,' he said, unfazed, 'I told you.' We followed him through back gardens, over broken down walls to the forward position, a trench behind a line of tall poplars.

'This is the frontline, the very frontline,' said Kovan breathlessly as we sat down behind the lip of the trench. You could hear the adrenaline in his voice. 'Soon the attack will start, when it gets dark.' The fighters milling around were less excited and gave us tea while insisting we didn't film them. We sat around for a bit, smoking, making small talk, joking around with a couple of female snipers and waiting for the fighting to begin. One female fighter waved at us as she walked a shaggy white sheepdog around the village on a long rope leash. We went over to say hello. 'His owners just abandoned him, poor thing,' she told us. 'So now we're looking after him.'

The sun was setting, and the machine gunners manning their positions behind a wall kept loosing off single aimed shots at Cava to keep the jihadists' heads down while the assault wave prepared for action. No foreign journalists had yet filmed the Kurdish fighters in a full-scale battle, due to their excessive regard for information security. We had a scoop here, one that would bring the war in Rojava the international attention it deserved. It was just while we were congratulating ourselves on this that the commanding officer strolled over, literally started in his tracks as he saw us, and ordered us to fuck off, his bushy grey moustache quivering with rage. No argument we made about the value of media attention would mollify him. An attempt to boost his ego by interviewing him failed; instead he gave us a long rant about how the war was all the fault of America, Britain and France, who he insisted were funnelling jihadists to Syria for some as yet undetermined purpose. He detailed a fighter to escort us away from the frontline. As soon as we walked away, dawdling, the attack began and the heavy machine guns and rifles a few metres behind us roared into life in concert. I clenched my fists with rage and frustration as we walked away from the fighting, so tantalisingly close.

A few hours later, these fighters had liberated Cava. We stood at the checkpoint and watched the sun, vast and golden, dip low over Ras al-Ain on the horizon. It was the end of our time in Rojava. For all their paranoia about the media, it was hard not to fall in love with the Kurds, fighting for their freedom for the first time in generations here on the farthest edge of Syria. As a fighting force, the Kurdish fighters, both men and women, are probably the most effective unit in Syria, with the closest adherence to Western human rights norms in the entire conflict. But the West, still committed to the rebels who have now been eclipsed by jihadist fighters, and to the myth of Syria's territorial integrity, refuse to deal with them, or allow them to attend the sputtering peace talks. And so the Kurds fight on alone, relying on their own improvised resources and total commitment to their cause. And in a strange way, they seem happier that way.

LEBANON

TRIPOLI
October 2013

I was strolling around the marketplace with Ziad and his bodyguard of Sunni fighters when they caught the Alawites, astray from their besieged hilltop eyrie of Jebel Mohsen. 'How many are there?' one of Ziad's men shouted. 'Three,' a fighter called back. One of Ziad's men gave a slow descending whistle in disbelief. 'Boss,' pleaded a teenage fighter, 'can I shoot them?' 'No, no, no,' said Ziad, ever the voice of reason, 'not on camera.'

Instead, the fighters surrounded the interlopers to warn them off ever coming back to the Sunni Bab al-Tabbaneh district. 'You know who this is? This is Haj Ziad. Go and tell your boss that we're letting you go this time, for Eid.'

The Alawites walked away briskly, grinning at their good fortune. Ziad turned to me. 'These men are spies from Jebel Mohsen, they sent them here to spy on us. But because it's Eid, because it's the holiday, we let them go.' And if it wasn't Eid, I asked, what would have happened then? 'If it wasn't Eid,' he said, 'then we would begin a new war.'

This was Syria's brutal civil war at work right in the heart of Lebanon, one city's mini-conflict dragging the entire tiny country right to the edge of the abyss, all but ignored by the media.

———————

The conflict between Tripoli's Sunni district of Bab al-Tabbaneh and the Alawite quarter of Jebel Mohsen dates back a generation to the Lebanese Civil War, when the Syrian regime of President Hafez al-Assad and its local Alawite allies crushed a Sunni rebellion in the coastal Lebanese city of Tripoli, culminating in the 1986 Tabbaneh Massacre of hundreds of Sunni men. Syrian troops only pulled out of Lebanon in 2005, and now that Hafez's son President Bashar al-Assad is facing his own bloody rebellion within Syria, a new generation of Tripoli's disenfranchised Sunnis are flocking to the black banner of Islamist revolt. Fighters who survived the 1980s are now grey-bearded commanders of their own militias, winning over young recruits with appeals to solidarity with the Syrian rebels next door and the promise of power and respect that only comes, here, to those toting automatic weapons.

Tripoli, essentially, is a safer mini-Syria, a place for journalists to mainline street clashes and sectarian hatred and still round off the evening with a sumptuous restaurant meal. A couple of weeks earlier I'd been in Syria's Hassakeh province with the Kurds fighting Arab jihadists; now I was hanging out with Sunni warlords who aspired to join their cause. Ziad Allouki is a controversial figure in Lebanon, not least for his willingness to send his men to fight against the Lebanese army, seen by Tripoli's Sunnis as puppets of the Assad regime next door, whenever they encroach upon his tiny fiefdom. A butcher by trade, Ziad has established total control of Tripoli's medieval market of Suq al-Qamr, a den of narrow winding lanes and alleyways ideal for guerrilla warfare. When he sits sipping coffee on a plastic chair in the middle of the *suq*, surrounded by his rifle-toting teenage retinue, grown men kneel before him, kissing his hand and demonstrating their fealty. 'There is no government here, no government,' Ziad told me, 'so I provide security for my Sunni Muslim people.'

The failure of the Lebanese state to disarm both Sunni and Shia militant groups has allowed commanders like Ziad to flourish in the security vacuum. With the Lebanese government essentially subordinate to the Shia Hezbollah militant group, whose presence in Syria is slowly turning the war's tide back in favour of the Assad regime, Tripoli's working-class Sunnis feel estranged from their own state, with young fighters eagerly declaring how ready they are to fight against their own army.

In his office in a small workshop, beneath a Jabhat al-Nusra banner, Abu Rami, a wiry, intense thirty-year-old commander allied with Ziad, fiddled with his pistol as he spoke to me. We'd spent days negotiating over whether I could film him and his men. I couldn't, it finally transpired. He was busy with other concerns. 'I have twelve fighters, and for me they live or die. Abu Omar here,' he said, waving his weapon at a thick-bearded young fighter who'd already shown off his bullet wounds from a night-long battle with the Lebanese army, 'he will turn himself into a bomb and explode himself as soon as I give the word.' The fighter nodded dispassionately; presumably they'd discussed this before. 'This is a message to Obama, to Britain, to France. Stop funding the Lebanese army, because they are liars. France gives them heavy machine guns and they test them on us, here in Tabbaneh. We are human beings, not dogs. We are Muslims, but this is an army of Syria. Bashar Assad created this army. All of the officers are Shia or Christians or Jews, and some Sunnis who are paid off by the regime. Look, you are sitting now with us and we are not hurting you, we receive you like guests. And they call us extremists, call us terrorists! Let the army fight Hezbollah then. They are the real terrorists, planting sleeper cells around the world and causing explosions here in Tripoli.'

Just two months earlier, a car bomb outside Tripoli's main Sunni mosque killed forty-two worshippers, raising sectarian tensions to their greatest height since the end of the civil war in the early 1990s. Since then, Lebanon has been plagued by a series of tit-for-tat car bombs across Beirut and the volatile Bekaa Valley, with prominent Sunni and Shia figures – and unfortunate civilian bystanders – paying the price of this descent into chaos. Tripoli's Sunnis blame both the Syrian regime and Hezbollah for carrying out the mosque attack, and castigate the Lebanese army for its inability to protect Sunni civilians at prayer. But if the army is incapable of or unwilling to defend Tabbaneh, commanders like Abu Rami and Ziad Allouki will gladly take their place, with angry teenagers flocking to their sides to fight beside them.

In the old stone building that functions as his secret base, beside the double mattress on the floor and the giant CCTV screen in the corner, Ziad's men chose rifles from the selection in the wardrobe, along with black vests emblazoned 'Mosque Patrol'. I watched them strap on their webbing, patting down their magazines just so and checking themselves in the mirror before heading out. It was Friday, and the local market's ancient mosque would be full of worshippers for noon prayers. In an effort to reassure the locals both of their security and his ability to provide it, Ziad would lead a handful of fighters as they patrolled the market's alleys, setting up a protective cordon of yellow police tape and gun-toting teenagers at the entrance to his fiefdom. Shopkeepers shouted out their blessings as he passed their stores.

What are you protecting the mosque from? I asked him. 'From explosives or any bomb from Syrian murderers, or any guys who want to put a bomb here. This mosque is Muslim Sunni.' The mosque, emblazoned with the flag of the Free Syrian Army, its entrance plastered with martyrdom notices for local fighters who had died in Syria, was within the terms of this conflict a juicy target.

'I'm worried,' said one shopkeeper, coming up to Ziad, 'it's Friday, and there are too many people here. If someone wanted to blow something up, it would be today.'

In a gift to lazy journalists, the frontline between the two warring Sunni and Alawite communities inside Tripoli is commonly held to be the broad thoroughfare of Syria Street, which divides the low-lying Tabbaneh neighbourhood from the Alawite hilltop of Jebel Mohsen above as it snakes its way to the border, some thirty miles away. In fact, Syria Street is firmly in Sunni hands and the real dividing line is a narrow street running parallel to it, though sadly with a less resonant name.

On each side of the sectarian divide, every building within view is pockmarked with bullet holes and rocket-propelled grenade scars from the almost weekly clashes.

Every window in every building on the frontline has been repurposed as a sniper position with heaped-up sandbags or breeze-block defences and, from time to time, a sentry keeping tabs on the enemy in their own sniper positions a street's width away. Army checkpoints and the recurrent patrols of rumbling armoured vehicles are deployed to keep the two sides from massacring each other outright. In the midst of all of this, small boys play with BB guns beneath the bullet-scarred walls and painted al-Qaeda flags, shouting *Allahu Akbar, Allahu Akbar* as they wave their plastic rifles in the air. 'We want to go up there to Jebel Mohsen,' one scrawny Sunni kid, about six or seven years old, told me. Why? I asked. 'So we can fuck their sisters.' His brothers, busy dealing grenades and pistol bullets to passing customers from a dark alley corner, both laughed and ruffled his long hair approvingly.

A couple of Ziad's fighters took me on a tour of their entire world, a claustrophobic warren of alleys and shops a few hundred square metres in extent. Armoured vehicles of the Lebanese army marked off the boundaries. 'To go any further would mean arrest,' they said, so they stood a short distance from the soldiers and pointed at them, while the soldiers affected not to notice the militants a few metres away, carrying their rifles openly in the street. The fighters took me through an archway and up a flight of stone stairs to a sort of flat-roofed ruin overlooked by Jebel Mohsen. 'There,' one said in broken English, 'Alawites, Bashar al-Assad. No good.' He stared at the bullet-riddled tower blocks overlooking us before shouldering his rifle and firing a few rounds in the vague direction of the Alawites. A headscarfed housewife scowled at us as we scurried back down the stairs before Jebel Mohsen returned fire. We walked back to Ziad slowly through the *suq*, the soldier on top of his armoured vehicle feigning interest in his smartphone, pretending not to have heard the shots directly overhead just a few seconds earlier.

Ziad was in an ebullient mood. We'd been hanging out for a week. He'd carefully steered us towards scenes that would display his power and largesse, and seemed to remain under the impression we were somehow in a position to supply him with heavy weaponry, or at the very least donate him our body armour. As soon as we reached his chair in the shuttered marketplace, he put down his *narghila* pipe and insisted we follow him, it transpired to our car.

His men opened the rear doors and piled in with their weapons, politely indicating we join them. Once they were comfortably seated. I asked Ziad where we were going. 'Just for a drive, it will be nice.' We got in, our companions' rifle muzzles gravitating discomfortingly towards the back of our heads as we jolted along the potholed road.

As we passed army checkpoints, Ziad gave the soldiers a slow regal wave from the front passenger window, which they returned. The army don't care, Ziad, I said. You and your men just drive right past them and they don't do anything. 'They're aware of our power and therefore they avoid getting into clashes with us. They tried us before and we did what we had to do.' Men like Ziad are the real power in Tripoli now, and I felt safe, protected even, in his company. That's how it works.

We parked up at a beachfront villa and the fighters jumped out beaming happily. It was a stormy day, and grey waves lashed cold spray at them as they posed for future martyr photos with the most pimped-out weapons. Under the black looming clouds, they set up bottles full of water against a nearby sandbank and took up position, taking potshots with the different assault rifles, cheering each hit and commiserating each near miss. It was fun, and Ziad was in a buoyant mood as he fired his M16, hitting the target with each shot. 'So, you see, sometimes we like things that come from USA!' he laughed, thrusting the rifle in the air for emphasis.

A cloud burst above us and we scampered into the unfinished villa for shelter from the rain, chatting idly and smoking, enjoying our day at the seaside. 'We do this once a month,' explained Ziad, 'practising sniping, practising for the fighting.'

One of Ziad's friends, another major commander, turned up in a people carrier and the two warlords kissed and hugged each other warmly. I asked him about the situation with Jebel Mohsen. 'If the army weren't there, we would finish this war tomorrow.' How, though? Would you get rid of them all? 'No no no,' he said, 'nothing like that. We would just reduce their numbers, to teach them a lesson.'

———

It was Eid, the feast of sacrifice, and the streets of Tabbaneh were awash with blood as men chose the fattest sheep from those tethered on display and butchers slit their throats. Small boys watched their death throes with wide eyes as they cradled their new toy Kalashnikovs. Little girls in party frocks munched pink candyfloss and skipped across the pools of blood. Ziad had a more impressive sacrifice planned, and a crowd had gathered by his butcher's shop by the time the truck trundled up, the white bullock in the back bellowing and straining against its leash. They dragged it from the truck and as it sank to its foreknees, its rear legs hoisted to a wall by a metal chain, a man strode forward and cut its throat with a deep sawing motion, the men and children all chanting *Allahu Akbar, Allahu Akbar* and filming its death on their smartphones. Within minutes, the bull had been carved up and bagged into kilo chunks and distributed to the crowd, Ziad hacking the bloody meat into portions with a cleaver. 'About one hundred families here will eat from this cow,' he said. 'The government give nothing to the poor people here, to the families. No government, no government here.' In some ways, you're the government here, I suggested. 'It is not exactly how you say,' he replied, 'I am in charge to help my people here, to help my Sunni Muslims.'

The Lebanese flag is nowhere to be seen in Tabbaneh, but the markers of pan-Sunni identity are everywhere. From the FSA flags fluttering from every corner, to posters of bin Laden, Zarqawi and al-Khattab, or the framed picture of the 'Sunni martyr' Saddam Hussein in Ziad's shop, a combative, defensive sense of Sunni-ness has enveloped Tabbaneh's urban poor. The black flags of jihad and of the Islamic State of Iraq and al-Sham (ISIS) fly high over Tabbaneh, and a vast banner facing Jebel Mohsen eulogises a local boy made good who blew himself up at a checkpoint for the rebel Jabhat al-Nusra brigade in Syria.

While most fighters in Tabbaneh seem ideologically aligned with the relatively moderate fighters of Syria's Islamic Front, many observers have claimed a growing sympathy for al-Qaeda ideology in Tripoli. When the al-Nusra front's emir al-Jowlani gave his first interview to Al Jazeera and remarked that Hezbollah's involvement in Syria had given his own group – now in the process of rebranding itself as the local franchise of al-Qaeda

– inroads into Lebanon, Tabbaneh's streets were lit up by a display of celebratory gunfire. When al-Qaeda suicide bombings against Shia targets in the capital of Beirut cause mass casualties, the Sunnis of Tabbaneh hand out sweets and fire long automatic bursts to express their pleasure. But then there are few enough reasons to be happy in Tabbaneh.

Tripoli was once a prosperous city, the main trading port for greater Syria, but as tiny Lebanon was carved away from Syria with independence in 1943, Tripoli lost its market as Beirut prospered. A mostly Sunni city, many in Tripoli feel closer ties to conservative rural Syria than to glitzy, cosmopolitan, decadent Beirut. There are no champagne-fuelled beach clubs in Tripoli, only poverty, and a growing sense that the sputtering conflict with their equally impoverished Alawite neighbours is just another front of the bloody war next door. 'Muslim Sunnis in any war, in any area, any country, we are brothers,' explained Ziad. 'We take our orders from God. Everyone here is ready to defend himself. Everyone you see here has a gun in his house, everybody here has an AK-47 or an M16, everybody here is armed. So if any fighting happens we can immediately go and defend ourselves.'

When clashes do break out, they have a carnival feel. One day, about a week after we arrived, the army arrested two Alawites they suspected of planting the car bomb outside the mosque, and Alawite snipers began firing at targets on Syria Street in response. Shopkeepers rushed out with their Kalashnikovs, gawping boys laughing and cheering as their fathers and uncles took potshots or fired long bursts at the hated Alawites on the hill above them. Commanders we'd met a few days earlier as small businessmen now positioned their fighters on street corners, and called in reinforcements on their mobile phones as their sons reloaded their weapons for them. Young lads took turns leaping from behind cover and emptying their magazines at unseen targets as their mates filmed them on their smartphones, videos that would later be uploaded on the Tabbaneh Facebook page. The Alawite return fire was more disciplined, single aimed shots, often with heavier weapons. The army kept driving past in their armoured vehicles, and the Sunni fighters shouted at them to do something. Eventually, commandos in full American uniform, the fruit of DC's military aid, deployed from an armoured vehicle to escort some women to safety from their house on the frontline. When they came under fire from Jebel Mohsen, the soldiers retreated quickly, slamming the heavy armoured doors behind them as they drove off again, spraying long bursts of heavy machine-gun fire at Jebel Mohsen in a last parting shot.

With the army's inability to prevent clashes made clear, both sides resumed combat once again, spectators bringing babes in arms to watch the fun, until the sun set and the streets fell quiet, but for the occasional sniper's shot. We'd all had fun, in a tragic, pointless way, and now it was time to go home and eat dinner in front of the TV.

In a district where men struggle to feed their families, the arsenals of costly automatic weapons and bulging plastic bags full of ammunition possessed by every household seem anomalous. I met a Sunni weapons dealer and small-time commander in his family's flat to ask how poor men could afford such expensive tools of war. 'The politicians are the ones handing them out, they are giving them to their groups,' he said. 'If we had the money we wouldn't buy guns, we would buy food and clothing. They hand out the weapons and from time to time they send people to check we haven't sold them for money for our families.' He showed me handfuls of bullets, their case heads painted emerald green, and told me they were made in Iran, supplied by the Syrian regime to Jebel Mohsen, and then sold by the Alawites to their Sunni enemies in a lucrative, ongoing trade. 'They give us weapons so the people of Lebanon can keep killing each other. If it goes on like this, soon we will see a different Lebanon. You will see it like it was in 1975. With the permission of God, we are prepared to go to war, and if we live, we live, and if we die, we die.'

I went to Abu Rami's office to say goodbye, and walked into a meeting of commanders. One of them had donated a machine gun to the Syrian rebels, and was enraged to discover that the middleman, another commander, had sold it on for his own profit. Rami (Rami is a common name there. Of the six people in the room, three were called Rami), a beefed-up Lebanese-Australian acting as enforcer for his brother, Tabbaneh's overall warlord Saad Masri, was delivering a stern lecture to the other commanders, as the aggrieved donor nodded and stroked his long beard with satisfaction. I sat in the corner quietly, drinking sweet coffee from a thimble-sized plastic cup and smoking. Abu Rami stared at the floor sheepishly, nodding in acceptance of his ticking off. When the meeting concluded, Rami picked up his pistol and tucked it into the waistband of his expensive jeans, hugging and kissing the other commanders and leaving with his bodyguards.

Abu Rami breathed out, lit a cigarette, ordered more coffee and began to relax. He started teasing Abu Omar and the two fighters pinched each other and slapped each other away, giggling like schoolboys. A truck drove past from the Hizb-ut-Tahrir office on the corner, fluttering ISIS flags and blaring *nasheeds*. I asked Abu Rami what he wanted to say to the world. He looked at me, coldly, suddenly serious. 'Five hundred journalists have come here and no one does anything. Five or six people are killed in Tabbaneh by the army every month, and no one does anything. Everyone is against us – the government, the Tripoli MPs, Hezbollah, Hariri … We have no bread, we have no clothes for our children, no electricity, no money, the rain leaks into our homes. So don't ask us any more why we are fighting. We are suffocating, we are ready to kill the army. We are ready to explode.'

EPILOGUE

Last week I was sitting in a house in Idlib, northern Syria with some rebel commanders. In the room beneath us, six captives lay locked in the commanders' personal dungeon. The rebels sat on their divans watching al-Arabiya, the satellite signal glitching horribly as they smoked and discussed the onscreen chaos in Libya. For most of the world, post-revolutionary Libya is a madhouse, a place of warring militias and armed anarchy. For these Syrian fighters, trapped by a far more brutal war, it must seem a kind of heaven. The house we sat in, like all the other houses in the village, belonged to Alawite farmers before the war. Now they'd all fled the rebel onslaught, and these fighters, themselves refugees, had moved in, sleeping in their beds, watching their TV, raising their families in houses that their owners must dream about nightly, wondering if they'll ever return to these concrete villas and almond groves in blossom.

The fighters were from the Wolves of al-Ghab brigade, a smallish unit of about 1,000 men spearheading the newly formed Syrian Revolutionaries Front's battle against the Islamic State of Iraq and al-Sham, rebels fighting other rebels. 'The fight against ISIS is harder than the fight against the regime,' said one commander, Abu Mahmud, 'because the regime never had the courage to come here and try to push into the town, but ISIS are constantly trying to do this, every night.' It was wet and dark outside. Lightning flickered on the mountaintops of Latakia to the west. Asad, a junior commander and *shari'i*, or Islamic judge, asked me a question from across the room, shouting over the noise of the TV: 'What will you do when the West puts us on the terrorist list?'

Three years ago, in Libya, rebels like these were keen to attract journalists like me, believing that publicising their struggle on television or in print would sway public opinion to their cause, and bring down war-winning airstrikes on their governments. It worked in Libya. In Syria, though the world wrings its hands, no one is prepared to intervene, fearing the same chaos as in post-war Libya; fearing that the rebels, if given Western arms, will become terrorists and use those arms against us. In Syria, rebels are fighting the

regime and each other, the country splintering into a patch-
work of tiny hostile fiefdoms as each commander builds his
powerbase, trading weapons, smuggling fuel, raising revenue
to feed his men and pay the bills for the five-star hotels in
Turkey from which they commute to the front, when they
must, joining their men for a day or two at frontline bases
like this. Foreign fighters, Sunnis from across the Arab world,
Europe and North America, Shias from Lebanon and Iraq,
have come here to replenish the ranks of locals killed in
the Syrian meat grinder, so that the war might last for ever.
No one here, not me, not them, is under the illusion that
anything I write or film might bring this war one hour closer
to a conclusion. I'm a tourist here in their misery, we all
know this. 'How much would your government pay for you
if we kidnap you?' one of the fighters asks idly.

Another fighter comes in, takes off his webbing and lays
down his rifle as he sits on the divan. A few hours earlier,
he'd shot one of his men in the legs in the village square for
robbing civilians at a checkpoint. These fighters had acquired
a poor reputation amongst Syrian civilians for looting and
banditry – the worst reputation in all of Syria. Now they're
trying to impose order and salvage their reputation, in the
hope the West will arm them. 'You didn't film me shooting
that donkey, the thief,' says the commander. No, I say, I wish
we had. Asad laughs. 'Then get your camera ready and we'll
shoot him again for you.' I actually consider this for a second.

Earlier we'd gone up to an olive grove on a muddy hillside and filmed them firing an anti-aircraft gun at the ISIS-held village of Khreba on a hilltop a few hundred metres away. Abu Mahmud's son, Mahmud, fired wild bursts at the village, aimed at nothing in particular. Perhaps every shot had missed, perhaps a stray round had torn through a house and killed a civilian: who knows? It felt like it was all done for the cameras. My presence here, I realised, may have killed someone, or got one of these fighters killed as they displayed their courage for my lens. I used to think my presence in wars like this could help the people living here. Now I realise it's all pure selfishness. I come to wars like Syria because I enjoy the risk, because the chaos staves off the emptiness I feel when safe at home in the West. I wanted to come here because no other journalists had in six months, because it was too dangerous, because of the risk of kidnap. Now I was here, I realised there was no point to any of it, not any more.

'When eleven people were killed in Ukraine, the whole of the West protested and said the killings must stop, and then it finished,' says Sheikh, a one-armed commander. 'But hundreds of thousands of people are killed in Syria and no one does anything, because we are Muslims, because you think we are terrorists.' That's not true, I say, though we both know it is.

I began writing this book at the beginning of the Arab Spring, when it looked like the rebels of Libya, the revolutionaries protesting in the streets of Cairo and Damascus, would be able to change their world for the better. While in Benghazi, I watched President Bashar al-Assad's keenly anticipated speech, when everyone expected him to announce reforms and avert a war, and instead he vowed to crush the demonstrators. That speech led all these men here, destroyed their homes, killed their families, made the owners of this house into refugees. It brought me here too. Rebellion seemed a wonderful thing once, a thing full of hope. But in Syria there is no hope.

There is a strength you need to fight on for a hopeless cause against overwhelming odds, or perhaps just a certain indifference to life. David, in Blue Nile, must know that his men will never reach Khartoum, that he will likely die in pain in the bush, and his children grow up fatherless in a squalid refugee camp. But he fights because he believes in the rebellion, and there is no other choice. In the Syria outside the walls of this smoke-filled room, the regime is winning, slowly, tightening the noose around rebel-held Aleppo, capturing towns and vital roads across the west of the country every day. Even when the war ends, if it ever ends, the killing will still sputter on. If the regime wins, the men I met will all be killed. If the rebels somehow win, the warlords the war has created will fight each other for the spoils, faction subdividing into small factions, and pitting former ally against ally. Perhaps I'll be here to witness it, perhaps the world won't care enough to send me. But just being here, and in Libya, and in Sudan, meeting these men, spending time with them, proves to me that people are capable of abandoning everything for a cause, ready to overturn their whole world, to bring the system they were raised in crashing down around them.

It may not be sensible, and the outcome of their rebellion may well be worse than the oppression that inspired it, but it's impossible not to admire them for it, revelling in their freedom like sleek, lethal, uncaged beasts. Beside theirs, our comfortable lives look so mean and constrained. For their confidence, even arrogance, in believing that by taking up arms they can alter the course of history, we should all look up to the rebels of the world.